Reproducing Narrative

For an Elizabeth and two Ians

Reproducing Narrative
Gender, Reproduction and Law

MICHAEL THOMSON

Ashgate

DARTMOUTH

Aldershot • Brookfield USA • Singapore • Sydney

Published by
Ashgate Publishing Limited
Gower House
Croft Road
Aldershot
Hants GU11 3HR
England

Ashgate Publishing Company
Old Post Road
Brookfield
Vermont 05036
USA

British Library Cataloguing in Publication Data
Thomson, Michael
    Reproducing narrative : gender, reproduction and the law
    1.Sex and law
    I.Title
    342'.08'78

Library of Congress Cataloging-in-Publication Data
Thomson, Michael, 1970–
    Reproducing narrative : gender, reproduction, and law / Michael
Thomson.
        p.   cm.
    Includes bibliographical references.
    ISBN 1-85521-929-8 (hardcover)
    1. Abortion–Social aspects.   2. Abortion–Law and legislation–
Language. 3. Human reproductive technology–Social aspects.
    4. Human reproductive technology–Law and legislation–Language.
    5. Women–Health and hygiene–Social aspects.   6. Women–Medical
care—Social aspects.   7. Discourse analysis.   I. Title.
HQ767.T56 1998
363.4'6–dc21   97-39111
                                                                                          CIP

ISBN 1 85521 929 8

Typeset by Manton Typesetters, 5–7 Eastfield Road, Louth, Lincolnshire, UK.

Printed in Great Britain by Galliard (Printers) Ltd, Great Yarmouth

Contents

Table of Cases

Table of Legislation

Table of Legislation

Acknowledgments

This book builds upon doctoral research conducted at the University of Birmingham between 1992 and 1995. This research, and hence this book, would have been immeasurably more difficult to complete without the supervision of Moira Wright. I would like to thank her for an approach to my work which continues to be constructive, insightful and above all supportive.

During the writing and rewriting of this book I have benefited greatly from colleagues and friends who have patiently read and reread chapters in their various stages. Whilst I owe a debt of gratitude to a number of people, I am particularly indebted to Sally Sheldon, who has had the misfortune of sharing a research interest and a corridor with me. Her encouraging comments, energy and patience have been truly remarkable. Katherine O'Donovan has been similarly generous in her willingness to discuss and comment upon my research. Didi Herman, Carl Stychin and David Feldman I would also like to thank for their comments and general encouragement.

Having completed my doctorate I moved in 1995 to the Department of Law at Keele University. The rewriting of this book and my general intellectual engagement with law has benefited from the supportive, intellectually stimulating and friendly environment that is maintained.

Ian Dorrington and Kirstie Best must be thanked for dealing admirably with me during this period. If I have remained sane, it is no small thanks to them. Both have also read and commented on various chapters and work in progress. Cath, Tim and Sarah, thanks for the most timely of breaks and the most perfectly mixed margaritas!

Sections of this book have appeared before. An earlier version of Chapter 2 appeared as 'Woman, Medicine and Abortion in the Nineteenth Century', *Feminist Legal Studies*, **2**, (1995), 159; an earlier version of Chapter 5 appeared as 'Employing the Body: The Reproductive Body and Employment Exclusion', *Social and Legal Studies*, **5**, (1996), 243; Chapter 7 was published at different stages of development as 'Legislating for the Monstrous: Access to Reproductive Services and the *Monstrous Feminine!*', in both *Women's Access to Health Care: Law, Society and Culture* (Feminist

Legal Research Unit, University of Liverpool, Working Paper No. 4, 1996) and *Social and Legal Studies*, **6**, (1997), 401; excerpts from Chapter 8 appeared as 'After *Re S*', *Medical Law Review*, **2**, (1994), 127; and with Ceri Widdett as 'Justifying Treatment and Other Stories: *Tameside and Glossop Acute Services NHS Trust v. CH (A Patient)*', *Feminist Legal Studies*, **5**, (1997), 77.

MICHAEL THOMSON

Introduction

Hutchinson Telecom, one of the growing number of telecommunication groups whose networks both visibly and invisibly inscribe our landscape, ran probably one of the most sophisticated advertising campaigns of the mid-1990s. In our culture of immediacy and image, Hutchinson played to our appreciation of the serial advertising campaign. This form of extended narrative moved on from selling coffee to selling mobile phones.

Hutchinson's immediate campaign saw black billboard posters appear across the country. Within weeks, the blank billboards transformed; great orange script compelled us to Laugh, Talk, Cry, Shout. No product information was provided. The company's name was barely discernible. The Hutchinson Orange campaign had caught the imagination. Great fecund orange/Orange airships soon floated above our cities, objects of war, defence and disaster from the past making visible the invisible networks of communication, discourse and observation that Hutchinson was soon to add to. As these aerial objects appeared, the television campaign was introduced: glossy, shot in black and white and accompanied by the minimalist music of Philip Glass. Introducing its thematic mantra, 'The future is clear, the future is Orange',[1] the commercial introduced the product. The first 30-second commercial provided us with the knowledge that the future was clear, the future was cordless. In a dense, almost subliminal, collection of images suggesting chronology, gestation, development and progress, a foetus/infant emerged. Obviously not *in utero*, and obviously many months old, the infant was shot as foetus. Moving in a fictional amniotic fluid, an umbilical cord was at times (tastefully) discernible. As our future was revealed to us, so the foetus/infant itself became cordless. Images of chronology, growth and progress remained evident in subsequent commercials, as did the minimalist, rhythmic, perhaps womb-like music.

This first commercial is heavily imbricated in existing cultural responses to reproduction. The commercial may be seen, for example, as part of a much more expansive contemporary denial or erasure of the woman in reproductive discourses.[2] Within the commercial, however, this is part of a broader denial. Within the commercial, the foetus/infant is also very much removed, sanitized, without context beyond the denial of its uterine environment. While I discuss the disappearance of the woman in Chapter 5, it is primarily the lack of any *narrative*, other than the narrative of disappearance, that concerns me here.[3] There is a heavy irony in this omission. Hutchinson's product works within a system of networks. Networks crisscross, providing lines of communication, of productivity and of surveillance. The body, and especially, as I will argue, the reproductive and foetal bodies are invested with similar networks. These are networks of narrative/discourse, networks of power/knowledge.

Questions of reproduction are commonly understood within the terms of reference which inform the Hutchinson commercial. Reproduction is understood as an acultural phenomenon unaffected by external narratives or external relations. The (reproductive) body in this context is understood as a given. This book contends, however, that reproduction, the reproductive body and foetal identity are transformed by and embody a complex system of externalities. Reproduction exists as a complex socioeconomic and political phenomenon.

This book may therefore be understood as being about externalities – about the external narratives that invest the reproductive/foetal body. Of these many narratives, there are two in particular I intend to consider, without wanting to suggest that these are exhaustive. The narrative I will focus on primarily is one of gender. Implicit in the analysis of this narrative is a particular understanding of gender. In referring to gender, I refer to a social relation, a structural code. As Thérèse de Lauretis helpfully explains: 'gender ... is both a socio-cultural construct and a semiotic apparatus, a system of representation which assigns meaning (identity, value, prestige, location in kinship, status in the social hierarchy, etc.) to individuals within the society'.[4] As such, this understanding of gender moves us away from a conception premised on biology:

> What popular wisdom knows ... is that gender is not sex ... but the representation of each individual in terms of a particular social relation which pre-exists the individual and is predicated on the conceptual and rigid structural opposition of the two biological sexes. The conceptual structure is what feminist social scientists have designated 'the sex–gender system'.[5]

What I want to argue is that within reproductive discourses and practices there are strong narratives of gender, narratives that may be read as representing a 'social relation'. Yet, importantly, it is not merely a question of representation. Discourse is productive. To put it another way, discourse does not only define or represent but also constructs and produces. This understanding of gender and discourse relies heavily on Michel Foucault's analysis of sexuality: 'Like sexuality ... gender is not a property of bodies ... but the set of effects produced in bodies, behaviours, and social relations ... by the deployment of a complex political technology.'[6] Recognizing that gender, like sexuality, is a set of effects arising from the deployment of political technologies, it becomes possible to talk to *technologies of gender*. This is where I want to locate reproductive discourses. These discourses exist as one of the many sites or technologies at or through which gender is constructed.

The second narrative is less global, less expansive. Having said that, it is also intimately tied to the first narrative. This second (and secondary) narrative concerns medical power. To be brief, it concerns a discourse of status enhancement, of fiscal and social upward mobility. The relationship between these two narratives will be unravelled through the course of the book. In looking at these two narratives, unravelling their interconnectedness, I do not want to suggest a complete picture, or even a history. What I want merely to provide is an illustration of a continuity of presence. That is to say, I want only to highlight recurring discursive themes.

Introducing this concept of narratives that may inscribe and indeed constitute the reproductive body, the book begins in Part I with an analysis of the nineteenth-century medical campaign to criminalize abortion. Chapter 1 locates the criminalization campaign within the context of the occupational assertion of medicine, its transition from occupation to profession. This chapter explores the *reproductive narrative* which was employed to validate the occupational closure of medical practice. Here I argue that, whilst the medical skill of the regular practitioners was no greater, no more advanced, than competing health care providers, opposition to abortion provided a means of forcing a differentiation between the regulars and the competing providers. The anti-abortion campaign facilitated a claim of cognitive exclusivity and allowed the regular physicians to seek legislative recognition and protection of this. Importantly, the political/campaigning regular practitioners broadcast a uniform ethical opposition to abortion even when many of the regulars advocated and practised abortion on medical and non-medical grounds. This occupational project was seen on both sides of the Atlantic.

Chapter 1, therefore, clearly introduces the manner in which narratives of desire (of parochial political ambition) may invest the body. While this first chapter introduces a relatively localized narrative, one which nonetheless has enduring relevance, Chapter 2 goes on to introduce the primary area of analysis, the relationship between reproductive discourses, gender and law. Introducing this relationship, or configuration, Chapter 2 further emphasizes the primacy within the medical anti-abortion campaign of non-medical issues. To highlight the role of gender within these discourses, medical opposition to abortion is juxtaposed with medical opposition to female

xvi   *Reproducing Narrative*

higher education, some areas of female employment and the question of women doctors. This juxtaposition reveals a continuity of argument. The anti-abortion argument, as well as reflecting parochial professional ambition, becomes understandable in terms of a broader opposition to a developing role for women. Opposition to abortion is seen, in part, as an opposition to a perceived redefinition of gender roles. The medical anti-abortion discourse is, therefore, located within the complex political technology which creates the set of effects known as gender. Ultimately, the chapter introduces and highlights the degree to which medical knowledge is deployed in the construction of gender.

The discursive patterns regarding gender highlighted in Chapter 2 are reconsidered in Part II in considering elements of the English abortion debate of the latter half of the twentieth century. Here I consider the female subject positions constructed within the parliamentary debates around the Abortion Act 1967, the Alton Bill 1987 and section 37 of the Human Fertilisation and Embryology Act 1990. The analysis employed places the narratives found within this legal discourse within a broader cultural context. This has two aims. In addressing legal discourses in this context, law is more readily understood as a (privileged) narrative, a cultural product. Law becomes very much part of the fictions we create or may create. Considering and understanding the female subjects of the parliamentary abortion discourses intertextually also animates the complexity of technologies of gender. Gender may be perceived as the product not only of the privileged discourses of science, medicine and law but also of less formal technologies. Gender may be understood as 'the product of various social technologies, such as cinema, as well as institutional discourses, epistemologies and critical practices'.[7] The two chapters within Part II, while recognizing law as a privileged discourse, locate some of the many sites, both social and institutional, within which gender is constructed. Importantly, these chapters aim to illustrate the fluidity of these spaces and the movement of ideas between them.

Part III extends the analysis of reproductive discourses beyond the scope of abortion. Chapter 5 provides an analysis of industrial foetal protection policies. The development of corporate policies and legislation broadcast as aimed at the exclusion of women from toxic workplaces on the basis of perceived foetal vulnerability is very much open to the analysis used above. Occupational health and safety provisions and their supporting discourses share many of the features of the abortion discourses considered in preceding chapters. Within these discourses are discernible strong narratives of gender. Traditional sexual divisions within the workplace appear actively maintained by the policies. The female body is constructed as pathological, or at least more susceptible to damage than the male body, defining areas of appropriate employment. Importantly, these areas defined as appropriate may be just as toxic as the industries from which the woman is excluded. They will also invariably be more poorly remunerated, with all that entails for the health of the woman and any family, whether potential or existing. There are very clear parallels with the medical opposition to female employment noted in Chapter 2. While asserting these continuities, Chapter 5 also highlights the shift in the subject of the discourses from the woman to the foetus. As the essentialist biologistic arguments of the past have become anachronistic and impermissible, forms or technologies of exclusion and gender definition have relocated. Narratives have shifted, inscribing not the woman but the emerging visual and cultural presence of the foetus.

This aspect of emerging foetal identity is returned to briefly in Chapter 6. In this and the following chapter, the developing medical techniques for artificially assisting conception are addressed in two distinct but interconnected contexts. In Chapter 6, the development of techniques for the management of infertility, and particularly the infertile woman, is considered within the context of a tradition of masculine creation mythology and desire. It is argued that the desire for a more assured role in reproduction (assured in part through the development of visual proof) has seen the emergence, not only of these technologies, but also of foetal identity and the marginalization, or invisibility, of the woman in reproductive discourses and practice. This has clear implications for the understanding of contemporary gender relations, and is more explicitly dealt with in Chapter 7.

In many ways repeating the methodology of Chapters 3 and 4, this chapter considers the female subjects constructed within the Human Fertilisation and Embryology Act 1990 and its enacting discourses. More specifically, in interrogating these discourses, Chapter 7 considers the association within the male imaginary of the female and the monstrous. This affinity in the male/medical imaginary goes some way to explaining the tradition of male creation mythology considered in Chapter 6 and the historical construction of the female body as inherently pathological – a theme which runs throughout the preceding chapters. The subject within these provisions is associated with the monstrous in sharing a cultural space defined by horror and fascination. In terms of horror, the 1990 Act in its enacting discourses and provisions reveals a horror of women's procreative capacity and, paradoxically, a fear of the circumvention of the paternal through technologies such as in vitro fertilization (IVF). Fascination is suggested in the recurring desire to know, understand and map the female reproductive system.

The argument that I hope to sustain is therefore composed of a complex series of interconnected ideas or strands. At its most immediate, this volume does no more than contend that reproductive discourses and practices are heavily imbricated in social, political and economic discourses. Beyond this, the body, and particularly the female reproductive body, is posited as a discursive construct, an embodiment of discourse both social and institutional. Where gender is traditionally perceived as a product of sexual difference, the figuring of the sexual body becomes understood as constructing and determining gender. Rationalizing the body and gender in this way, the construction of the body through biomedical and medico-legal reproductive discourses is understood as a technology of gender. Recognizing this, and showing an awareness of the genealogy of the configuration of reproduction, gender and law, provides a position from which contemporary medico-legal considerations of reproductive issues and possibilities may be read. This assertion is tested in the final chapter.

Notes

1   Perhaps a sign of the success of the campaign, in October 1994, *Panorama* ran one of it features under the title, 'The future is clear, the future is woman'!
2   In advertising itself, similar images are popular. During the course of the Hutchinson commercials, Spa attempted to sell their mineral water using a similarly distorted image of a foetus/infant. Projected in its fictional amniotic fluid, the suggestion of purity and security was clear. The controversial Benneton campaign, devised and shot by the Italian photographer Olivieri Toscani, provides perhaps another example; see p. 64.
3   See pp. 132–3.
4   T. de Lauretis, *Technologies of Gender: Essays on Theory, Film and Fiction* (London: Macmillan, 1987), 5.
5   Ibid.
6   Ibid., at 3 (quotations omitted).
7   Ibid., at ix.

PART I

1 The Doctor, the Profession, his Patient and her Abortion

The hospital was a temple ... and inside it was a God. (W. Channing, *Introductory Lecture, Read Before the Medical Class of Harvard University, November 5, 1845* (Boston, 1845), 5–21)

Mrs Cadwallader: He is a gentleman. I heard him talking to Humphery. He talks well.

Lady Chettam: Yes Mr Brooke says he is one of the Lydgates of Northumberland, really well connected. One does not expect it in a practitioner ... . For my part I like a medical man more on a footing with the servants; they are often all the cleverer. (G. Elliot, *Middlemarch* (London: Everyman's Library, 1990))

Of any of the known measures that can be employed to procure abortion, danger, more or less considerable to health is a consequence, and lest this danger should not be great enough, legislators, with their usual barbarity, have stepped in and converted this measure of security into a crime. (J. Bentham, *The Theory of Legislation*, ed. C.K. Ogden (London: Routledge & Kegan Paul, 1931), 493–4

Introduction

In the modern mind, abortion is imagined as an exclusively medical and legal matter. Indeed, the doctor is arguably the figure who is most clearly animated within our understanding of abortion.[1] Through medicalization it is now almost impossible to imagine a legislative context for abortion other than one which passes control to the medical profession.[2] The degree to which abortion has become consumed within a more general medicalization has limited our understanding of reproductive choices. Yet, beyond these parameters, before and outside this medical model, there are possibilities. We have evidence and rumours from history, from other societies and from the fringes of our own society.[3] Such possibilities, however, remain distant.

This chapter and the next assess the criminalization and medicalization of abortion in the nineteenth century. They assess the medical campaign which led to this limiting of possibility. Given the almost absolute nature of the medical model, it becomes essential to understand its genealogy. Reading the medical campaign of this period within these initial chapters, the dominant model is revealed as built upon two (interconnected) discourses which concern occupational status and gender definition. This first chapter moves outside the traditional and popular understanding of the medical campaign as a scientific commitment to the sanctity of life, or as a manifestation of the regard had for the health of the woman. Rather, it aims to show the campaign as primarily motivated by the occupational aspirations of medicine. Abortion is identified as central to the energetic campaign waged by the regular physicians in the nineteenth century to create a single market for health care. In these terms, abortion emerges as pivotal in the professionalization of medicine in the nineteenth century.

This analysis of the manipulation of the issue of abortion introduces the disparate and numerous ways in which the body, and specifically the reproductive body, is inscribed with meaning and power. The body exists as an object of knowledge and as a subject for the exercise of power: 'The body is … located in a political field, invested with power relations which render it docile and productive, and thus politically and economically useful'.[4] Within this chapter women's reproductive systems are understood as politically useful to an emerging occupation. Subsequent chapters will consider the enduring *usefulness* of women's reproductive systems, predominantly in the construction of gender identities and inequalities.

In order to appreciate the process of professionalization and the role of abortion in medicine's occupational assertion, it is first necessary to understand the structure and stature of medicine before this occupational project.[5] The following section will provide an outline of the legislative and social status of medical practice in the nineteenth century. Following this, a review of contemporary analysis of *the professions* provides a theoretical framework through which a subsequent discussion of the medical campaign for abortion law reform may be understood. In this final section the campaign in both the United Kingdom and the United States is considered.

Medicine in the Nineteenth Century

Status and Structure

In the case of the murder of Sir Reuben Levy, Lord Peter Wimsey, Dorothy L. Sayer's otherwise unshakable fictional detective, doubts the findings of his investigations. The possibility that Levy has been murdered by his rival, the eminent surgeon Sir Julian Freke, Kt, GCVO, KCVO, KCB, MD, FRCP, FRCS, shakes Lord Peter. He refuses to disclose to his companion his suspect's identity: "I say I *may* be wrong – and I'd feel as if I'd libelled the Archbishop of Canterbury."[6] While this point is perhaps being made a little flippantly, Lord Peter's association of the eminent surgeon with the eminent theologian reflects the exalted, almost deified, status of medicine in the twentieth century. Lord Peter's parallel is explained by Elliot Freidson:

> If we consider the profession of medicine today, it is clear that its major charac-
> teristic is preeminence. Such preeminence is not merely that of prestige but also
> that of expert authority. That is to say, medicine's knowledge about illness and
> treatment is considered to be authoritative and definitive … . Medicine's official
> position is akin to that of state religions yesterday – it has an officially approved
> monopoly of the right to define health and illness and to treat illness.[7]

Such a social position is a phenomenon largely particular to the twentieth century.[8] Medicine has only recently been widely perceived as a prestigious, scientific, effective and justly remunerated occupation. In the United Kingdom and the United States the transition of medicine from craft or trade to its current status has broad parallels.

In the United Kingdom, and Europe generally, in the eighteenth and nineteenth centuries the dominant health care occupations worked within the guild, or corporation, structure. Three guilds existed, comprising physicians, surgeons and apothecaries. These guilds provided a limited means of pursuing the collective interests of medicine. They took responsibility for teaching and to some extent exercised control over the conduct and practice of the occupations. The existence of the guilds demarcated areas of practice without delimiting the overall structure of medicine. The members of the Royal College of Physicians, for example, whose charter dates from 1518, had a monopoly on the practice of 'physic' – the practice of internal medicine. Surgeons, on the other hand, were responsible for the outward disorders:

> the pestilence, syphilis, and such other contagious infirmities, letting of blood in
> all cases, and drawing of teeth, customable diseases, as women's breasts being
> sore, a pin and web in the eye, uncomes of hands, burnings, scaldings, sore
> mouths, the stone, stangury, sanceline and morphew, and such other diseases,
> apostemations, and agues: all wounds, ulcers, fractures, dislocations and
> tumours.[9]

Where physicians were concerned with the inward and surgeons with the outward ailments, apothecaries exercised a monopoly, within the guilds, in the preparation and supply of medicines. John Willcocks, writing in 1830, described how an apothocary's 'proper practice consists in preparing with exactness, and dispensing, such medicines as may be directed for the sick by any physician lawfully licensed to practise physic. [The apothecary is] also at liberty to administer medicines of their own authority, and without the advice of a physician.'[10]

While delimiting areas of practice the law did not, however, prescribe other models of health care. Consequently, the regular physicians[11] still worked in competition with folk or irregular practitioners. This led to inconsistencies in the regulation of medicine: 'Quacks, "empirics" and drug peddlers practised freely with no legal sanction against them, while a physician in London could be disciplined by his College for preparing and selling a prescription to his patient.'[12] This situation, the legally defined spheres of practice for the three guilds, is illustrated in a case of 1828 where a member of the Royal College of Surgeons was unsuccessful in his claim for medical charges against a patient he had treated for typhus. His failure resulted from the judicial belief in typhus being a medical and not a surgical disease, and hence not within the province of the surgeon. Best CJ informed the court:

> I cannot admit that the legislature intended to give surgeons the privilege of practising in physic as well as surgery ... . For some disorders relief is sought from medicine, for others from topical applications. A different education is necessary to prepare men to undertake the cure of either of these descriptions of complaints ... . The first description belongs to the physician and the apothecary; the second to the surgeon.[13]

Notwithstanding the existence of the guild structure the provision of medicine in the eighteenth and first half of the nineteenth centuries was in a state of near chaos.[14] The situation in the United States in this period was similar in its chaotic state, while markedly different in structure. As a colony, the United States had attracted few guild-trained physicians, and consequently a formal guild structure never developed. Health care originated as a domestic rather than an occupational skill; therefore anyone claiming medical talent could practise outside any institutional controls of the sort that existed in the United Kingdom and Europe.[15] American physicians, while distinguished minimally by the legislature, had no powers of exclusion, and no powers to enforce the higher fees they generally charged. Equally importantly, nineteenth-century practitioners were far from trusted by the public and, indeed, were viewed by many as menaces to society.[16]

Deregulation and Disquiet

From the limited position noted above, the occupational status of the regular physicians was weakened further on both sides of the Atlantic in the nineteenth century. In the United States, the dawn of the nineteenth century brought with it a deregulation of health care. The spirit of liberalism and democracy, and laissez-faire economics, led to the removal of the scant regulations that had marginally distinguished regular physicians from other health providers. The dominant medical model became part of the unregulated free market in health care provision. In the United Kingdom, similar pressures emerged. Yet here the drive for the free market did not see a deregulation as it had done in the United States. Rather, new economic and governmental policy acted as an obstacle to occupational closure through licensing laws. These external pressures were further compounded by internal disquiet.

The occupational status of medicine in both the United States and the United Kingdom suffered during this period as schisms developed within regular medicine. The drastic and seemingly mediaeval treatments that had been employed up to the nineteenth century became increasingly challenged from within the regulars' ranks. The medicine that had relied upon purging and bleeding faced growing opposition. In contrast to the brutal techniques of the traditional regulars, a number of new models of treatment developed. The majority of these were non-invasive, relying on mild treatments such as natural diets, the ingestion of herbal extracts, and baths. By mid-century, an increasing number of physicians, influenced by new scientific knowledge, challenged the heroic practices of the established practitioners.[17] In the United Kingdom, these growing internal divisions were exacerbated by opposition to existing status differentials.

Prior to the Industrial Revolution, divisions within health care were strongly class-based. Whilst the middle classes were treated by surgeons and apothecaries, the wealthier classes patronized physicians. The social status of the practitioners was the product of the social evaluation placed on their work, without regard to its demonstrable effectiveness.[18] Social identity reflected the standing of patients, leaving physicians as the 'first class of medical practitioners in rank and legal pre-eminence'.[19] As John Keown notes:

> [Physician's] higher social status was not ... matched by professional competence: their expertise was limited to writing complicated prescriptions and they depended on their cultured gentility and patron's ignorance to build up a practice ... . The examinations which were set by the Royal College of Physicians were designed not so much to test medical knowledge as to ensure the admission of only those candidates with the appropriate social background.[20]

Appropriate social background was ensured not only by the Royal College but also by Parliament. Parliament reserved the practice of physic to 'those persons that be profound, sad and discreet, learned, and deeply studied'.[21] The College made further attempts to ensure this by only allowing full membership (fellowship) of the College to graduates of Oxford and Cambridge. This approach existed notwithstanding the fact that medicine was not regularly taught at Oxford or Cambridge until mid-century. The classics, philosophy and literature were at the heart of the physician's education.[22] Highlighting the non-medical nature of the physician's training, the *Gentleman's Magazine* in 1834 drew attention to the distinguishing characteristics of the physician: 'Large attainments as a scholar ... sound religious principles as a Christian ... practical worth and value as a good member of society, and ... polished manners as a well-bred gentleman.'[23]

The emergence largely from the continent of new scientific knowledge (knowledge that had already challenged the efficacy of traditional methods) began to challenge this internal structure. As science grew in importance within medicine so the importance of social status declined. The new majority began to fight for the status and power that had previously been the preserve of the old physicians. This fight was fuelled by both social and material ambition. Having spent one thousand pounds on his training, the general practitioner nonetheless was not differentiated by the public from the herbalists, druggists and midwives with whom he competed.[24] The effect on the material livelihoods and social status of the regulars was dramatic. This was seen in both the United States and the United Kingdom where many regulars were driven from practice into trade.[25]

Returning to the health care market as a whole, as has already been suggested fiscal reward was not the sole concern of the regulars. Social status was also an issue of great concern. The regulars of both the United States and the United Kingdom were traditionally relatively wealthy and educated members of the middle classes.[26] In sharp contrast to this, those offering alternative models of health care were generally from the working classes. Compounding this, it was generally women who were seen to challenge the regulars' market. In the United States, the ranks of the irregular health providers involved not only the working class and women but also slaves.[27] As the number of irregulars increased, the regular physicians saw themselves as threatened by association within the unregulated health care market.

Licensing Status

With this confluence of concerns the old school regulars perceived the need to improve the occupational and therefore social status of medicine. Such change could only be facilitated through the use of licensing laws, yet licensing laws could only be attained upon the regulars asserting their supremacy over competing models of health care. This created an obvious dilemma, as Kristin Luker writes: 'Physicians faced the paradox that they could not obtain licensing laws until they were "better" than the competition, but becoming "better" depended on having licensing laws.'[28] As she continues: 'The way in which physicians solved this problem was to bring them to the center of the abortion debate.'[29] Yet it is arguable that Luker has underplayed the causative relationship – a relationship which is examined in this chapter. Luker's statement suggests an existing pro-life/pro-choice debate, a debate possibly of the ferocity that we understand today. It also, more importantly, suggests a lack of tactical intent on the part of the regular physicians. Luker's expression suggests that the regulars were inadvertently manoeuvred into the centre of an existing debate, rather than instigating the debate and constructing themselves at its centre. Yet prior to the construction of abortion as a means of improving medicine's occupational status, little by way of a debate or issue existed. Rather the abortion issue appears to have arisen out of the medical campaign. To an extent Luker recognizes this when she states:

> · within [the] complex backdrop against which the first ... debate on abortion emerged, we can trace a more direct social struggle. The most visible interest group agitating for more restrictive abortion laws was composed of elite or 'regular' physicians, who actively petitioned state legislatures to pass anti-abortion laws and undertook through popular writings a campaign to change public opinion on abortion. The efforts of these physicians were probably the single most important influence in bringing about nineteenth-century anti-abortion laws.[30]

Explicit in Luker's statement is the fact that public opinion did not oppose abortion, at least not before quickening. Yet in the first half of the nineteenth century the public was not alone in what at best may be called its quiet acquiesence. Neither government, church nor press opposed abortion before quickening, or at least not absolutely: 'In the early decades of the nineteenth century, when politicians, clergy, and press were silent on the question of abortion, then doctors began a concerted campaign, directed at fellow practitioners, legislators, religious leaders, and the public at large, to put abortion on the national agenda.'[31]

Of the institutional responses, the passivity of organized religion appears most difficult to marry with contemporary institutional attitudes towards abortion and supports this view of medicine's involvement.[32] Whilst organized religions are closely associated with the abortion issue today, the evolution of anti-abortion attitudes owes relatively little to the influence or the activities of organized religion.[33] Religious indifference, like governmental indifference, became a target for medical criticism.[34] Similarly, the press became a target for the medical campaign, not simply in its acquiesence but in its failure to prohibit the advertising of 'female medicines'.[35] Support was given to moves to prosecute such advertisers,[36] and the existence of these adverts was seen as: 'an episode at once disgraceful and nefarious'.[37] The presence of advertisements for cures for 'female irregularities' was seen as contradictory to the high moral quality of the press. The *British Medical Journal* regarded their presence as 'an ugly blot on the deservedly high character of our press in general',[38] while the *Lancet* remarked: 'The consequence is that our apostles of purity are too often the purveyors of filth and the vehicles of indecency.'[39]

The breadth of the regulars' campaign – against fellow doctors, politicians, clergy, press and general public – suggests the construction of an 'issue' rather than, as Luker suggests, an involvement in a pre-existing campaign. Whilst I want to move on to argue that the anti-abortion stance was motivated by political objectives, I do not want to suggest that the medical campaign is reducible solely to issues of occupational enhancement. There is a greater complexity evident. Opposition to abortion was motivated, not only by concerns for status enhancement, but also by broader medical and social anxieties regarding gender and class. These seemingly disparate anxieties became inextricably entwined (with each other and with abortion) in the process of medical assertion and professionalization. The physicians, in their campaign to criminalize abortion, corporealized the preoccupations of civic governance and their own parochial professional concerns. The female body became the repository for social concerns, contemporary anxieties and the professional aspirations of physicians. Chapter 2 will consider the role of these broader concerns and anxieties in the regulars' campaign. More immediately, the following review of the nature of professionalization provides a theoretical framework for a more detailed analysis of the regulars' anti-abortion campaign.

The Professionalization of Medicine

> The practice of medicine has from time immemorial been shared by orthodox and unorthodox attendants. (F. Cartwright, *A Social History of Medicine* (London: Longman, 1977), 40)

Traditional sociological analysis of the professions and of professionalization has utilized functionalist and 'trait' paradigms. Parsonian analysis, for example, may be understood as stating that illness creates a situation with certain psychological tensions and that men create norms to reduce these tensions. These norms are orientated towards maximizing the performance of socially useful tasks and, therefore, are fundamental for maintaining the social system. In the case of the medical profession, the social function is the prevention of 'too low a general level of health' and thereby the prevention of dysfunctional incapacitation of members. Illness itself, in this perspective, is defined as those conditions which incapacitate men for meeting their social responsibilities.[40]

Such systems of analysis, however, have done little to question the political and dynamic nature of these occupations, providing 'little more than professional ideology cloaked in value-neutral garb'.[41] The 1970s, however, saw a radical reconceptualization in sociological understanding of the professions: the profession became understood, not in terms of altruism or service, but in terms of power. This has provided the focal point for a new critical sociology of the professions.[42]

Terence Johnson, in his work, *Professions and Power*, saw professionalization as a structural means of controlling occupational activities. Whilst Johnson developed an increasingly structural interpretation within his subsequent work,[43] his central assertion (professionalization as a strategy for occupational control) has remained pivotal in the sociology of the professions. Eliot Freidson, for example, has distinguished the attainment of the right of an occupation to control its own work through legitimate organized autonomy as the primary feature of a profession.[44] Professionalization has also been defined as a process of exclusionary closure designed to control occupational supply. Such control, or management, of the supply facilitates the enhancement of the market value of that occupation.[45] The process of occupational closure has also been seen as a means of social closure and social advancement.[46] Within these paradigms the concept of power remains focal.

Yet how is this power achieved? How, for instance, did medicine attain the licensing laws and occupational closure it enjoys today? The answer appears to lie in the concept of special knowledge: 'Professional movements [are] essentially organizational projects, aimed at a specific form of monopoly based on a complex model of market organization and control ... . Professionalization is essentially about market power and the construction of a formal knowledge base.'[47] It is arguable, however, that knowledge has a more causative role. Maglia Larson has argued that knowledge facilitates the attainment of power: 'I see professionalization as a process by which producers of special services sought to constitute *and control* a market for their expertise ... . Professionalization is thus an attempt to translate one order of scarce resources – special knowledge and skills – into another – social and economic rewards.'[48] Professionalization may therefore be seen as a process of market manipulation, a 'professional project':[49] occupational closure attained through the reification of special knowledge. This reification was essential to the emergence of the medical profession. It facilitated the elimination of the considerable and diverse competition and the concomitant creation of a single market for medical services. The pursuit of professional status necessitated the soliciting of legislative sanctions against competition within the health care market. As noted, sanctions in the form of licensing laws would only accrue to the regulars upon distinguishing themselves from their competitors. This was achieved through medicine unifying 'its cognitive base and establish[ing] cognitive exclusiveness'.[50]

What this chapter argues is that this cognitive exclusiveness was achieved, in part, through the anti-abortion stance of regular medicine in the nineteenth century. Regular practitioners asserted their proficiency through a general adherence to a scientific model. Abortion was very much part of this – notwithstanding a lack of any real coherent clinical approach. Campaigning for abortion law reform facilitated a claim to superior scientific knowledge. The regulars could also claim to follow the Hippocratic oath. Thus they presented themselves as demonstrably both scientifically more knowledgeable and more morally rigorous than their competitors.[51] In this way the abortion issue provided a basis which was lacking in their general medical knowledge and skills, for in that the regulars were largely indistinguishable from the quacks: 'The established physicians of the [nineteenth century] as a group ultimately lacked a basis upon which to solidify their elite status, because they could not do what they claimed to do. They could not cope very well with the human diseases of the day.'[52] In addition to this, many of the remedies utilized by the regulars were similar to, if not the same as, those used by the irregulars. Indeed, whilst the regulars vehemently opposed quack theories, many of the irregulars advocated courses of treatment which were actually less detrimental to health than the regulars' own. Campaigning for reform of the abortion law therefore provided a means of opposing the practices of the irregulars, a means which because of these similarities had previously been illusory. The general inability to prolong life left the issue of abortion, understood in terms of the assertion of biomedical expertise over questions of the inception of life, as perhaps the only vehicle for occupational enhancement.

Abortion and Professionalization

Men interested in establishing their professional authority … encouraged other men to assert their political authority over women's role in reproduction by criminalising the means of controlling birth, each acting to preserve life in the social order as they knew it. (R. Siegel, 'Reasoning from the Body: A Historical

Perspective on Abortion Regulation and Questions of Equal Protection', *Stanford Law Review*, **44**, (1992), 261, at 318)

To begin mapping the social investment of questions of reproduction, and the female reproductive system specifically, this chapter attempts to introduce aspects of the biopolitical and medical changes that occurred in the nineteenth century. To achieve this, I have begun by sketching the occupational status and knowledge of medicine in the eighteenth and early nineteenth centuries. I have also asserted that, prior to the medical campaign to criminalize abortion, it was largely tolerated both by a sizable number of doctors and by the institutions of the state. Having subsequently outlined a sociological analysis of the professions, the aim now, using this outline, is to demonstrate the degree to which the opposition of regular medicine to abortion was associated with, and used to achieve, status enhancement.

The United Kingdom

Although the collegiate guild structure had been in existence since the sixteenth century (at least in the case of the Royal College of Physicians), the overall cohesion and structure of medicine, as has already been noted, was very limited at the beginning of the nineteenth century. While local medical societies had existed towards the end of the eighteenth century, the Provincial Medical and Surgical Association, which was to become the British Medical Association, was not constituted until 1832. However, this did not prevent some regulars attempting to effect abortion legislation. Indeed, the influence of medical involvement can be detected in the initial statutory treatment of abortion in Lord Ellenborough's Act of 1803.

Before 1803, only abortion after quickening – the point at which the woman first experienced movement of the foetus – was punishable by law. This was largely a matter for the ecclesiastical courts and was seldom considered by the common law courts.[53] During this period an abortion after quickening was treated as a misdemeanor. The 1803 Act made abortion a felony. While section 2 of the Act made abortion before quickening punishable for the first time, it was punished less severely than abortion after quickening. The provision of the Act had clearly followed the condemnation of abortion by medical men.[54] Medical influence in the legal regulation of abortion became more obvious, however, with the enactment of subsequent statutory provisions.

After Lord Ellenborough's Act, the law regulating abortion was left untouched by the legislature until 1828. Lord Lansdowne's Act of that year removed an anomaly created by Lord Ellenborough's Act that had meant only attempts made after quickening with poison were criminal.[55] Instrumental attempts after quickening were left unpunished, although this was not so before quickening.[56] The influence of the medical profession in effecting the 1828 changes is suggested in an article published in 1832 in the *Legal Examiner*: 'Now medical men found great fault with this statute, on the ground that medicines administered internally, rarely produced abortion, when the child is what is vulgarly called quickened. But the effect can be infallibly secured by instruments.'[57]

The heavy penalties provided for by the 1803 Act, however, were left substantially unchanged. Abortion was to remain a capital offence until the Offences Against the Person Act 1837. Like the preceding Acts of 1803 and 1828, the 1837 Act was consolidatory legislation. Its aim was largely to rationalize the law relating to criminal offences against the person. The Act also came in the footsteps of the 1836 report of the Criminal Law Commissioners.[58] The report had strongly criticized the provision of the death penalty for a broad range of offences. The Commission noted that the death penalty frustrated attempts to secure conviction, undermining any deterrent effect such a penalty may hold. With specific reference to the provisions of the Lansdowne Act, the Commission noted how prosecutors were reluctant to follow a capital charge, juries were unlikely to convict and judges were correspondingly willing to interpret the law in the defendant's favour.[59]

Although after 1837 abortion was no longer a capital offence, the Offences Against the Person Act removed the distinction that had previously been upheld between pre- and post-quickening abortions. In effect, the law was extended. While abortion was no longer a capital offence, the penalties provided by the Act remained draconian. The law provided, with the discretion of the court, for those found guilty under the act 'to be transported beyond the seas for the term of his or her life, or for any term not less than fifteen years, or to be imprisoned for any term not exceeding three years'.[60] The possibility of transportation for life was to remain until the Offences Against the Person Act 1861. The 1861 Act, which presents the law in its present form,[61] provides a maximum penalty of life imprisonment.[62] The Act also explicitly provides for attempted self-abortion,[63] and liability for obtaining or supplying means knowing they are to be used contrary to the Act.[64] Referring to the anti-abortion legislation introduced between 1803 and 1861, Keown notes:

> The gradual extension of the law and its persistent severity can be seen not only as a reflection of the harshness of the contemporary criminal code as a whole but also as a response to proposals for reform, advanced by the emerging medical profession, which were incorporated into a programme of consolidation of the criminal law.[65]

Medicine had vociferously and successfully lobbied Parliament for reform of the law. While calls for reform may have included genuine concern for the safeguarding of foetal and maternal life, such concern appears inconsistent with the medical skill and practice of the period. Why was abortion being opposed in the name of securing maternal health when, for much of the period in question, childbirth and abortion carried similar risks of maternal fatality?[66] Why was it opposed when new medical knowledge had made terminations safer than at any time before? Why was there opposition when it was clear that most regulars condoned abortion when medically indicated,[67] and some when non-medically indicated?[68]

As has already been suggested, the answers appear to lie in the assertion of special knowledge, the construction of medical knowledge as qualitatively superior to that of competing schools and, indeed, the knowledge of the pregnant woman. Regular medicine energetically opposed abortion and the quickening doctrine in order to assert new medical knowledge. It allowed regulars to distinguish themselves from the irregulars. Implicit in this opposition was the emergence of a new reproductive ethics. The rise of bioethics may be seen as integral to the rise of the medical profession, as Berlant has written: 'Medical ethics can be an organizational tool for organizing physicians for monopolization ... they are appropriate for ordering the conduct of physicians, redefining the organization of the profession as nonmonopolistic and legitimizing licensing privileges.'[69] The ethical stance against abortion was clearly part of the process of redefinition. Opposing abortion became an assertion of moral superiority and a means of attaining internal cohesion. Medical responses to the legislative tolerance of the popular theory of quickening provides a clear illustration.[70]

The common law reliance upon the quickening doctrine and its legislative validation in the Acts of 1803 and 1828 became a focus for medicine's professional project. The legislature's support for the theory was strongly challenged. Beck and Dunlop, for example, claimed of the legislature that 'They tempt to the perpetration of the same crime at one time which at another they punish with death.'[71] Rather more acerbic, Michael Ryan exclaimed, three years after the introduction of the 1803 Act,

> The law of this empire is extremely defective on abortion, for it abounds with the greatest absurdities. Its intention is humane and excellent, but it is based upon erroneous physiological principles. It enacts, for instance, that the embryo is not animated until after quickening, that is until half the period of uterogestation has lapsed, tho' the foetus is alive from the very moment of conception.[72]

In the year before the legislature was to invalidate the doctrine with its repeal in the Offences Against the Person Act 1837, the medical jurisprude

Professor Thomson remarked how 'extraordinary' the 1803 distinction had been, given medical knowledge at that time. The provision represented 'a singular instance of the difficulty of rooting out prejudice from the mind'.[73] As a corollary to this, he professed the need for the legislature to heed medical opinion in questions of physiology: 'This distinction with respect to the periods in which criminal abortion is effected, demonstrates, very strongly, the necessity of lawyers and statesmen consulting medical men, prior to framing Acts which involve physiological questions.'[74]

This call for deference to medical opinion reflected the deeper intent of medicine: not solely to create a single market for health care, but also to be able to define that market. The role of ethics in social, economic and political assertion becomes clear. This ability to define is central to the nature of professions:

> It is part of being a profession to be given the official power to define and therefore create the shape of problematic segments of social behaviour; the judge determines what is legal and who is guilty, the priest what is holy and who is profane, the physician what is normal and who is sick.[75]

Opposition to the quickening distinction fostered this ability to define. Yet, while embryology and reproductive ethics had been used to define, it also became used to discriminate. Once medicine had persuaded the medical and non-medical worlds that the ability of the pregnant woman to sense the movements of the foetus marked no significant stage in embryonic development, and that an abortion carried out at any stage of pregnancy was a heinous crime, 'an evil of the highest magnitude',[76] medicine began a campaign of association. In a clear move to force occupational closure, to assert one market for health care, the regulars broadcast as synonymous the moral and criminal offence of abortion and the practice of medicine by the irregular practitioners. Medicine was clearly attempting to 'translate one order of scarce resources – special knowledge ... into another – social and economic rewards'.[77] With medical criticism of abortion and the quickening doctrine becoming realized in legal changes (medical knowledge therefore receiving a degree of state validation), the association between abortion and quack, or irregular, practioners grew. More specifically, abortion and the continued failure of the legislature to proscribe unqualified practice were increasingly projected as synonymous. Importantly, this very clear association was pursued regardless of the lack of homogeneity in the regular physicians' attitudes towards and practice of abortion. Regular physicians' involvement in abortion was, however, the subject of occasional censure: 'There is a class of physicians who treat this subject with so much indifference that they sanction rather than discountenance the crime. In mild terms they object to employing the means to produce an abortion, and yet suggest the remedies by which it may be accomplished.'[78]

On the rare occasions when the stark dichotomy of regular and irregular was recognized as fictitious, criticism was levelled against those who occupied the seldomly acknowledged twilight between regular and irregular, physician and quack:

> There is still another class of medical men, standing on the boundary between legitimate medicine and quackery, who both advocate and practise abortion. They assume a sanctimonious air and a clerical dress, and under this specious guise practise the black art of the abortionists. They are found in the most respectable medical circles, and make their professional associations subserve their base purposes.[79]

An almost militant stand against abortion was, therefore, advised to distinguish the regulars. The political manipulation of abortion is graphic:

> Every physician should resolve not only to discourage this crime, but in all cases where the evidence is positive, expose irregular doctors, druggists, and female accoucheurs who engage in the business. Every *true physician* should be upright, just, and honest, and thus secure an honourable position amongst all good citizens.[80]

Rather more energy, however, was expended on the public campaign tying abortion to the practice of medicine by the irregulars. The *Lancet*, for example, took a rather confrontational and vitriolic stance. An editorial that had followed the prosecution of two irregular practitioners for abortion employed the language of vice, infamy and disgrace. The journal warned:

> there hangs upon the skirts of our noble profession a pestilent race ever ready to pander to vice, and who seem to wield the broken scraps and fragments of medical knowledge, picked up in the by-ways of life, with no other purpose than illicit gain, and with no other effect than ruin and misery to their victims.[81]

Graphically, the article highlighted the evils of abortion as the direct consequence of the free market in medicine. It continued:

> It is not to be endured that the defect of our laws or their lax administration should tolerate the reckless assumption of medical practice by the ignorant and the unprincipled, who by parading the false insignia and titles of our profession are thus confounded in the eyes of the public with honourable men, and permitted to vilify and discredit an honourable profession.[82]

Abortion was broadcast as not only the product of an unregulated market, but also as an independent and extensive trade, 'a regularly established, money making business carried on by ... Herods of both sexes'.[83] One correspondent, who signed himself 'Disgusted', remarked forcefully: 'There is no question that the large majority of these people make their living by preying upon the fears of erring women.'[84] The perceived lucrative nature of providing abortion services was frequently used to bolster charges of immorality and probably reflected one of the regulars' primary concerns. A report in the *British Medical Journal* in 1870 regarding 'mock confinements and abortion mongering' appears typical of such reports:

> We know that there are many abortion mongers who depend entirely for their living on this vile traffic in which they are engaged, and whose practices remain secret. Some of them obtain large sums from their victims; and, as both are equally criminal, it is to their mutual interest to preserve silence, however serious may be the consequences which ensue.[85]

Reflecting the desire for occupational closure, and the association constructed between abortion and the irregulars, medicine was also keen that in the reporting of abortion cases the courts and the media ensured that they reported accurately, not referring to all abortionists as 'doctors'. Subsequent to the reporting of the case of Henry Timson at the Old Bailey, for example, the *Lancet* remarked:

> It would be satisfactory were officers of justice to take the trouble to refer to the authorised Medical Register before accepting the claim of every ignorant quack to the honourable titles of the profession; and we may mention for the police courts that there is ... now an authorised annual list of medical students, by reference to which the magistrate might distinguish the rowdies who occasionally claim the title from the real Simon Pures.[86]

The way in which the regulars constructed abortion and the practice of medicine by the irregulars as almost synonymous allowed the regulars to 'blame' the legislature for the alleged prevalence of abortion. After the physicians had campaigned to convince the non-medical world that abortion was 'a grave crime',[87] 'a pestilent traffic',[88] and 'one of the most despicable, loathsome, and enormous of human crimes',[89] the regulars offered the legislature an easy way of tackling the problem, a way favourable to their professional concerns. Designing abortion and quackery as inter-related, emphasizing the 'correlation between vice, depravity, crime, and the practice of medicine by unqualified persons',[90] implicitly allowed the legislature to legislate against abortion by legislating against the irregulars:

We have, in the first place, again to express our reluctant opinion that society and the Legislature, which foster and sanction the illegitimate and irresponsible practice of medicine, are deeply to blame. If the practice of medicine in every form by the unskilled, the illiterate, the unscrupulous, be tolerated, is it not hypocrisy to wonder that the appliances of medicine are systematically perverted to the foulest and most abominable ends?[91]

The solution was simple: 'The first and foremost urgent remedy then is to suffer no one to practise medicine whose qualifications have not been approved by competent means, and whose conduct is not guaranteed by his education, his social position, and the controlling influence of professional and public observation.'[92] Even after the passing of the 1861 Act, the law was seen as offering too little by way of intervention. Commenting on the case of a Mr Humpage in 1862, it was dramatically remarked: 'The tribe of miscreants who profit by the felonious traffic in "female irregularities" are stained with the darkest hue of criminality; and of all the mysteries of this modern Babylon, there is none that requires more than this trade the searching intervention of justice'.[93] Warning of the 'horrible abyss which threaten[ed] to engulf so many more and an increasing number of victims', an editorial in the *Lancet* provided probably the most forthright and graphic call for legislative action:

> The practice of foeticide *must be put to a stop*; the trade in abortion *must have an end* … . The whole system is bad – the system of allowing any ignorant knave to practise what delusion or bestiality he chooses, and any ignorant old woman to term herself a midwife. It is evidently amongst these people that the active instruments of mischief lie.[94]

Illustrating the functional nature of 'medical ethics', the journal juxtaposed with these bestial 'ignorant knaves' the gilded regulars:

> The code of medical ethics, the high sense of honour pervading the legitimate ranks of the profession, as well as the ordinary rules of mortality, effectually prevent, of course, all pandering upon the part of medical practitioners, either to the depraved sentiments of the higher classes, or to the criminal desires of the lower ranks. The evil lies at the door of a loathsome parasitical race which preys upon the follies and vices of mankind. They are slayers of the body and polluters of the mind. They are of the hybrid growth of rampant, barefaced charlatanry, and vicious desires.[95]

Presented with this dramatic and almost theatrical Jekyll and Hyde duality in the provision of health care and its effects upon the nation's health, the article challenged those who supported a free market in health care. It concluded with a call 'for some direct interference of the Legislature for the purpose of arresting the crying shame'.[96]

Yet criticism was made, not solely of the general laissez-faire policy towards health care, but also of the failure of the legislature to accord the medical colleges some degree of autonomy, of self-governance. Freidson's emphasis on the right of an occupation to control its own work becomes apposite.[98] Commenting on the case of a successful prosecution for criminal abortion, a leading article in the *British Medical Journal* called for medical reform: 'Criminal abortion is, we fear, a much more common crime than many of the good and just amongst us may suppose; and we therefore deeply deplore that the medical colleges cannot rid the profession of miscreants who are found out in the commission of this sinful and horrible practice.'[98] Criminal abortion therefore provided a vanguard for calls for occupational autonomy in terms of the ability of the profession to define behavioural standards, as well as the dominant medical model. Abortion facilitated demands for far-reaching reform: 'No one can save the medical profession from sharing in the disgrace of such discoveries, till there is a legal register of qualified practitioners, and a medical council, with power to erase from it the names of delinquents.'[99]

The nature of the medical campaign is perhaps most clearly illustrated by the way in which the use of abortion in an attempt to achieve occupational enhancement overtly surpassed any 'ethical' objection to abortion. Indeed, questions of reform appear generally to have been of far greater concern to the medical body than the issue of abortion *per se*.[100] This former assertion is strongly evidenced in the open construction of abortion as an 'opportunity' for reform:

> We would earnestly say to our colleges, that an opportunity presently exists, such as never before existed for obtaining a useful measure of medical reform; and that with such scandals ... damaging our social reputation, it becomes a duty to meet each other in the spirit of the most liberal concession as regards our class interests, and to rally ... in obtaining at least an instalment of reform in the present parliament.[101]

The article concluded that this opportunity should be pursued regardless of whether or not practitioners actually ethically objected to abortion. This call for a 'brotherly and patriotic spirit of mutual *concession*'[102] belies the monolithic and unified image which the profession attempted to broadcast externally. It belies the simple, clear and universal ethical objection to abortion that was claimed by the profession. This is emphasized by the suggestion that questions of detail be dealt with privately, within the purely medical environment:

Nothing will tend more to the accomplishment of reform than our pouring petitions in profusion upon the table of the House of Commons. By signing such a form of petition as we published last week, no one will compromise his individual opinions upon matters of detail; and those who have strong views upon any matters of special difficulty, can easily make them known through the medical journals, or through the medical committees.[103]

As a result of this professional lobbying, Parliament enacted the Medical Act 1858. In part the Act responded to the regulars' objective of occupational enhancement by establishing a register of qualified practitioners, although it did not proscribe the practice of quack medicine. While these associations and criticisms failed to secure occupational closure, within this period, they did secure legislation which was seen as limiting the irregulars' scope of practice. Section 59 of the Offences Against the Person Act 1861 prohibits the supplying or obtaining of the means of abortion. Importantly, this provision translates into law the regulars' perception of abortion as the irregulars' primary means of economic survival. Similarly, the enactment of section 58 of the 1861 Act provided that pregnancy need not be a necessary element of an offence under the Act when committed by a third party. This provision has been interpreted as reflecting a general belief in the dangers posed to women by abortion: 'The reason assigned for the punishment of abortion is not that, thereby an embryo human being is destroyed, but that it rarely or never can be effected ... without the sacrifice of the mother's life.'[104]

John Keown asks why, if women were perceived as the victims of abortion, was self-abortion criminalized?[105] Yet, arguably, it would be more revealing to ask why, if the dangers of invasive abortion techniques were the primary consideration of the legislature, was attempted self-abortion when the woman was not pregnant kept outside the criminal law? If a woman's health is to be protected, should not attempted abortion be an offence regardless of whether a pregnancy existed or not? Arguably there is a removal of the woman from much of the discourse surrounding abortion. This removal and the translation of this into statute, illuminates the primary focus of medicine and the legislature: the abortionist/quack, rather than the act of termination. While the profession had failed to achieve occupational closure, the enactment of these provisions was a move towards this professional aspiration – prohibiting a procedure which it was believed irregular practitioners were finding profitable – and increasingly so.[106]

Following the enactment of the 1861 Act, opposition to abortion did not, however, cease. As the 1861 Act had failed to proscribe the practice of medicine by the 'unqualified', the regulars maintained a campaign highlighting the immorality and danger in a 'free trade in physic'. In one example, in discussing the death of a woman from Brighton after 'taking ergot of rye for the purpose of procuring abortion',[107] the *British Medical Journal* reported: 'Several questions of interest turned up during the enquiry. Who supplied the medicine? Who prescribed?'[108] As a rather secondary consideration it was asked: 'What are the symptoms of a poisonous dose of ergot?'[109] Recoding self-interest as public interest, the journal concluded:

> Science comes forward ... and informs justice that a great wrong has been done; that a deadly medicine has been prescribed by a soi-disant 'doctor', of 'clerical appearance', 'the family physician', who is not found ... . Altogether, the affair is just another of the daily occurring proofs of the unsatisfactory condition of the healing art in relation to the public.[110]

The woman, her circumstances and their wider social setting are of little or no concern to the reporter. In the final year of the nineteenth century medicine was still using abortion as a means of seeking occupational closure and enhancement. Commenting on the case of an elderly woman referred to only as 'White' who was convicted of the murder of Alice Birmingham, an editorial in the *Lancet* concluded:

> In a country in which every quack may practise general medicine or surgery until he kills someone there is no logical reason why a woman who cares to run a small risk should not do the same in a special department without her qualifications or her methods being subjected to the smallest inquiry.[111]

In the nineteenth century, therefore, the medical profession, in the process of occupational assertion, managed to effect considerable changes to the law regulating abortion. This success entrenched within the law the ideology of the regulars and the deference to medical opinion that the regulars had sought. While there appeared a degree of genuine ethical objection to the common law status of abortion,[112] this appeared secondary to more parochial considerations, as McLaren writes: 'The early abortion laws were more a consequence of the medical and legal professions' attempts to serve their own interests than to affect directly fertility.'[113] Opposition to abortion based on 'knowledge' of the embryo became a means of self-interested differentiation. This occurred notwithstanding the rather amorphous nature of health provision at the time, and the fact that both regular and irregular practitioners provided abortions.[114] To seek to criminalize abortion became, nonetheless, a means of criminalizing alternative models of health care. The origins of the 1803 Act and subsequent attempts to shape legislation may therefore, in part, be located within 'the effort launched by doctors, as part of the process of their professionalization, to eliminate both rival practitioners such as midwives and their non-scientific concepts such as quickening'.[115] The same process of assertion, and the same means of assertion, were evident in the United States in the nineteenth century.

The United States: the Example of Ohio

In the landmark case of *Roe* v. *Wade*,[116] the Supreme Court recognized three possible justifications for the enactment of restrictive abortion provisions in the nineteenth century. Initially, Blackmun J, who delivered the opinion of the court, considered the argument that 'these laws were the product of a Victorian social concern to discourage illicit sexual conduct'.[117] This possible motivation was rejected out of hand by the court, Blackmun J remarking that: 'no court or commentator has taken this argument seriously'.[118] Secondly, the court considered, more favourably, that the provisions were the result of legislative paternalism, safeguarding the health of women against a procedure which at that time posed considerable risks to the woman's health. As the court noted, it could be argued that the 'real concern in enacting a criminal abortion law was to protect the pregnant woman, that is, to restrain her from submitting to a procedure that placed her life in serious jeopardy'.[119] Lastly, the court considered that: 'a purpose of these laws, when enacted, was to protect prenatal life'.[120] The court considered these histories, but it left the issue unresolved. It did, however, recognize a state interest in the foetus, suggesting at least a superficial support for the last of these rationales.[121] Yet, as in the United Kingdom, the passage of restrictive abortion provisions in the United States was intimately tied to the occupational concerns of medicine.

According to James Mohr, 'Prior to the physicians' crusade [in the nineteenth century] most states had taken a cautious, ambiguous, or defensive attitude towards abortion.'[122] Whereas at the opening of the nineteenth century most states did not directly criminalize abortion, by its close abortion was almost uniformly illegal.[123] Although there existed a uniformity in this respect, there appeared little consistency in the severity of the punishment provided for by legislation, or in the treatment of the common law immunities.[124] As in the United Kingdom, and as already noted, the primary group campaigning for restrictive legislation were the emerging regular physicians.

The rise in power of the Republican Party facilitated the success of the regulars' campaign. With the Republicans' predisposition to rationalization and bureaucracy, and their susceptibility to the influence and teachings of experts and professionals, state legislatures reacted sympathetically to the regulars' claims. In the first half of the century, the regulars worked covertly, predominantly working with the legislatures reforming state criminal codes. Only in the second half of the century did the campaign enter a more public arena, as Reva Siegel notes:

By 1859, medical opponents of abortion had secured a resolution from the American Medical Association condemning abortion as an 'unwarranted destruction of human life', and under the leadership of Horatio Storer, elite physicians launched an aggressive public campaign dedicated to saving the nation from the evils of abortion.[125]

Horatio Storer, the son of Dr David Humphrey Storer, professor of obstetrics and medical jurisprudence at Harvard and president of the American Medical Association (AMA), was to play a pre-eminent role in the criminalization of abortion. Storer served as secretary to the AMA in 1865, and as its vice-president in 1868. In 1864, the AMA established a prize and the promise of publication for 'the best popular tract upon the subject of induced abortion'.[126] Perhaps unsurprisingly, Horatio Storer's submission, 'The Criminality and Criminal Evils of Forced Abortion', was awarded the gold medal for 1865. The prize committee, comprising Boston's elite physicians, had been chaired by D. Humphrey Storer, Horatio's eminent father.[127] The essay was published in book form by the AMA under the title, *Why Not? A Book for Every Woman*.[128] The range of the book was important. While permeated throughout by 'scare propaganda'[129] aimed at women, the extended essay also addressed male policy makers. *Why Not?* was well received both medically and in the popular press, and sold well for five years. This was followed by *Is It I? A Book for Every Man*.[130] In 1868, reflecting the breadth of the campaign, Storer co-authored, with Franklin Fiske Heard, a third volume: *Criminal Abortion: Its Nature, Its Evidence and Its Law*.[131] This third volume, unlike the preceding volumes, was intended for a legal readership. *Criminal Abortion* examined the law relating to abortion in considerable detail, coupling law with the statistics available to bolster Storer's previous contentions.

These volumes were designed as the Gospel of a united profession. Yet, as in the United Kingdom, medical commentators were repeatedly demanding the censure of those regulars willing to provide abortion services and encouraging fellow doctors to testify against abortionists. Indeed, the report delivered by the AMA's Committee on Criminal Abortion, which was appointed to investigate criminal abortion 'with a view to its general suppression', recognized three causes of this 'general demoralization'.[132] The Committee reported that amongst 'the agents alluded to is the fact that the profession themselves are frequently supposed careless of foetal life'.[133] Yet Storer's tracts were peppered with allusions to unity. Unity was suggested with Storer's repeated claims to be 'viewing the matter from a professional standpoint' and informing his readership that 'the views I represent are those accepted by the physicians of our time most competent to judge'.[134]

The nexus between abortion and professionalization was as direct in the United States as in the United Kingdom. When the secretary of the AMA requested state-of-the-profession reports from affiliated societies in 1879, nine of these state organizations mentioned anti-abortion campaigns as among their professional activities.[135] A more specific example may be found in the creation of the Baltimore Medical Association, a response by the regulars to their dissatisfaction with the organization and, more importantly, professionalism of the Medical and Chirurgical Faculty of Maryland, a regular society affiliated to the University of Maryland School in Baltimore.[136]

The aims of the new Association were aided greatly by the successful election of Dr Eli Henkle to the State Senate in the winter of 1866. In the first year in office, Henkle introduced a bill 'for the protection of the public against medical imposters'.[137] The bill aimed at providing a licensing procedure involving a board of medical examiners to ensure the quality of the state's practitioners. This would of course involve only the licensing of regulars, the appointees of the board of medical examiners being 'respectable physicians, graduates of some recognised school of medicine'.[138]

In the lower house the bill was amended by the addition of two new sections. Section 16 created harsh penalties for the performing of an abortion, and barred advertising and commercial dealings in abortion services or abortifacients. Section 17 called for the new bill to be law immediately upon its passing through both houses. After considerable debate in the house of delegates, the proposals were passed and the bill became law.[139] In essence, Maryland's first anti-abortion statute was intimately tied to the provision of monopolistic occupational closure. Indeed, the provisions appear secondary to the licensing aim of the legislation. Importantly, the legislation is also suggestive of the success of the Maryland regulars' campaign which had used the evils of abortion to illustrate the need for an end to the laissez-faire free market approach to the provision of health care.[140] The influence and success of the medical campaign to criminalize abortion and the emerging deference to (official) medical opinion are possibly most clearly witnessed in the example of Ohio.

The pattern of medical lobbying and legislative action in the state of Ohio lends insight into the process of adoption of anti-abortion policies in the United States in the nineteenth century. As in other states, and as in the United Kingdom, pressure for change originated with the regulars. In 1867, two anti-abortion statutes were enacted in the state of Ohio as a direct result of the lobbying and advocacy of the state's physicians. The quickening requirement that had been enshrined in prior legislation was removed by the first Act. The Act made it a 'high misdemeanour' to attempt, advise or devise instruments for abortion which caused the death of an 'embryo, or foetus, or mother'.[141] The Act provided for a custodial sentence of between one and seven years on conviction.[142] It had replaced an 1834 statute which had made a pre-quickening abortion a misdemeanour (punishable by up to one year's imprisonment and/or a fine up to $500) and a post-quickening abortion a high misdemeanour punishable with the same sentence as under the 1867 Act. The second Act was adopted to 'prevent the publication, sale or gratuitous distribution of drugs, medicines and nostrums intended to prevent conception, or procure abortion'.[143] The Act may be seen as a precursor to what became known as the Comstock Act, federal legislation enacted in 1873 which had classified information regarding contraception and abortion as obscene and prohibiting the passing of such information through the mail system.[144]

The Senate special committee which had introduced the legislation published a report in conjunction with the Acts which clearly illustrates the influence of the state's physicians.[145] Importantly, the report also illustrates the multiplicity of concerns, primarily regarding gender, race and class, which motivated the enactment of anti-abortion statutes and which the physicians had manipulated in ensuring their passage. The special committee opened their report by reflecting a concern which probably had most impact on the legislatures – the question of 'race suicide'. The committee recoiled at the 'alarming and increased frequency' of forced abortion which reduced 'the number of children born alive of native American parentage'.[146] By 'native American', the committee and the physicians were referring, not to the indigenous people, but, as revisionists, to the white Anglo-Saxon protestants (WASPs). In a time of increased immigration, with an increasing percentage of the country's population originating from eastern Europe, the Mediterranean countries, Ireland and further afield, the WASPs feared for the racial 'purity' of the country and their economic and social position. This concern had featured in Horatio Storer's texts, and the committee acknowledged that its understanding of the question of abortion had much to do with the AMA and Storer's extended essay, *Why Not?*[147] Storer's influence can be felt throughout the report. The Acts' removal of the quickening distinction, for example, was justified by the committee on medical grounds, relying on Storer's interpretation of the foetal–maternal relationship. The committee quoted directly from Storer's earlier work, *On Criminal Abortion in America*.[148] Yet, apocalyptically, the committee concluded its report with a return to the concern of 'race suicide'. Drawing heavily on Storer's *Why Not?*, the committee claimed that those wives who aborted 'avoided the duties and responsibilities of married life [and were] living in a state of legalised prostitution'. In such a state they denied their racial instincts and placed the health and ultimately the destiny of the race in danger.[149]

The experience of Ohio reflects the influence the medical profession had attained within the legislature. Their campaign against abortion was rewarded by laws which made illegal what was believed to be the economic basis for the practice of medicine by the irregulars. Attaining the moral high ground with the new ethics of reproduction not only allowed the regulars to suppress the irregulars and quacks, but also concomitantly elevated the stature of regular medicine. Legislative deference to the regulars enhanced their status and no doubt helped to facilitate the licensing laws and occupational closure that were to come in the early years of the twentieth century.

Abortion, however, was not to be made uniformly illegal. By the turn of the century, only six of the American states were not to include a therapeutic exception in the formulation of their abortion laws.[150] These clauses typically exempted doctors from prosecution where the abortion was performed to preserve the life of the pregnant woman. Two of the provisions stated that the doctor must be a regular; Maryland's provided for the opinion of a 'respectable' physician.[151] No review procedures were provided for, and only 10 states required consultation with another doctor.[152] The failure of most states to require consultation gave more discretion to individual doctors than even the campaigners had sought. In 1871, the AMA Committee on Criminal Abortion recommended, *inter alia*, that it 'be unlawful and unprofessional for any physician to induce abortion or premature labor, without the concurrent opinion of at least one respectable consulting physician, and then always with a view to the safety of the child – if that be possible'.[153] In this respect, the regular physicians had attained a considerable degree of empowerment. None of the provisions described what constituted a threat to the mother's life. Medical opinion was therefore left largely unregulated, restrained only by the general requirement that the doctor be acting in good faith.[154] The failure of legislatures to define what constituted a threat to the life of the woman reflected, in part, successful medical opposition to legislative control over the profession. Some of the physicians campaigning against abortion opposed legislature which would define exactly what was entailed in the therapeutic exception. Indeed, some of the most ardent activists tended to feel that, on balance, it was better to tolerate, and expect, some abuse in the practice of abortion than to abdicate too much control outside the profession.[155]

The physicians' opposition to abortion therefore appears to be contingent. This contingent nature supports the assertion that a predominant (but by no means sole) rationale for opposition to abortion was the enhancement of the profession. Opposition to abortion appears to be contingent upon the result of opposition favourably shaping the terrain between profession, legislature and public. Where this geography becomes antagonistic to the movement of the profession, dogmatic and entrenched opposition becomes much more fluid: 'In short, the opposition of the regulars to abortion could become quite tempered when it appeared that abortion could be suppressed only at the cost of increased social and legislative control of the medical profession.'[156]

The existence of the therapeutic exception nonetheless had important ramifications. It encapsulated the enhanced status of the physicians, created an exclusive market in some states for the regulars and signalled the entrance of regular (male) medicine into a sphere which up to that point had largely been women's. Within the various state legislatures the profession began almost immediately to consolidate its control over the provision of medical care generally and women's reproductive health care in particular.[157]

Conclusion

The regulars' campaign against abortion in the nineteenth century may be seen as considerably more complex than the Supreme Court's historical reasoning in *Roe* suggests. The overlooked issue of the parochial professional ambitions of an emerging occupational group appears central to legislative changes. The legal regulation of abortion was transformed through medicine's occupational project. Medicine in turn was transformed by the successes of its campaign. Deference, both institutional and social, to medical knowledge and expertise was attained by occupational envy and ambition recoded as moral, ethical and humane concern regarding abortion. The effects of this on health care provision for women have been manifold. Expertise in questions pertaining to abortion quickly became translated into a general expertise in obstetrics and gynaecology and, in order to legitimize control, the necessary construction of the female reproductive system as inherently pathogenic. This has had enduring consequences.

This chapter has detailed the way in which the nineteenth century saw medicine assert itself through the question of abortion. As suggested in the examination of the regulars' campaign both in the United Kingdom and, more graphically, in the state of Ohio, the medical campaign to criminalize abortion was a complex recognition of anxieties prevalent among the middle and upper classes of the time. It is arguable that anti-abortion legislation was attained in part through such legislation being presented as a panacea for these anxieties, as Siegel notes: 'Doctors presented the protection of unborn life as a *means* to various social goals as much as an end in its own right.'[158] The following chapters, building upon this analysis, will consider the extent to which the attainment of *social goals* remains imbricated in the determination of reproductive regulatory provisions. As will be illustrated, within this complexity a central place must be given to issues of gender and, more specifically, the social goal of defining and entrenching appropriate gender roles.

Moving to assert this centrality, Chapter 2 considers the presence of the issue of gender within the campaign just considered. While it is clear that gender may be understood as a socio-cultural construct which the physicians manipulated, it is also clear that this issue was of genuine concern to the physicians both at a personal level and at a collective occupational level. The majority of medicine's competitors were, as has been noted, women. The presence of gender within the regulars' campaign therefore proves interesting in a number of ways. It is interesting in its manipulation by the regulars, in the way it reveals broader social concerns which the regulars were relying on and, finally, in the way this is addressed in the regulation of reproduction.

Notes

1   Although this primacy is arguably under threat from the increasing *media/cultural presence* of the foetus.

2   L. Gordon, 'Review of James Mohr's *Abortion in America: the Origins and Evolution of National Policy*', *Journal of Social History*, **13**, (1980), 514.

3   See R.P. Petchesky, *Abortion and Woman's Choice: The State, Sexuality and Reproductive Freedom* (London: Verso, 1986); B. Malinowski, *Sex, Culture and Myth* (London: Dell, 1967); K. Luker, *Abortion and the Politics of Motherhood* (Berkeley: University of California Press, 1984); J. Mohr, *Abortion in America: The Origins and Evolution of National Policy* (New York: Oxford University Press, 1978); A. McLaren, *Reproductive Rituals: The Perception of Fertility in England from the Sixteenth Century to the Seventeenth Century* (London: Methuen, 1984); G. Devereux, 'A Typological Study of Abortion in 350 Ancient and Pre-Industrial Societies', in H. Rosen (ed.), *Abortion in America* (Boston: Beacon, 1967); H. de Laszlo and P.S. Henshaw, 'Plant Materials Used by Primitive Peoples to Affect Fertility', *Science*, 119, (7 May 1954), 629.

4   B. Smart, *Michel Foucault* (London: Tavistock, 1985), 75.

5   While I aim to consider the use of the issue of abortion by physicians as a means of social and economic advancement, this process of advancement, of professionalization, is itself the product of a *complex network* of influences. As Ivan Waddington illustrates, stressing the interrelationships that have existed between the development of the medical profession and a range of other processes: 'changes in the occupational structure and class structure, the development of a more prosperous society, increasing levels of centralisation of administration, and many other processes [are all] associated both with the development of English society, as an increasingly complex, modern, urban industrial society, and with the emergence of medicine as a modern profession' (I. Waddington, *The Medical Profession in the Industrial Revolution* (Dublin: Gill and Macmillan Humanities Press, 1984)).

6   D.L. Sayers, *Whose Body?* (London: T. Fisher Unwin, 1923), 133.

7   E. Freidson, *Profession of Medicine: A Study in the Sociology of Applied Knowledge* (New York: Harper and Row, 1970), 5.

8   An exception to this was evident in the seventeenth and eighteenth centuries where, according to Mohr, physicians in the United States had enjoyed an elite status. These physicians were 'generally learned men from families of solid social standing and they were looked up to in the colonies of North America' (Mohr, *supra*, at 32).

9   J.W. Willcock, *The Laws Relating to the Medical Profession* (London: 1830), 56.
10   Ibid., at 67.
11   That is, those formally trained in and subscribing to the dominant allopathic model of medicine. Allopathy refers to the curing of a diseased action by inducing another action of a different kind. Allopathy therefore exists as the opposite to homeopathy.
12   M.J. Peterson, *The Medical Profession in Mid-Victorian London* (Berkeley: University of California Press, 1978), 5.
13   Willcock, *supra*, ccxx.
14   Peterson, *supra*, at 5.
15   Luker, *supra*, at 16.
16   Mohr, *supra*, at 31.
17   See 'Effects of Blood-Letting', *BMJ* (31 May 1873), 617; W. Rothstein, *American Physicians in the Nineteenth Century: From Sects to Science* (Baltimore: Johns Hopkins University Press, 1972), 177–90, also George Elliot's *Middlemarch*.
18   See Freidson, *supra*, at 16, 21–2.
19   Willcock, *supra*, at 30.
20   J. Keown, *Abortion, Doctors and the Law* (Cambridge: Cambridge University Press, 1988), 160.
21   14 & 15 Henry VIII.
22   Waddington, *supra*, at 3.
23   *Gentleman's Magazine*, new series, 1 (March 1834), 334.
24   Keown, *supra*, at 161.
25   E.C. Atwater, 'The Medical Profession in a New Society, Rochester, New York (1811–1860)', *Bulletin of the History of Medicine*, **XLVII**, 3, (May–June 1973), 221–35. See also Peterson, *supra*, at 284. Matters were compounded in the United States. Not only was the number of irregulars growing but also the number of regulars. In the United States, an estimated 400 new medical schools opened during the nineteenth century. While numbers increased dramatically, the standard of graduates went into a corresponding decline. The new medical schools existed on a fee-paying basis. They were dependent on these fees for their economic survival and were therefore unwilling to fail students who could be relied upon to furnish them with regular fees. As a consequence, many of the medical schools existed as little more than degree mills, fees buying medical diplomas. See Mohr, *supra*, at 33.
26   See Luker, *supra*, at 27, and Keown, *supra*, at 160–61.
27   Luker, *supra*, at 16.
28   Ibid., at 18.
29   Ibid.
30   Ibid., at 16.
31   R. Siegel, 'Reasoning from the Body: A Historical Perspective on Abortion Regulation and Questions of Equal Protection', *Stanford Law Review*, **44**, (1992), 261, at 282.
32   As McLaren has written: 'The shift in public attitudes towards embryonic life would later be attributed to religious preoccupations with the sanctity of foetal life, to new scientific appreciations with the process of gestation, and to a growing emotional and sentimental concern for the child. But significant, also, were the pragmatic concerns and professional interests of lawyers and doctors seeking to implement laws that would best serve their needs' (*supra*, at 144).
33   Mohr, *supra*, at 195.
34   See, for example, 'This Week', *BMJ* (2 May 1863), 459.
35   See, for example, the 11-article campaign run in *The Lancet* between December 1898

and July 1899: 10, 17, 24 and 31 December 1898; 21 January, 4 February, 11 and 25 March, 1 April, 8 and 15 July 1899.

36 See, for example, 'Abortion Advertisements', *BMJ* (26 February 1898), 578; 'Abortion Advertisements', *BMJ* (12 March 1898), 739; 'Abortion Advertisements', *BMJ* (19 November 1898), 1572; 'The Sale of Abortifacients', *BMJ* (2 December 1899), 1583.

37 'Immoral Advertisements', *The Lancet*, **II**, (1896), 829.

38 'The Traffic in Abortifacients', *BMJ* (14 January 1899), 110.

39 'Immoral Advertisements', *supra*, 836.

40 J.L. Berlant, *Profession and Monopoly: A Study of Medicine in the United States and Great Britain* (Berkeley: University of California Press, 1975), 7.

41 R. Abel, 'The Rise of Professionalism', *Journal of Law and Society*, **6**, (1979), 82. See also T. Johnson, *Professions and Power* (London: Macmillan, 1972), 26.

42 A. Witz, *Professions and Patriarchy* (London: Routledge & Kegan Paul, 1992), 40.

43 T. Johnson, 'Professions in the Class Structure', in R. Scase (ed.), *Industrial Society; Class, Cleavage and Control* (London: Allen & Unwin, 1977); T. Johnson, 'The State and the Professions: Peculiarities of the British', in A. Giddens and G. Mackenzie (eds), *Social Class and the Division of Labour: Essays in Honour of Ilya Neustadt* (Cambridge: Cambridge University Press, 1982).

44 E. Freidson, *Professional Dominance: The Social Structure of Medical Care* (New York: Atherton Press, 1970); also Freidson, *Profession of Medicine, supra*.

45 F. Parkin, *Marxism and Class Theory: A Bourgeois Critique* (London: Tavistock, 1979).

46 N. Parry and J. Parry, *The Rise of the Medical Profession* (London: Croom Helm, 1976).

47 Witz, *supra,* at 56.

48 M.S. Larson, *The Rise of Professionalism: A Sociological Analysis* (London: University of California Press, 1977), xvi–xvii.

49 Witz, *supra*, at 57.

50 Ibid.

51 Luker, *supra,* at 27.

52 Mohr, *supra*, at 32.

53 See B. Dickens, *Abortion and the Law* (Bristol: MacGibbon and Kee Ltd, 1966).

54 Keown, *supra*, at 28.

55 Section 1.

56 Section 2.

57 'Law Lecture', *Legal Examiner*, **3**, (1832–3), 279, at 286.

58 'Second Report From His Majesty's Commissioners on Criminal Law', *Parliamentary Papers XXXVI*, (1836), 183.

59 'Correspondence', *Parliamentary Papers XXXVII* (1837), 31, at 41. See also 'Another Abortionist', *The Lancet*, **I**, (1899), 468.

60 Section 6.

61 Subject to the defences provided for by the Abortion Act 1967.

62 Section 58.

63 Ibid.

64 Section 59.

65 Keown, *supra*, at 27.

66 As Mohr writes, 'Child-birth was just as subject to shock and infection as abortion ... it is difficult to imagine that the death rate from abortion ... exceeded the death rate from child-birth', (Mohr, *supra*, at 30).

67   Although there was agreement that there did exist medically determinable criteria for the induction of an abortion, there existed confusion as to what these were; see, for example, 'Induction of Abortion', *The Lancet*, **I**, (1881), 428.

68   See Mohr, *supra*, at 40 and 49–83.

69   Berlant, *supra*, at 127–8.

70   See T. Denham, *An Introduction to the Practice of Midwifery* (London: J. Johnson, 1794), vol. I, 268; S. Farr, *Elements of Medical Jurisprudence* (London, 1788), 23–4. 'The Remarkable Trial ... of William Pizzy and Mary Codd', *Edinburgh Medical and Surgical Journal* (1810), 248; also T. Percival, *Medical Ethics: Or, a code of Institutes and Precepts Adapted to the Professional Conduct of Physicians and Surgeons ... To Which is Added an Appendix Containing a Discourse on Hospital Duties* (Manchester, 1803), 80.

71   T.R. Beck and W. Dunlop, *Elements of Medical Jurisprudence* (London: Anderson, 1815), 140.

72   M. Ryan, *A Manual of Midwifery* (London: Longman, 1806), 66.

73   A.T. Thomson, 'Lectures on Medical Jurisprudence', *The Lancet* (1836–7), 625, at 626.

74   Ibid.

75   Freidson, *Profession of Medicine, supra*, at 206.

76   Dr. Hutchinson, 'Medical Jurisprudence', *London Medical and Physical Journal* (January 1820), 97.

77   Larson, *supra*, at xvii.

78   'This Week', *BMJ* (2 May 1863), 459, at 460.

79   Ibid.

80   'Criminal Abortion', *BMJ* (26 September 1868), 342 (emphasis added). See also 'Criminal Abortion', *The Lancet*, **I**, (1884), 577; 'The Crime of Procuring Abortion and its Penalties in England and Other Countries', *The Lancet*, **II**, (1893), 153, at 154.

81   'The Charge of Criminal Abortion Before the Lambeth Police-Court', *The Lancet*, **I**, (1853), 432.

82   Ibid.

83   'More Abortionists', *The Lancet*, **I**, (1861), 294, at 295.

84   'Advertising Abortionists', *The Lancet*, **II**, (1896), 1720. See also 'The Frequency of Criminal Abortion', *The Lancet*, **II**, (1853), 101, at 101–2; 'This Week', *BMJ* (2 May 1863), 17. However, the incidence of abortion in this period is hard to gauge. While many within medicine testified to the great extent to which the practice of abortion was carried out, others were more cautious. See, for example, A.T. Thomson, 'Lectures on Medical Jurisprudence, Lecture XVII: Pregnancy', *The Lancet*, **I**, (1836–7), 625.

85   'Mock Confinements and Abortion', *BMJ* (1870), 88.

86   'Abortion Mongers', *The Lancet*, **II**, (1869), 484; see also 'Abortion Producers', *The Lancet*, **I**, (1875), 521.

87   'Attempt to Procure Abortion by Mechanical Means', *London Medical Gazette*, **2**, (1846), 831.

88   'The Traffic in Abortifacients', *BMJ* (14 January 1899), 110.

89   'More Abortionists', *The Lancet*, **I**, (1861), 294, at 295.

90   'Criminal Abortion', *The Lancet*, **I**, (1861), 272.

91   'The Practice of Procuring Criminal Abortion', *The Lancet*, **I**, (1853), 475. See also 'Criminal Abortion', *The Lancet*, **I**, (1861), 272; 'Correspondence on Criminal Abortion', *Provincial Medical and Surgical Journal*, **8**, (1844), 80, at 81.

92   'The Practice of Procuring Criminal Abortion', *The Lancet*, **I** (1853), 475. Interest-

ingly, immediately following the article were two editorial notices reflecting the strong occupational anxieties which plagued medicine. The first was a call for opposition to duties imposed by an amendment to the Compulsory Vaccination Bill. The editorial claimed such an amendment was 'degrading and galling in as much as it arbitrarily imposes duties and responsibilities without providing compensation'. Secondly, there was notice of the formation of a 'steering committee' to help push through the Medical Reform Bill. The aim was to facilitate 'The emancipation of the profession from the degradation and injustice of bad laws'.

93　'Abortion and its Procurers', *The Lancet*, **II**, (1862), 627. These sentiments were expressed equally unequivocally the following year, when it was suggested that these 'slaves of vice … should be ground into the mud by the sternest tread of the iron heel of law when once they have been hunted from their holes' ('Alleged Abortion-Mongers', *The Lancet*, **I**, (1863), 614).

94　'More Abortionists', *The Lancet*, **I**, (1861), 294.

95　Ibid.

96　Ibid.

97　Freidson, *Professional Dominance, supra.*

98　'The Criminal Production of Abortion by Persons Calling Themselves Surgeons Shows That a Medical Reform Act is Required as a Measure of Public Safety', *BMJ* (13 May 1853), 410.

99　Ibid.

100　For example, Keown writes: 'A survey of the *British Medical Journal* from 1857 to 1862 reveals that the B.M.A. was more concerned with the issue of medical reform in general than with abortion in particular' (Keown, *supra*, at 181).

101　'The Criminal Production of Abortion', *supra*, at 410.

102　Ibid. (emphasis added).

103　Ibid.

104　'Trial of William Russell for the Murder of Mary Wormsley. No. 2', *Legal Examiner*, **2**, (1832), 10, at 10–11.

105　Keown, *supra*, at 38.

106　Ibid., at 46.

107　'Free Trade in Physic', *BMJ* (1864), 446.

108　Ibid.

109　Ibid.

110　Ibid., at 446–7.

111　'Another Abortionist', *The Lancet*, **I**, (1899), 468.

112　Keown, *supra*, at 22–4.

113　McLaren, *supra*, at 148.

114　Of the distinction between the *medical* practitioner and the *quack* practitioner, Irvine Loudon has stated: 'At each end of the spectrum the two are easily distinguished; in the centre they mingle imperceptibly' (I. Loudon, *Medical Care and the General Practitioner* (Oxford: Clarendon Press, 1986), 13).

115　McLaren, *supra*, 129. Although McLaren has correctly located medical opposition to abortion within the context of professional aspirations, the projected dichotomy of opposition to 'rival practitioners' and 'non-scientific concepts' suggests a failure to recognize the importance of opposition to the latter in attempts to achieve occupational closure. Put more plainly, opposition to the 'non-scientific' may be read as primarily a position assumed in order to oppose rival practitioners. The two are not divisible.

116　410 US 113 (1973), 35 L Ed 2d 147.

117   Ibid., at 174.
118   Ibid.
119   Ibid. Yet, as Mohr states, new medical techniques, especially in the closing quarter of the century, meant abortion was probably markedly safer than before: 'at the very time abortion might theoretically have become an obviously safer procedure than it had been earlier in the century, it came instead to be perceived as more dangerous than ever' (Mohr, *supra*, at 239).
120   410 US 113 (1973) 35 L Ed 2d at 175.
121   The court was of the opinion that, 'as long as at least potential life is involved, the State may assert interests beyond the protection of the pregnant woman alone' (ibid.).
122   Mohr, *supra*, at 224.
123   As Mohr states, 'Every state in the Union had an anti-abortion law of some kind on its books by 1900 except Kentucky, where the state courts outlawed the practice anyway' (ibid., at 229–30).
124   See J.S. Witherspoon, 'Reexamining Roe: Nineteenth-Century Abortion Statutes and the Fourteenth Amendment', *St. Mary's Law Journal*, 17, (1985), 29, at 53 n.70.
125   Siegel, *supra*, at 286.
126   *Transactions of the American Medical Association*, XV, (1864), 35, 50.
127   Mohr, *supra*, at 158.
128   H. Storer, *Why Not? A Book for Every Woman* (Boston: Lee and Shephard, 1865).
129   Mohr, *supra*, at 158.
130   H. Storer, *Is It I? A Book for Every Man* (Boston: Lee and Shephard, 1867). Although again well received in the popular press, it proved less influential than its predecessor. (See Mohr, *supra*, at 158).
131   H. Storer and F. Fiske Heard, *Criminal Abortion: Its Nature, Its Evidence and Its Law* (Cambridge, Mass.: 1868).
132   *Transactions of the American Medical Association*, XII, (1859), 73–8.
133   Ibid., at 75–6.
134   Storer, *Is It I?*, *supra*, at 10–11, 38–9.
135   S.E. Chaille, 'State Medicine and State Medical Societies', *Transactions of the American Medical Association*, XXX, (1879), 355.
136   Ibid.
137   *Journal of the Proceedings of the Senate of Maryland, 1867* (Annapolis, 1867), 233.
138   *Laws of the State of Maryland, Made and Passed at a Session of the General Assembly 1867* (Annapolis, 1867), 339–44.
139   With the amendments made in the lower house, the bill when passed became retitled as 'An Act for the Protection of the Public Against Medical Imposters and for the suppression of the Crime of Unlawful Abortion' (ibid., at 339).
140   Ironically the Bill was ultimately unsuccessful in terms of providing a system of licensing. The Bill had been passed without an enabling clause. Henkle attempted unsuccessfully to pass the Act again in 1868, although delegate Hammond was later successful in his bid to pass it without the first 15 sections. In effect, the appended abortion provisions were ultimately the only provisions to have been secured. See Mohr, *supra*, at 213–14.
141   Act of 13 April 1867, *1867 Ohio Laws*, 135–36.
142   This Act was repealed by Amended Substitute House Bill No. 511, 1972, *1972 Ohio Laws*, 2032 (vol.134).
143   Act of 16 April 1867, *1867 Ohio Laws*, 202–203.
144   Comstock Act, ch 258, 17 Stat. 598 (1873) (repealed 1909).
145   1867 *Ohio Senate J. App.* 233.

146   Ibid., at 233, 235.
147   Ibid.
148   H. Storer, *On Criminal Abortion in America* (Philadelphia: J.B. Lippincott & Co., 1860).
149   *Ohio Senate J. App., supra,* at 235.
150   Luker, *supra,* at 32–3.
151   Ibid., at 33.
152   Ibid.
153   *Transactions of the American Medical Association,* **XXII**, (1871), 38–9.
154   Luker, *supra,* at 35.
155   Ibid., at 33.
156   Ibid.
157   Siegel, *supra,* at 315.
158   Ibid., at 317.

2 Woman, Medicine and Abortion in the Nineteenth Century

[It was] as if the Almighty, in creating the female sex, had taken the uterus and built up a woman around it. (Professor Hubbard, cited in M.L. Holbrook, *Parturition Without Pain: A Code for Escaping from the Primal Curse* (New York, 1882), 14–15)

That one truism says it all – women are made and meant to be not men, but mothers of men. (President of the British Medical Association, Withers Moore, 'The Higher Education of Women', *BMJ*, 14 August 1889, 295 at 299)

Introduction

In the opening chapter I considered the influencial role of the medical profession in shaping nineteenth-century abortion laws. Medicine's involvement, as was illustrated, may be assessed in terms of a desire for occupational enhancement. Abortion constructed as a medical as well as a social issue allowed medicine to promote its parochial professional concerns:

> It appears that a central (though not exclusive) concern of the profession in both the restriction of the law in the nineteenth century and its relaxation in 1967 has been self-interest ... two central concerns of the profession are freedom from control and the prevention of encroachment upon its sphere of influence by the medically unqualified ... [Both] of these concerns have been prominent in the development and operation of the laws relating to abortion from 1863.[1]

While recognizing that women's reproductive choices are affected by a complex network of institutions and social forces,[2] the present chapter remains within the parameters of medical practice and influence. It will suggest that medicine's response to abortion was not motivated solely by professional self-interest: as will be argued, opposition to abortion in the nineteenth century resulted, in part, from a desire to maintain existing gender relations. Yet the analyses presented in these first two chapters should not be read separately. They are not alternative or competing accounts. The professionalization of medicine and the issue of gender are intimately linked. Medicine's occupational project is imbricated in questions of gender at a number of levels. At a very immediate level, many of the groups with whom the regular physicians were competing were dominated by female health care providers. Similarly, using abortion as a vehicle to achieve fiscal and social rewards meant that the regulars could tap existing concerns and fears. The arguments as to gender used within the campaign to criminalize abortion may therefore evidence both political manipulation and genuine social concern.

When considering medical involvement in gender relations in the nineteenth century, it is important to note that medical opposition during this period worked within the framework of *True Womanhood*.[3] *True Woman* was characterized by inherent ('biological') features or traits. These, it was believed, defined her social and economic role, her 'appointed sphere of action'.[4] As this chapter will demonstrate, the stance taken by the medical profession may be understood as part of a broader opposition to the emergence of Woman beyond the confines of this appointed sphere – beyond church, home and family. Allowing women to control their reproductive lives threatened to introduce new avenues of experience and purpose beyond those provided by childbirth and child rearing. Contextualized in this way the abortion issue becomes part of a much broader picture of gender relations.

At this point it is worth clarifying my use of the term 'Woman'. This is used to denote a constructed social being rather than a tangible biological reality. In other words, as Carol Smart has noted, written in this way, Woman denotes a recognition of the 'distinction between Woman and women. This is familiar to feminists who have, for some centuries, argued that the *idea* of Woman (or sometimes the *ideal* of Woman) is far removed from real woman'.[5] While I refer to *True Woman*, *Womanhood* and *Woman* and recognize their proximity, I want True Woman to denote a gender position specific to the nineteenth century. The use of Woman denotes a continuity in the representation of a perceived inherent essence – although specific details of this representation will differ with historical location. I shall use this distinction in the remainder of the book. While gender is the primary focus for this chapter it is important to recognize that medical involvement in the abortion issue may also be located within the historic transformation in the nature of governance, the emergence in the seventeenth and eighteenth centuries of what Michel Foucault has called *biopower*. This needs to be explained further.

Foucault's Biopower

> There was ... the emergence, in the field of political practices and economic observation, of the problems of birthrate, longevity, public health, housing and migration. Hence there was an explosion of numerous and diverse techniques for achieving the subjugation of bodies and the control of populations, marking the beginning of an era of 'bio-power'.[6]

From the exercise of absolute power by or in the name of the sovereign, there emerged in the seventeenth and eighteenth centuries a shift in the nature of governance. From a modality characterized by the expression of absolute power, governance became more *pastoral*. This new modality of power was characterized by *(micro)technologies* directed towards the administration of populations.[7] Technologies of government moved towards the management and regulation of the processes of life, the population and its demographic characteristics. Marking this shift was the 'proliferation of political technologies ... investing the body, health, modes of subsistence, and habitation, living conditions, the whole space of existence'.[8] As such, the juridical punishment of transgression became largely subsumed by dispersed regulatory and corrective mechanisms seeking to achieve a normalization of life.[9] Foucault's concept, however, involves a bifurcation. Biopower focuses on both the body and on the population, as Paul Rabinow explains:

> Historically, practices and discourses of biopower have clustered around two distinct poles: the 'anatomopolitics of the human body', the anchor point and target for disciplinary technologies, on the one hand, and a regulatory pole centred on population, with a panoply of strategies concentrating on knowledge, control and welfare, on the other.[10]

Importantly, (bio)power may be understood as productive. Bodies are constructed, through discourses and practices, to fit properly within certain social structures. Techniques of power operate on the body, transforming, dividing and investing it with capacities and training it to perform certain functions.[11] Following this, as Foucault observed, we need to ask: 'What mode of investment of the body is necessary and adequate for the functioning of a capitalist society such as ours? ... One needs to study what kind of body the current society needs.'[12]

The body may thus be understood as the product of need. Yet, as some commentators have suggested Foucault perhaps fails to consider, the female and male *publicly viable bodies*[13] are subject to differing transformations, divisions and investments.[14] Accepting that women have traditionally been assigned different roles and habitats to men, the nature of women's embodiment differs. The investment of the female body has reflected both the needs of a new economic order and the needs and desires of a sex which has defined women's physiology, personhood and gender.

This chapter therefore has two objectives. Primarily, it aims to place opposition to abortion in the nineteenth century within the context of general gender relations and anxieties. Arguably encompassing this, it also aims to place the medical campaign within the context of both the broader concept of biopower (the move to regulate and manage the movement, passions and reproduction of populations) and the more specific 'anatomopolitics' of the body (the disciplines and techniques focused upon individual bodies, their forces and capacities). To locate the medical anti-abortion campaign in this context, this chapter highlights the continuities that existed between the medical discourses that opposed increased female entry into education and employment, and those used in seeking the criminalization of abortion. This assessment introduces the (productive) narratives of gender which, it will be suggested, undergird many reproductive discourses. Before moving on to this, it is first necessary to outline the intellectual/social terrain medicine was situated in during this period and also to briefly sketch the general response of medicine to the question of *True Womanhood* mentioned briefly above.

The Nineteenth Century and the Biomedicalized Woman

The nineteenth century saw industrialization alter the social and geographical structure of society. In this period of change, science emerged as the basis for a new rationalism. Foucault's theorization of the shifts in the modality of power that had occurred during and before this period also lend support to our understanding of this. With the 'investment of the body, its valorization and the distributive management of its forces'.[15] knowledge of the body became privileged. The classical *episteme* became displaced, epistemological primacy shifting as the nature of power shifted: 'the emergence and diffusion of technologies of power exercised over life, notably the technologies of discipline and confession and their associated methods of examination, techniques of subjection and objectification, and procedures of individualization, provided the appropriate conditions in which the human sciences could emerge'.[16]

This shift marked the conditions of possibility that fostered a flourishing in the epistemic and therefore cultural importance of medicine and the human sciences. An increasingly secular (western) world had found a new truth. As has already been noted, medicine's social function and status became 'akin to that of state religions yesterday'.[17] Scientific arguments were used to rationalize and legitimize almost every aspect of nineteenth-century life. This was most clearly the case where social change challenged existing social arrangements.

The period being discussed saw economic and social forces within the industrializing world begin to compromise traditional gender roles, particularly in the middle classes. Women had begun to question or challenge their confined and limited participation in society. In response, biological and medical arguments were employed to cement previously largely unchallenged gender roles 'inevitably and irreversibly in the prescriptions of anatomy and physiology'.[18] Women's status became a product and design of nature, mapped upon, and decipherable from, the body. Social gender differences became recoded as 'the mark of the differences of organization, which nature has conferred, in order that each may hereafter be in accord with her reproductive laws'.[19] Nature defined gender roles: 'implant[ing] in each sex the peculiarities which are responsible for things as they are and, for the most part, must continue to be'.[20] The desired virtues of nineteenth-century Woman ('a spirit of obedience and submission, pliability of temper, and humility of mind'[21]) became located in bioscience. *True Woman* became rationalized, validated in her manifestation as the *Biomedicalized Woman*.

Perhaps the most potent symbol of this recoding was the complex and extreme investment of the female reproductive organs. The uterus, and later the ovaries, were seen as 'the *controlling* organ[s] in the female body'.[22] The ovaries and the process of ovulation were seen to 'give woman all her characteristics of body and mind'.[23] Medicine became empowered to define roles, as behaviour could be deemed *unphysiological*. Gender untypical or undesirable behaviour could be deemed adverse to the reproductive system and hence adverse to every aspect of the person. Medical knowledge of (or medical narratives about) the female reproductive system became a disciplinary power, a technology of gender. Woman had become a prisoner of her reproductive organs and their physiological processes. Such was the strength of this hysterization and its disciplinary effects that it provoked the lament: 'It is almost a pity that a woman has a womb.'[24]

Biomedicine, therefore, provided a means of bolstering increasingly challenged gender role definitions. The hysterization of women's bodies was an integral part of biopower, the extension of power over bodies, part of the 'whole series of power networks that invest the body, sexuality, the family, kinship ... and so forth'.[25] Hysterization facilitated the drawing of reproduction, and particularly women's bodies, into a more visible arena. Women's bodies were 'integrated into the sphere of medical practice, by reason of a pathology intrinsic to it; whereby it was placed in organic communication with the social body'.[26] Placed within this social organic communication, Woman became more clearly defined and definable. She became regulated and disciplined, her body a point of definition. The female body became construed in a way that facilitated its existence within the emerging social and economic structures. This process is clearly illustrated in the responses of biomedicine to increasing female access to education and employment.

Medicine, Education and the Biomedicalized Woman

The closing quarter of the nineteenth century saw opportunities in higher education burgeon with the foundation of women's colleges on both sides of the Atlantic. With this breach of established gender divisions there developed the idea of an internal war waged between the uterus and the brain.[27] Women were constructed as 'not physiologically rich enough to bear the expense of being trained for motherhood, and also that of being trained for competition with men in the severer exercises of the intellect'.[28] Her body was seen as an enwombed microsystem possessing a finite *vital force*. Energy spent in one area was so used at the expense of another. A woman pursuing educational or intellectual activities necessarily did so with the consequence of diverting this vital force, or energy, away from her uterus, and therefore away from her achievement of *True Womanhood*.

The physical effects of education on a woman were twofold. Following literary tradition, her body revealed betrayal.[29] She became less rounded, more angular: 'Where before her beauty was suggestive and elusive, now it is defined ... . The haze, the elusiveness, the subtle suggestion of face are gone.'[30] More palpably a symbol of her deviance would be the loss of her breasts, embodiments of her natural nurturing role. G.S. Hall believed the first symptom to afflict an educated woman was the loss of her 'mammary function'.[31] This was followed by the loss of the breasts themselves, as Arabella Keneally remarked: 'her modesty has been put to the necessity of puffing and pleating, where Nature had planned the tenderest and most dainty of devices'.[32] More generally, education damaged a Woman's health. Such women risked a variety of ills, including sleeplessness, reflexive vomiting,[33] nymphomania,[34] insanity,[35] sterility[36] and paralysis.[37] This spent her vital energy before it could fashion, and enter, succeeding generations. Education involved a 'large outlay of vital capital' and therefore proved 'antagonistic to reproductiveness',[38] it was 'the very apotheosis of selfishness from the standpoint of every biological ethic'.[39]

Education, with its clearly detrimental effects upon female health, was seen as a major factor in the perceived deterioration in the health of the nation's middle-class women. These women were seen as too physically weak, or prone to disease, to pursue education. Indeed, it was asked whether it was 'altogether wise to urge these ill-developed, anaemic-looking girls to compete for academic laurels with their brothers on such a narrow basis of bodily health?'[40] Such was the general inevitability of ill health that the nation's men lamented the days when women had more readily recognized and fulfilled their *natural role*:

> Our great-grandmothers got their schooling during the winter months and let their brains lie fallow for the rest of the year. They knew less about Euclid and the classics than about housekeeping and housework. But they made good wives and mothers, and bore and nursed sturdy sons and buxom daughters and plenty of them at that.[41]

This nostalgia for a more bovine woman was reinforced by the belief that education would 'desex' women. The loss of the breasts and the ability to lactate was coupled with an inability to produce healthy offspring:

> She will not have the strength to bring forth; her reproductive system will more or less have been atrophied; she will have lost her womanhood's proper power. With the power, she will have largely lost also her inclination; of 'Love's sweet want', as Shelley calls it, she will know little, for ... she will have lost sensuality of a proper commendable kind. Unsexed it might be wrong to call her, but she will be more or less sexless. And the human race will have lost those who should have been her sons.[42]

Such ills inevitably became generationally compounded: 'She would become weak and nervous, perhaps sterile, or more commonly, and in a sense more dangerous for society, capable of bearing only sickly and neurotic children – children able to produce only feebler and more degenerate versions of themselves.'[43] The fear of the degeneration of the race confirmed the stance of those opposed to women entering higher education. Primacy had to be given to the health of future generations: 'We want to have body as well as mind, otherwise the degeneration of the race is inevitable.'[44] The social responsibility of women was too great to be subordinated to personal desires for education.

The opposition to education was not, however, absolute. A woman could embark upon academic pursuits so long as they enhanced her duties within her 'proper and God-given sphere'.[45] A woman was given leave to pursue any education which would allow her to be a 'wise and loving mother', and therefore a 'source of every good to her child'.[46] This reflected the belief in Woman's primary 'mission to make home happy and to educate and train their children'.[47] Education that moved beyond facilitating the maternal role threatened to impede the fulfilment of this duty. Some, recognizing the need for an educated wife and mother, called for the improvement of female further education. Yet this was possible 'without granting them degrees [as] the sexes should be kept separate, and their education should be distinct, their aims in life being different'.[48] Similarly, it was suggested that 'Women should be admitted to the examination in Art, not in anything else, and successful candidates should receive, not degrees, but certificates of having passed.'[49] Education which recognized the separation of the sexes of course meant that the physical burdens which usually befell the educated woman were eschewed.

Women who sought escape from their prescribed role, one of giving birth, nurturing and bovine placidity, therefore faced considerable opposition from the biomedical experts.[50] Their behaviour became prescribed through the ability of medicine to deem behaviour physiological or unphysiological. Women who pursued inappropriate education were destined to damage their already precarious health, lose their breasts, lose their femininity and, most importantly, they would be guilty of causing weakness and disease in their children. Medicine religiously delimited the life options of women. Those options were decipherable from the body, from the breasts, and the ability to produce healthy progeny – a narrative of appropriate gender behaviour read from the body. Medicine defined and delimited, by the construction of an inherent female pathology, a narrative of weakness and disease. The same arguments utilized to oppose women's entry into higher education, most notably those concerning the degeneration of the race, were mobilized against women who sought employment.

Female Employment and Medical Opposition

Opposition to the entry of women into what had previously been exclusively male areas of employment was diffuse and powerful. The catalyst for intervention appeared not, as is commonly perceived, to be concern created by harsh working conditions, but the question of immorality. Horror was expressed at the close proximity of the sexes. This propinquity in mines and factories was believed to threaten moral and spiritual degradation. The evangelical Tory and social reformer Lord Shaftesbury, for example, warned of the effects 'not alone upon themselves, but upon their families, upon society, and ... upon the country itself.' He continued: 'It is bad enough if you corrupt the man, but if you corrupt the woman, you poison the water of life at the very fountain.'[51] This justification for opposition was discernible in responses to the 'indescribable immodesty and immorality' of female labour in the chain and nail-making industries in the Black Country:

> In these counties it is the custom to employ both male and female labour in the work of forging nails and chains, but no steps are taken to separate the sexes, and women and girls of tender years work in more than semi-nude conditions

among men and boys equally little clad. As a consequence, it is found that the greatest immorality, depravity and pauperism prevails.[52]

Recognising the issue of immortality, Susan Atkins and Brenda Hoggett argue that the primary motivation for opposition derived from the threat female employment was perceived to pose to the home: 'concern was expressed at the ... immorality of married women who, it was alleged, left their homes and families, neglected their domestic duties and forced their menfolk to seek the comforts of public houses.'[53] In an attempt to safeguard the home, access to employment was restricted. This was justified on the basis of a Woman's natural role as reproducer. In 1918, for example, the Report of the Women's Employment Committee of the Ministry of Reconstruction called for a reduction in the number of hours worked by women in factories and shops. The committee's rationale was the belief that every possible incentive should be afforded to married women for them to return to the home: 'As a general principle we would suggest that the only differentiation between women and men which could be justified is such as has its basis in the need of preserving women's powers unimpeded for those primary activities which are connected with the family and the home.'[54]

Within this framework of opposition the medical profession played a significant role, lending the cause the mantle of objective, rational, scientific proof. The medical opposition to the employment of women was on the basis of its causing foetal disability, or death, and increasing what had been a diminishing infant mortality rate. Foetal death, or disability, arose from strenuous work while the woman was pregnant. Cases were reported of foetuses being born *blighted* as a result of the pregnant woman's *insistence* upon working. In one such case, the foetus was removed 'quite flat, of about the thickness of a penny piece, and like the rest of the mass quite blanched'. The child miraculously lived for two days. The cause of the foetus's death was held to be the woman's employment: 'The mother, who assists her husband in a pork shop, has been actively engaged during her pregnancy, and in the habit of lifting heavy weights, and resting them against the abdomen.'[55] Yet the effect of employment upon foetal health was seen as a secondary danger, usurped by the dangers posed to the infant by the working mother. The infant mortality rate of the time was held to be largely due to the effects of women being removed from the home. The Registrar-General's statistics for infant mortality were held clearly to support the doctors' case. The statistics pointed to Salford, Blackburn, Bolton, Huddersfield and Manchester as showing the highest rates of infant mortality. In each of these towns there was held to exist 'an undue proportion of females doubtlessly engaged in factory labour'.[56] The removal of the mother from the home was seen as perhaps a greater cause of infant death than the appalling slum conditions of many urban areas: 'The mortality of Salford and Nottingham depends, not alone on unhealthy slums, but to a great extent on the employment of women away from their homes – a system which, as at present conducted, involves the artificial rearing of their infants.'[57] The removal of the mother resulted in 'injudicious feeding', which was perhaps the ultimate cause of an infants death. It was imperative to provide 'infants with the food nature intended they should have; any cause which took the mother away from the home at a time when she should be suckling her child must prejudicially affect the health of that child and thus predispose it to fatal diseases, which under more favourable dietetic conditions, it might of resisted or overcome'.[58]

Legislation was demanded. While many asked for the statutory postnatal month of confinement to be extended to three months,[59] some went so far as to call for a legislative ban on the employment of women with children younger than three years of age.[60] With a lack of efficient contraception, the exclusionary nature of this proposal is evident. Women are isolated as the producers of labour, 'not men, but the mothers of men',[61] their only access to employment vicarious, through their male progeny. Medical knowledge, therefore, supported and scientifically validated phallocentric 'desire lines' of division. By gendered scientific construal, or mapping, of the body, biomedical reasoning attempted to maintain the stark dichotomy of the gendered public/private divide. As a poignant precursor of present-day exclusionary reasoning in foetal protective policies, the rights of the child were evoked:

> The 'liberties' of a baby would not be infringed upon … . On the contrary, the Government would insist on the infant having its right, and that right is its mother's breast. Infants cannot raise a public agitation; and their private complaints are soon stilled by syrups, when they are put out to nurse whilst their mothers are still at work. In short, they are the very class that must be helped by laws, and that at the same time need not and cannot be consulted as to their desire for such legislation.[62]

Woman was therefore reduced, not to something as complex as a reproducer, but to a breast, that symbol of femininity and barometer of *Womanhood*. The right of the child to its mother's breast negated any right of the mother to seek employment outside the private sphere of the home. Yet, as with education, opposition to female employment was not absolute. Women were encouraged to pursue careers that were deemed *suitable*. The Society for Promoting the Employment of Women suggested: 'Book-keeping, law copying, photography, pattern staining on furniture, wood engraving, lithographic training, music copying, plant preserving, heraldic painting, modelling [and] watch engraving.'[63] The type of job deemed suitable could be read from the body. Traditionally male jobs were precluded by physical and mental inferiority or incapacity. Women were more suited to genteel pursuits, employment that would not detract from, or corrupt, their femininity: 'All the hard work in this world is for men's stalwart arms to accomplish. Women can be very much better employed in offices of charity, training the young, filling all hearts and adorning all homes.'[64]

The mobilization of biomedical opposition to female employment was intimately tied to the medical profession's parochial concerns. As women entered education and employment they threatened to breach the male domain of medicine. This threatened not only gender security but also, to an extent, the foundations of the profession which was establishing itself in part in its differentiation from other female forms of health care. Opposition to female employment in medicine therefore involved a more intense reading of the body, providing much stronger and vitriolic characterizations of women as unfit for pursuits beyond the home and family.

Male Medicine and Female Doctors

When the limited emancipation of women in the second half of the nineteenth century allowed women to seek medical education and employment, medical opposition to female employment intensified. No other issue of the period appeared to consume so much energy. The arguments that had previously been mobilized to oppose female education and employment were again utilized. The intensity of the arguments this time, however, reflected the unease with which doctors met women encroaching upon male medicine, and the threat of the revival of the 'old midwives'.[65] Parochial professional concerns melded with both the increasing 'anatomopolitical' interest in the body and the intent of securing challenged gender roles. While the same arguments were used, often more aggressively,[66] the justifications for exclusion became both more sophisticated and more sophistic.

Again the most frequently voiced objection to women doctors reflected the prevalent belief in the existence of separate 'distinctive spheres'.[67] The importance of the Woman's sphere was extolled, and the pre-eminence of this sphere to her life was characterized as the primary justification for opposing her entry into medicine: 'The objections to woman as practitioner of medicine rest upon higher grounds than her intellect and tact. Hitherto the chief goal of a woman, determined by her natural and irrepressible instincts, has been wife-hood; her chief crown maternity.'[68] The opposition to female doctors on the basis of the recognition of natural gender roles developed to centre upon the interdependence of the sexes through their complementary roles, as Jonathan Hutchinson warned:

The sexes have hitherto worked together in mutual dependence and mutual help; each taking separate and well defined shares in the duties of life. It is open to society, if it like, to alter this, and to place them as rivals in the same pursuits; but if this is done, it will surely be to the detriment of both, and to the special loss of the weaker one.[69]

Portraying gender relations as placed under threat by the pursuit of medicine by women allowed the use of warnings of an apocalyptic nature. The 'unnatural and preposterous attempt on the part of one or two highly strongly minded women'[70] threatened the very basis of society. While some merely foresaw that 'The relationship between the sexes would lose half its charm if the "softening veil" of simplicity and privacy were rudely withdrawn from the life of young women',[71] others predicted the destruction of family and nation: 'Upon the just exercise of the domestic virtues ... the moral stability of society mainly rests. In direct proportion as woman is true and apt to the holy duties of home and hearth, the moral life of families and nation exists.'[72] As with other areas of opposition, the rationalism of science depoliticized and legitimized the exclusion of women from the medical profession. Science explained the physiological bars that existed, the 'peculiar hindrances, moral and physical to the successful pursuit of medicine by women'.[73] These ranged from an innate frailty[74] to a naturally inferior intellect. A history of female intellectual inferiority gave anthropological witness: 'If one could find a race who, in whatever age, in whatever country they might be found, always occupied an inferior intellectual position, we should be justified in presuming that there was a mental inferiority. And such is the position of women.'[75] Temperamentality, frailty and illogicality combined to create a creature achingly unsuitable for medicine:

the preponderance of the emotional qualities in woman's nature, I submit, ill adapts her for the performance of those duties which are entailed upon those who enter into the profession of medicine. In the profession of medicine, what is so much desired is the clear exercise of the logical faculty. Hence I think that the whole history of our race shows that, in this matter of the possession of logical or scientific faculty, women have not yet shown that they possess any power of coming to the front.[76]

Medical study was constructed as not only contrary to the natural, God-given and physiologically prescribed role of Woman, but also as destructive to her femininity. Medicine threatened to 'injure the delicacy, refinement and higher feelings of women'.[77] As medicine and society lauded femininity and frailty as all that was virtuous in Woman, anything which was seen to corrupt this was to be avoided. As Septimus Sibley warned:

It is scarcely possible for a woman to go through a course of medical education without losing that simplicity and purity of character which we so much value; there are subjects which cannot be discussed with freedom between the sexes, and there are many matters with which women had better not be acquainted ... . In the truest interest of women it is better that they should not practise the medical profession.[78]

As with higher education, if a woman persisted in her folly she risked androgyny or masculinity. A female doctor would without doubt be 'indelicate and coarse ... pitilessly unsexed'.[79] A woman could not study or practise 'without assuming the habits, dress, and manners of the opposite sex'.[80] In attempting the challenge of medicine she was 'compel[l]ed ... to unsex herself or neglect[] her professional duties'.[81]

The continuity with which male medicine opposed an expanding female role reconstructs the social context within which opposition to abortion evolved. The discourse of hysterization placed women in a more regulatory relationship with the social body. Integral to this, the body contained gender differences. Gender could be defined through the ability to regulate behaviour, prescribing actions as physiological or unphysiological. The unphysiological threatening not only health but also *Womanhood*. Abortion, however, more than any other issue, acted as a confluence for many of the concerns and anxieties of the period. Concomitantly, the body evolved as the point at which these anxieties were translated and diffused.

Birth Control, Abortion and the Biomedicalized Woman

Opposition to birth control and abortion shared many of the common elements discernible in medical opposition to female entry into education and employment. The medical campaign relied again on the concepts of *True Womanhood* and the existence of distinct spheres of action for the sexes. Perhaps most importantly, however, opposition again focused upon the effects of birth control and abortion on succeeding generations. Yet opposition here appeared more dynamic than that noted above. This is no doubt due in part to the involvement of the abortion issue in the occupational project of medical professionalization. In seeking the criminalization of abortion, the medical campaign relied both on traditional physiological warnings and on more overtly social and political anxieties. Opposition to abortion, for example, was a more open defence of existing gender roles and relations. Medicine fostered a belief in a causal link between increasing attempts by women to avoid their 'highest and holiest privilege'[82] and the emerging feminism. H.S. Pomeroy, for example, saw abortion and feminism as almost synonymous: 'It is impossible to treat the sin against parenthood without touching upon what is called the Woman Question.'[83] Abortion was so inextricably linked with feminism that any emancipatory call was construed as a call to abort: 'Many ... connected with the Woman's Rights Movement, and at least some of the advocates of higher education for women ... indirectly at least, have aided and abetted the sin against maternity.'[84] By constructing a fictional nexus between abortion and feminism, doctors could infuse opposition to abortion with the strength of feeling, fear and opposition created by the question of emancipation.

Yet medical opposition to abortion may be located within the context of biomedical opposition to birth control in all its manifestations.[85] Birth control generally was seen as unnatural, an interference, not only with the 'Longing[s] of every normal woman',[86] but also with divinely dictated processes: 'Interference with Nature so that she may not accomplish the production of healthy human beings is a physiological sin of the most heinous sort, for, from a physical standpoint, reproduction is the first and foremost aim and object of Nature.'[87] The woman who prevented pregnancy was therefore seen to commit a grave sin 'because she shirk[ed] those responsibilities for which she was created'.[88] As 'unnatural' and 'unphysiological', such interference was destined to be accompanied by physical *reflexes*. This was exaggerated by the fact that a woman's good health was seen as dependent upon regular pregnancy: 'Every married woman, until the so called turn of life, should occasionally bear a child ... as the best means of insuring her health.'[89] Any contraceptive method would therefore have almost unspeakable consequences, as 'any infringement of [natural law] must necessarily cause derangement, disaster or ruin'.[90] The only possible method of prevention was, therefore, 'total abstinence from coition'.[91]

Opposing birth control as a violation of marital obligation, and utilizing warnings of the dire physiological effects upon women, allowed the realignment of marital obligations into therapeutic terms. Arguments which may have begun to appear anachronistic were transformed, recoded. Marital obligations became written upon, and therefore decipherable from, the body. Reading the body, of all the methods of birth control abortion was deemed the one which afforded the direst consequences, the most 'tremendous penalties'.[92] As Horatio Storer, whose influencial role in abortion law reform was discussed in the previous chapter, warned: 'intentionally to bring [a pregnancy], when begun, to a premature close, [is] disastrous to a woman's mental, moral and physical well being'.[93] Abortion was commonly labelled as a cause of death or insanity. Insanity was either a consequence of a physical injury or the product of guilt and remorse:

Mental derangement has generally occurred as a result of local injury, and the serious impairment of general health directly traceable to the criminal act [of abortion]. In a few cases it has operated directly as a moral cause, as, for instance, when the unfortunate sufferer has borne a child which has been permitted to remain with her long enough to show the unhappy mother the priceless value of the gift she had previously refused to accept. In these cases the immediate cause of insanity is remorse.[94]

As with opposition to female entry into higher education and certain areas of employment, medical opposition highlighted the physiological effects of abortion on *Womanhood*, femininity and the family. Abortion acted to replace 'delicacy, refinement and chastity' in the nation's women with 'unblushing effrontery, unchastity and utter heartlessness'.[95] Aborting an unwanted pregnancy undermined a woman's ability to fulfil her maternal, wifely and domestic duties, and propelled her towards an early and pitiful death:

She becomes unmindful of the course marked out by Providence, she overlooks the duties imposed on her by the marriage contract. She yields to the pleasures – but shrinks from the pains and responsibilities of maternity; and, destitute of all delicacy and refinement, resigns herself, body and soul, into the hands of unscrupulous and wicked men. Let not the husband of such a wife flatter himself that he possess her affection. Nor can she in turn ever merit the respect of a virtuous husband. She sinks into old age like a withered tree, stripped of its foliage; with the stain of blood upon her soul, she dies without the hand of affection to smooth her pillow.[96]

As this rather dramatic narrative suggests, and as with earlier oppositional discourses, concern for the home was central. Abortion, it was warned, necessarily left the relationship between husband and wife irreconcilably injured. A woman who sought an abortion became alienated 'from that respect without which her husband can possess no affection; in short [it produced] such results that the happiness and morality of the home life would be undermined'.[97] As a 'high moral tone' in the family was the 'basis of all civilized communities', abortion with its deleterious effects upon the morality of the home became 'a canker at [civilization's] root that would ultimately cause destruction to our race and the downfall of this great nation, as other vices have been the ruin of other nations in the past'.[98]

Fostering the construction of a relationship between a changing female role and abortion, the incidence of abortion was seen to reflect a growing self-indulgence, a simple egoism, in the country's women. The woman who choose to abort her pregnancy was seen to lack 'even a shadow of a sufficient reason' for her action.[99] Rather, she was motivated by her 'love of fashionable life',[100] by her 'desire ... for a life of luxury and display'.[101] Augustus Gardner saw not merely the pursuit of fashion as the cause of abortion, but also 'arrant laziness [and] sheer, craven, culpable cowardice'. If not lazy and loving of fashion, the woman who aborted was alternatively cast as 'ignorant and evil-minded'[102] and as a woman who had 'abandoned [her] maternal duties for selfish and personal ends'.[103] While medicine suggested indulgence and selfishness, and created a politically charged association between feminism and abortion, the primary tool used in opposition was probably the apocalyptic warnings of *race suicide*. This strategy, as has already been noted in Chapter 1, was employed on both sides of the Atlantic.

In perhaps one of the clearest embodiments of Foucault's concept of *biopower*, the state was modelled as having a legitimate, almost proprietary, interest in the nation's children. Marriage was seen as part of a social contract with the state which necessarily involved the production of children: 'marriage is a civil contract, the fruits of which vastly concern the public welfare, bearing as they do on the present and future generations'.[104] Consequently, a woman had a duty to fulfil her reproductive role:

> If you are not willing to accept the cares, labors, responsibilities, and duties of married life why did you enter into that state? You were not forced into it; but you voluntarily and deliberately assumed that relation, and now you have no right to attempt to escape from what you tacitly promised the State, by whose authority you legally came together as husband and wife, you would perform.[105]

By the depicting of marital sex as the means whereby citizens were produced, this area of private life was recast as a matter of intense public regulatory interest. Sex, while confined to the home and the procreative couple, emerged as a governmental matter, 'a public issue enmeshed in a web of discourses, forms of knowledge and analysis'.[106] The wives of the nation became literally objectified as the *Nation's Wives*. This dynamic regulatory interest was most clearly illustrated in connection with the fears that emerged over the health of the nation, and more particularly the health of the middle and upper classes.

In the United Kingdom in the second half of the nineteenth century, concern emerged over the low birth rate,[107] and higher than average sterility amongst the 'better classes'.[108] In America in the 1860s and 1870s, census returns began indicating that non-American born nationals had a birth rate considerably higher than the 'native' (WASP) Americans.[109] This declining fertility was understood as 'the result mainly of the practice of criminal abortions'.[110] These birth rate fears gave an added dimension to the opposition of birth control. Not only did the married middle-class woman owe a duty to fulfil her child-bearing capacity/destiny to God, her husband and her own health, she also now had a duty to her class and race. Birth control, and specifically abortion, had become more clearly enmeshed in the language of politics and governance.

It is here that abortion provided a focus for a multiplicity of concerns reaching beyond gender. The use of contraceptives and abortion, coupled with the perception of increasing immigrant birth rates, was seen to doom the 'better classes' or 'natives' to 'rapid extinction'.[111] Abortion had become a 'leprosy on the body politic'.[112] In America, consideration of birth rates was predominantly motivated by the fear of differential birth rates and miscegenous decay. In Britain, motherhood and fertility became a focus for a nation in flux, a nation threatened from within and without. By the end of the nineteenth century, Britain faced a number of crises: its imperial supremacy was being challenged abroad, while at home feminism, an emergent working class and Ireland were all points for concern. Compounding this situation, falling birth rates, high infant mortality and poverty all fuelled a rising fear of national degeneracy.

These fears were translated into a belief in the need for women to follow their natural 'racial instinct'.[113] Failure of the middle classes to procreate would lead to their being outbred by the 'wrong' sorts, by 'the ignorant, the low lived and the alien'.[114] In the United States, a failure by women to change their ways would result in men taking the future of the 'race' into their own hands, an image of violence and misogyny: 'The wives who are to be mothers in our republic must be drawn from trans-Atlantic homes. The Sons of the New World will have to re-act on a magnificent scale, the old story of unwived Rome and the Sabines.'[115] Whilst misogyny appears a strong motivating force, the theory, and use, of race suicide arguments appears inextricable from a number of diverse cultural issues. As noted above, the social changes shaping the nineteenth century involved not only industrialization, its geographical effects and the changing shape of the family, but also immigration, the emergence of feminism, growing class antagonism and world power shifts. With society in such a labile state, 'race' became an issue as a product of insecurity. Birth rates, as indices of racial health and competition, became one manifestation of a new racism. The (aborting) female body therefore became invested with a new significance, as Laqueur helpfully concludes: 'Women's bodies in their corporeal, scientifically accessible concreteness, in the very nature of their bones, nerves, and, most importantly, reproductive organs came to bear an enormous new weight of cultural meaning.'[116]

Conclusion

Race suicide arguments and warnings regarding gender stability and mental and physical degeneration constituted important elements of the medical profession's campaign against women and abortion. The female body absorbed, and was transformed by, social anxieties, fears and desires. A multiplicity of concerns invested and transformed the female body, ensuring its imbrication within the emerging social structure. The female body became that which the current society needed.[117] Opposition to abortion, and the consequential investment of women's bodies, ensured that the childbearing, nurturing, home-centred role retained its primacy. Within this context, physicians may be seen as actively participating in the creation and shaping of the ideology of female maternalism and domesticity. In this respect, the medical campaign is indistinguishable from medical opposition to female education and employment. Perhaps more importantly, it is indistinguishable from the general pattern and processes of gender relations in the nineteenth century.

A recognition of this cultural and political history of medical opposition to abortion encourages a reappraisal of present-day medical attitudes to abortion and an increasing range of reproductive issues. The nineteenth century saw biomedical justifications for prohibiting abortion as both secondary to, and constituted by, political concerns. Primacy must be given within this to the desire to assert and affirm appropriate gender behaviour. A rereading of the 1967 abortion legislation, current medical attitudes to reproductive rights and freedoms, and the emergence of *foetal rights*, each discussed in the following chapters, illustrates the perennial nature of the desire to define the role of women in this way. Implicit in this is the suggestion of an enduring 'anatomopolitical' interest in the female body. Medical knowledge of the reproductive body in particular endures as a disciplinary power and, as will be argued, a *technology of gender*. While science may have escaped, to a large extent, the subjectivity of the nineteenth century, the biomedical body remains essential to the nature of governance and a forum for the construction and justification of social gender differences.

The degree to which this assertion is true is explored in the remaining chapters. Part II takes a historical leap to consider the discourses around the enactment of the Abortion Act 1967. It is important to stress at this point that an attempt is not being made to achieve or suggest an (orthodox) history. What is intended is to look at a number of reproductive discourses and to suggest a recurring narrative. While it is recognized that the way the body was talked about and understood shifted dramatically in the period between the discourses under consideration, focus will be placed only on the continuity of the issue of gender. That is to say, I will explore the degree to which biomedical and medico-legal discourses remain technologies of gender (re)producing what is perhaps the most significant of the cultural codes that shape the spaces we live in.

Notes

1 J. Keown, *Abortion, Doctors and the Law* (Cambridge: Cambridge University Press, 1988), 159.
2 R.P. Petchesky, *Abortion and Woman's Choice: The State, Sexuality and Reproductive Freedom* (London: Verso, 1986), 72.
3 See C. Smith-Rosenberg and C. Rosenberg, 'The Female Animal: Medical and Biological Views of Woman and Her Role in Nineteenth-Century America', *Journal of American History*, **60**, (1973), 332. Petchesky, however, emphasizes the medical role as more creative than merely affirmative: 'physicians more than any other group [were] the social agents who, through their popular writings as much as their medical treatise, propagated the Victorian ideology of "true womanhood"' (Petchesky, *supra*, at 82).
4 C. Beecher, 'The Peculiar Responsibilities of American Women', in N.F. Cott (ed.), *Root of Bitterness* (New York: Dutton, 1974), 173–4.
5 C. Smart, 'The Woman of Legal Discourse', *Social and Legal Studies*, **I**, (1992), 29 at 35. It is worth adding Smart's qualification that the concept of 'real woman' is itself problematic: 'The claim to an absolute reality located in the body of women against which the excesses of patriarchy can be measured has become less tenable'. See also S. Sheldon, '"Who is the Mother to Make the Judgement?": The Constructions of Woman in English Abortion Law', *Feminist Legal Studies*, **1**, (1993), 3.
6 M. Foucault, *The History of Sexuality, Volume One* (London: Penguin, 1990), 140.
7 M. Foucault, 'Governmentality', *M/F*, **3**, (1979), 5.
8 Foucault, *The History of Sexuality*, *supra*, at 143–4.
9 B. Smart, *Michel Foucault* (London: Tavistock, 1985), 103.
10 P. Rabinow, 'Artificiality and Enlightenment: From Sociobiology to Biosociality', *Incorporations, Zones*, **6**, (1992), 234.
11 Foucault, *The History of Sexuality*, *supra*, at 25.
12 M. Foucault, *Power/Knowledge: Selected Interviews and Other Writings 1972–1977*, ed. C. Gordon (Brighton: Harvester Press, 1980), 58.
13 The phrase is Rosalyn Diprose's; see R. Diprose, *The Bodies of Women: Ethics Embodiment and Sexual Difference* (London: Routledge & Kegan Paul, 1994).
14 See Z. Eisenstein, *The Female Body and the Law* (London: University of California Press, 1988), 10–11; R. Braidotti, *Nomadic Subjects: Embodiment and Sexual Difference in Contemporary Feminist Thinking* (New York: Columbia, 1994), 61.
15 Foucault, *The History of Sexuality*, *supra*, at 139.
16 Smart, *supra*, at 105.
17 E. Freidson, *Profession of Medicine: A Study in the Sociology of Applied Knowledge* (New York: Harper & Row, 1970), 5.
18 Smith-Rosenberg and Rosenberg, *supra*, at 333.
19 W.F. Wade, Ingleby Lectures, 'On Some Functional Disorders of Females', Lecture I, *BMJ* (5 June 1886), 1053

20   W.F. Wade, Ingleby Lectures, 'On Some Functional Disorders of Females', Lecture II, *BMJ* (12 June 1886), 1095.

21   *The Young Ladies' Book* (New York, 1830), 28.

22   F. Hollick, *The Diseases of Women, Their Cause and Cure Familiarly Explained* (New York: T.W. Strong, 1848), 42.

23   G.L. Austin, quoted in B. Ehrenreich and D. English, *For Her Own Good: 150 Years of the Expert's Advice to Women* (London: Pluto Press, 1979), 108.

24   Monograph on the uterus given by Professor Byford, the University of Chicago's professor of gynaecology in the 1860s, cited in A. Douglas Wood, '"The Fashionable Diseases": Women's Complaints and their Treatment in Nineteenth-Century America', *Journal of Interdisciplinary History*, **IV**, (1973), 25.

25   Foucault, *Power/Knowledge, supra*, at 122.

26   Foucault, *The History of Sexuality, supra*, at 104.

27   Medical concern over education was not restricted to its possible effects on women. At a time of increasing working-class organization, its possible liberating effect produced concern; see, for example, G. King, 'Education in Parochial Schools: Its Influence on Insanity and Mental Aberration', *BMJ* (14 September (1855), 855 at 856.

28   W. Moore, 'The Higher Education of Women', *BMJ* (14 August 1886), 295 at 297.

29   See S. Sontag, *Illness as Metaphor* (London: Penguin, 1991), 44.

30   Dr Arabella Keneally, quoted in Ehrenreich and English, *supra*, at 117.

31   A.R. Burr, *Weir Mitchell: His Life and Letters* (New York: Duffield and Co., 1929), 374.

32   Ehrenreich and English, *supra*, at 116.

33   J. Martin, 'Injury to Health From the Present System of Public Education', *BMJ* (16 February 1884), 311 at 311–12.

34   King, *supra*, at 856.

35   Sir J. Crichton-Browne, 'Sex in Education', *BMJ* (7 May 1892), 949 at 952–3.

36   Moore, *supra*, at 298.

37   'University of London', *BMJ* (16 May 1874), 661.

38   Moore, *supra*, at 296.

39   Ehrenreich and English, *supra*, at 116.

40   Miss Chreiman, 'The Physical Culture of Women', *BMJ* (19 January 1889), 139.

41   W. Goodell, *Lessons in Gynaecology* (Philadelphia: D.G. Brinton, 1879), 353.

42   Moore, *supra*, at 299.

43   Smith-Rosenberg and Rosenberg, *supra*, at 340.

44   T.S. Clouston, *Female Education from a Medical Point of View* (Edinburgh, 1882), 19.

45   H. Storer, *Is It I? A Book For Every Man* (Boston: Lee and Shephard, 1867), (1974), 89–90.

46   H. McCormack, *Moral–Sanitary Economy* (London, 1853), 8.

47   'University of London', *BMJ* (16 May 1874), 661.

48   Ibid.

49   Ibid.

50   The prescribed role of women in the nineteenth century appears to have been so constricting and limiting as to create a situation where disease was seen as an alternative role. Carol Smith-Rosenberg states: 'This was a period when ... social and structural change had created stress within the family and when, in addition, individual domestic role alternatives were few and rigidly defined. From this perspective hysteria can be seen as an alternative role option for particular women unable to

accept their life situation' C. Smith-Rosenberg, 'The Hysterical Woman: Sex Role Conflict in Nineteenth-Century America', *Social Research*, **XXXIX**, (Winter 1972), 652 at 655, 678).

51 Speech to the House of Commons, 7 June 1842, cited in I. Pinchbeck, *Women Workers and Industrial Revolution 1750–1850* (London: Frank Cass, 1969), 267.

52 'Hygiene of Female Workers', *BMJ* (26 September 1884), 578.

53 S. Atkins and B. Hoggett, *Women and the Law* (Oxford: Blackwell, 1984), 12–13.

54 *Report of the Women's Employment Committee of the Ministry of Reconstruction*, Cd 9239 (London: HMSO, 1918).

55 'Case of Blighted Foetus', *BMJ* (3 January 1857), 12.

56 'Infant Mortality and Female Labour in Factories', *BMJ* (19 January 1884), 134.

57 W. Stanley Jevons, 'Married Women in Factories', *BMJ* (14 January 1882), 63. The primacy of female removal from the home as a cause of infant mortality was reiterated by George Reid, who claimed: 'Whatever the secondary cause might be, the main cause of the increased mortality was undoubtedly the employment of women in factories' (G. Reid, 'Legal Restraint Upon the Employment of Women in Factories Before and After Childbirth', *BMJ* (30 July 1892), 275 at 278).

58 Reid, 'Legal Restraint' *supra.*

59 Ibid.

60 Jevons, *supra*, at 63.

61 Moore, *supra*, at 299.

62 Jevons, *supra*, at 63.

63 'The Employment of Women', *BMJ* (22 August 1863), 224.

64 McCormack, *supra*, at 7.

65 'Medical Women', *BMJ* (14 October 1871), 454.

66 This aggression is, in a way, reflected in the combative language used. The opposition to women was framed in the language of warfare, for example: 'The walls of our modern Jericho will not fall before the sound of a voice, however fluty or nicely modulated' ('Minerva Medica', *BMJ* (23 September 1871), 356); or: 'The Queens University, it is anticipated, will be the next to follow suit [in admitting women] and, these fortresses having surrendered at discretion, it is impossible that others can long sustain the siege' (*BMJ* (21 October 1876), 537). The vocabulary, employing the words and imagery of siege and surrender, reveal for us the insecurity, and corresponding combativeness, of the profession.

67 General Council of Medical Education and Registration, 'Discussion of the Admission of Women to the Medical Profession', *BMJ* (3 July 1875), 9 at 10.

68 'Female Physicians', *BMJ* (26 July 1862), 96.

69 J. Hutchinson, President's Address, 'A Review of Current Topics of Medical and Social Interest', *BMJ* (19 August 1876), 231 at 232.

70 'The Female Doctor Question …', *BMJ* (22 November 1862), 537.

71 'Medical Education for Women', *BMJ* (30 April 1870), 445.

72 'Female Physicians', *BMJ* (26 July 1862), 96.

73 General Council of Medical Education and Registration, *supra*, at 16.

74 In the course of questioning which areas of medicine a woman could manage, surgery was ruled out: 'Surgery they can hardly follow; for like Rosalind, they would faint, we fancy, at the very sight of blood' ('Shall We Have Female Graduates in Medicine'), *BMJ* (2 August 1856), 653 at 654).

75 A.H., 'Mr Huthinson's Address', *BMJ* (23 September 1876), 414.

76 General Council of Medical Education and Registration, *supra*, at 10.

77 'Medical Act Amended …', *BMJ* (8 July 1867), 65.

78   S.W. Sibley, 'Remarks on Some Current Medical Topics', *BMJ* (1 September 1877), 283.
79   'Women Doctors', *BMJ* (28 May 1870), 559.
80   'Female Physicians', *BMJ* (26 July 1862), 96.
81   Ibid.
82   H.S. Pomeroy, *The Ethics of Marriage* (New York: Funk and Wagnalls, 1888), 95.
83   Ibid., at vii.
84   Ibid., at 137–8.
85   Indeed, any failure to procreate was opposed. The 'Maiden' woman was not exempt from this, opposition manifesting again in biomedical 'evidence' of the ills likely to befall her. See Smith-Rosenberg and Rosenberg, *supra*, at 336.
86   E.S. Chesser, *Woman, Marriage and Womanhood* (London: Cassell and Co., 1913), 43.
87   Pomeroy, *supra*, at 97.
88   L.F.E. Bergeret, 'Clinical Lecture on Conjugal Onanism and Kindred Sins', *Philadelphia Medical Times* (1 February 1872), 162.
89   H. Storer, *Is It I? A Book for Every Man* (Boston: Lee and Shephard, 1867), 115–16.
90   H. Storer, *Why Not? A Book for Every Woman* (Boston: Lee and Shephard, 1865), 36.
91   Storer, *Is It I?*, *supra*, at 76. See also Geo. Steele Perkins, 'The Traffic in Abortifacients', *BMJ* (25 February 1899), 506. Yet see n.85.
92   Storer, *Why Not?*, *supra*, at 81.
93   Storer, *Is It I?*, *supra*, at 76.
94   *BMJ* (26 September 1868), 351.
95   'American Opinion on Artificial Abortion', *BMJ* (19 February 1870), 189.
96   W.L. Atlee and D.A. O'Donnell, 'Report of the Committee on Criminal Abortion', *Transactions of the American Medical Association*, **XXII**, (1871), 241.
97   Steele Perkins, *supra*, at 596.
98   Ibid.
99   A. Nebinger, *Criminal Abortion; Its Extent and Prevention* (Philadelphia: Collins, 1876), 11. Nebinger believed women sought abortions because of the 'inconvenience incident in pregnancy, fear of the pains and risks of labor; but mainly … to avoid the labor and expense of rearing children, and the interference with pleasurable pursuits, fashions and frivolities' (ibid.).
100   E. Hale, *The Great Crime of the Nineteenth Century* (Chicago: C.S. Halsey, 1867), 10.
101   'The Traffic in Abortifacient', *BMJ* (14 January 1899), 110 at 111.
102   Ibid.
103   'Rethinking (M)otherhood: Feminist Theory and State Regulation of Pregnancy', *Harvard Law Review*, **103**, (1990), 1325 at 1333 (quotation omitted).
104   D.M. Reese, 'Infant Mortality in Large Cities; The Sources for its Increase, and Means for its Diminution', *Transactions of the American Medical Association*, **X**, (1857), 91 at 101–2.
105   D.H., 'Procuring Abortion: A Physician's Reply to the Solicitations of a Married Woman to Produce a Miscarriage for Her', *Nashville Journal of Medicine and Surgery*, **17**, (1876), 200 at 201.
106   Smart, *supra*, 96.
107   The birth rate of the upper classes was believed to be 'about half, or even less than half' of that of other classes: 'A Low Birth-Rate', *BMJ* (24 September 1892), 705.
108   J. Matthews Duncan, 'The Sterility of Women', *BMJ* (24 February 1883), 343 at 344.
109   Between 1800 and 1900, the white fertility rate in the United States decreased by 50

per cent. The number of children born to married women dropped dramatically, from 7.04 to 3.56: J. Smith, 'Family Limitation', in N. Cott and E. Pleck (eds), *A Heritage of Her Own* (New York: Simon & Schuster, 1979), 226.

110   Nebinger, *supra*, at 6–7.

111   A. Gardner, *Conjugal Sins Against the Laws of Life and Health* (New York: J.S. Redfield, 1870), 5.

112   M.A. Pallen, 'Foeticide or Criminal Abortion', *Medical Archives*, **3**, (1869), 193 at 195.

113   E.S. Chesser, *From Girlhood to Womanhood* (London: Cassell and Co., 1913), 122.

114   J. Mohr, *Abortion in America: The Origins and Evolution of National Policy* (New York: Oxford University Press, 1978), 167. This reflects the broader eugenic base of 'race suicide' arguments: 'it was aimed at the defence of the WASP establishment against rising immigration and proletarianization, a goal that would be taken on more directly by early-twentieth-century eugenicists' (Petchesky, *supra*, at 79).

115   E.H. Clarke, *Sex in Education: Or a Fair Chance For Girls* (Boston: J.R. Osgood and Co., 1874), 63.

116   T. Laqueur, 'Orgasm, Generation and the Politics of Reproductive Biology', *Representations*, **14**, (1986), 1 at 18.

117   Foucault, *Power/Knowledge*, *supra*, at 58.

PART II

3   The Abortion Act 1967:
        Supporting Narratives

Abortion is no longer a single issue but rather a code word for a whole range of issues. ('The Bishop's Plan for Prolife Activities', *America* (27 December 1975), 454)

By the 1960s 'permissiveness' had become a political metaphor, marking a social and political divide. But it was a charged and emotive term, obscuring, in its ambivalence, more than it illuminated. Those who were supposedly chief advocates of the 'permissive society' would rarely have used the term; while for the defenders of traditional (and largely authoritarian) values, 'permissiveness' became an almost scatological word of abuse, a phrase which welded together a number of complex, and not necessarily connected changes, into a potent symbol of unity ... by erecting that symbol of sexual relaxation, of loose moral standards, of disrespect for all that was traditional and 'good', it became easier ... to recreate a sense of crisis around social changes and the beginnings of a mass support for authoritarian moral solutions. (Jeffery Weeks, *Sex, Politics and Society* (London: Longmans, 1989), 249)

Introduction

Peter Greenaway's controversial 1993 film, *The Baby of Macon*, is based broadly upon a remark made in Greenaway's preceding film, *The Cook, the Thief, His Wife and Her Lover*: simply that the good of the world are seldom rewarded, the bad are seldom punished, and the innocent are always abused.[1] To Greenaway the film represents an attempt to resolve 'intriguing and damning questions about the nature of abuse, symbols, reality, history, film, cinema, ways, methods and techniques of telling a story'.[2] At its most immediate, *The Baby of Macon* considers a legend of the creation, and ultimate destruction, of a child–saint represented through the medium of a play performed in the 1650s in Italy. The film/play tells the tale of a child born to a woman misshapen, disfigured and bald through disease, famine and age. The birth of this *perfect* child to this woman, and in a time of misery and barrenness, gives the child magical, miraculous significance. The miraculous child becomes a point of conflict: 'The child means potency, wealth and power for those who can exploit him.'[3] The initial conflict arises between mother and daughter, the daughter imprisoning her mother and claiming the child as her own progeny – a virgin birth. The claims of the daughter are easily accepted; how could a woman so old, so destroyed, produce this flawless, miraculous child?

The child then becomes a locus for conflict between sister/'mother' and the Church. The child is seen as a projection of superstition, its status unverified by the new rationalism of the Church, the Church's following threatened by this miraculous child. In the Church's inevitable victory, the miraculous child becomes an instrument of pecuniary gain, hair, teeth, faeces and vials of tears and urine being auctioned for their sacred and curative powers. Ultimately, the child is destroyed at the hands of its sister/ 'mother'. The child is graphically and brutally ripped apart, dismembered, by its faithful following. The 'mother', by religious decree, is in turn subjected to a fatal mass rape: 'deflower[ed] according to various bogus religious examples of sado-masochistic martyrdom'.[4] The biological parents perish.

Greenaway's parable acts as a commentary on the manipulation and corruption of the child by the media and society. Not least of Greenaway's inspirations was the high-profile work of Italian photographer, Olivieri Toscani, probably best known in the United Kingdom for his controversial Benneton advertising campaign:

> The film arose from the consideration of many propositions, many of them formal and iconographic, but of not small significance were two images – the infamous contemporary poster of a seconds-old newborn child covered in blood and mucous, and – more obscurely – an Elle fashion-magazine front-cover featuring a beautiful model far too young to be the mother of the beautiful blue-eyed child she was holding to her coutured breast in the image of a Nativity painting.[5]

Whilst manipulation and corruption are central to the film, Greenaway is equally concerned with our associated inability to disentangle fact from fiction, media falsity and spectacle from (other) truths and realities. *The Baby of Macon* challenges the fictions through which desires, greed and struggles for power may be rationalized: 'there is deliberate, organised confusion as to what is real, what is theatrical, who is an actor, who is a member of an audience, what is a ceremony in the theatre and what is the theatre-play in the church'.[6] In the final brutal rape, for instance, theatre becomes reality/cinema: 'The actress playing the sister is forced to suffer the humiliations of her stage character.'[7]

As has been suggested in the first two chapters, the discourses and politics of reproduction may be read in these terms. The female reproductive system is a point of conflict and of manipulation. Similarly, like Greenaway's perception of the child, the foetus is subject to a complex iconography, both secular and sacred. While the discourses to be considered in this and the following chapter will again concern primarily the figure of the (aborting) woman, there is an implicit foetal presence. This presence becomes much more explicit in abortion and other reproductive debates subsequent to the Abortion Act 1967 and will be considered in Part III. Nonetheless, given this implicit presence, it is at this stage worth expanding upon the investment of both the woman and the foetus.

Like the child–saint in Greenaway's parable, the foetus is shrouded, swaddled, by narrative. It has become almost an object of theatre, subject to falsity and distortion. In 1965, Lennart Nilsson published in *Life* magazine his foetal photographs: 'Drama of Life Before Birth'.[8] The photographs were to become illustrative material for most works on reproduction that were to follow. They were also used in a pro-life postcard campaign during consideration of the Alton Bill in 1988. The photographs were structured, presented and narrated as *life*, as 'human embryos in their natural state'. A supporter of the Alton Bill in the Commons described the photograph selected for the campaign as 'a beautiful photograph of an eighteen-week foetus. It was clear [and] precise in colour'.[9] In reality, they were images of death – still, breathless and void of life – autopsied embryos.[10] In both the physical and the narrative there has been a 'deliberate, organised confusion'. The foetus has become a discursive object, around it is spun a complex series of narratives, fictions and desires.

This is explained further, and with a less narrow focus, in considering a related work by Greenaway. In a curatorial exhibition, *The Physical Self*, at Boymans van Beunigen National Gallery Collection in Rotterdam in 1991, Greenaway presented 400 images of the human body from the last 600 years. He placed Olivieri Toscani's raw newborn image as the first hanging of the exhibition.[11] According to Greenaway, the picture's 'transparently uncensored – and as it was perceived – sensational honesty conceived of in a publicity context put many of those fine and beautiful Christian propaganda pictures of the Nativity, and those well-wrought advertisements of the virgin Birth into all manner of new perspectives'.[12] The honesty of Toscani's image illuminated the power of historical propaganda, of historical 'stories'. A new image is required to prompt our understanding that what is within our field of view is not merely the physical but also the narrative, the connotation.[13] The narrative constructs our visual landscape and the *possi-*

bilities of that landscape. The same power infects the law, as Katherine O'Donovan has observed: 'Old stories can retain a powerful hold. Stories affect the creation of law and its application. Such laws remain with us and mediate our perception of realities and truths. The stories influence what we see and what we can see.'[14]

Within the intercourse between reproduction and law the role of 'stories' is conspicuous. In the nineteenth century, abortion became enmeshed in a story of developing gender roles, racial (and racist) concerns and a shifting world power structure.[15] It also emerged as central to the story told by an occupation desperately seeking status enhancement, spinning a narrative that would validate, indeed, demand occupational closure.[16] As conspicuous as the stories that are told are the stories that are not told. In the debate preceding the Abortion Act 1967, the denial of a historical narrative is as poignant as the new stories that were spun. In the discourse (medical, parliamentary, legal and journalistic) – the chiaroscuro out of which the 1967 Act emerged – history was denied. In the extensive debates in the Houses of Parliament no reference was made to the emergence of prohibitive abortion legislation in the nineteenth century. Not even was there the purblind account of paternalistic medicine that the United States Supreme Court was later to narrate in the *Roe* v. *Wade* decision.[17] In many ways, law denies itself knowledge by the constraints it imposes upon its own narrative; in other words, its knowledge is limited by what it allows itself to know. In consideration of the abortion issue, it denied and denies itself knowledge of the complexity of motives that shaped legislation in the nineteenth century. During the second reading of David Steel's Private Member's Bill, the bill that was to go on to become the Abortion Act 1967, opponent William Wells, Member of Parliament for Walsall North, epitomized this historically sanitized approach. Wells warned: 'The path which this Bill seeks to tread would reverse the trends that we have tried painfully to build up in this and in other countries for respecting all human life as something sacred in itself.'[18] The complexity of motive that had shaped the anti-abortion campaign in the nineteenth century did not fall within the consideration of Parliament. Most importantly, the motives and desires that by 1967 would have appeared anachronistic and impermissible were not considered by the legislature.

Although the Abortion Act was constructed without an explicit recognition of the campaign waged by the emerging medical profession in the nineteenth century, many of the assumptions, preoccupations and aims of the reformers were similar. With the focus provided by an understanding of the campaign of the preceding century it becomes possible to disentangle (to decode) the language utilized within the discourse around the passage of the Act. As this chapter and the next will illustrate, once the language has been decoded the parallels between the campaigns are revealed. Whilst a belief in a woman's 'proper and God-given sphere',[19] frailty and the overriding importance of her reproductive system appeared no longer as explicit, covertly the debates, and ultimately the Act, still appear to be predicated on them. To substantiate this assertion, it is intended to provide a consideration of the female subjects created within the parliamentary discourses: the present chapter will interrogate the discourse of those who supported David Steel's bill, while Chapter 4 will move on to subject the opposing narratives to the same analysis.

In reading these narratives within the law's discourse, it is worth reflecting briefly that feminist jurisprudence in recent years has highlighted, paradoxically, the blindness of law to gender[20] and, simultaneously, the gendered nature of law.[21] Critiques have posited law as essentially male (or *phallocentric*), suggesting either a male universal subject[22] or the construction of law as masculine within individual laws.[23] In her consideration of the Abortion Act, Sally Sheldon conceptualizes the legal subject as an internal construct of a given law.[24] She contends that 'Law creates its own fiction of the subject it seeks to regulate', and that, recognizing this, it is possible to '"deconstruct" the 1967 Act to reveal the legal subject created within it'.[25] This section seeks not only to consider the *fiction* of Woman[26] within the 1967 Act, and the discourse around its enactment, but also to question why this fictionalization occurs. It is suggested that the fiction, and the commonalities in the proponents' and opponents' positions, reflect not merely women as the subject of regulation but, mirroring nineteenth-century concerns, the control of women as a means of controlling gender relations, the family and the structure of society.

Before embarking on the project outlined above, it is worth providing an idea of the parameters applied. While it is intended to concentrate on the question of construction and regulation in this central section, it should not be assumed that this was the sole concern of legislators or campaigners. Nor, indeed, would it be wise to attempt to claim, or suggest it is possible, that there exists one story or *history* of the development of abortion law, or indeed of our attitudes to abortion. Rather, it may be suggested that there exist *histories* of development. These histories provide hermeneutic tools, uncovering and exploring 'different layers of understanding'.[27] The analysis provided here is intended to fall within this recognition of 'multiple standpoints, multiple truths, multiple sites of power/knowledge'.[28] To explain this a little further with a pertinent example. As has already been recognized, women's reproductive rights and freedoms are a result of a complex network of interactions. Women's reproductive options in both the long term and the short term are determined by the interplay of numerous and disparate interests, including religion, medicine, law, the economy and the family.[29] As with the criminalization of abortion in the nineteenth century, the professional self-interest of medicine again played a crucial if not determinative role in the twentieth century. This role has been considered elsewhere, and the complexity of interests that structure reproductive options illustrated.[30] Most notably, this other history illustrates the enduring role of the medical profession in shaping the landscape of reproductive discourse or, as O'Donovan may state, telling 'The stories [that] influence what we see and what we can see.'[31] While recognizing the role of the medical profession, this chapter, as has already been noted, seeks primarily to discuss the construction of Woman within the primary debates around the enactment of the Abortion Act 1967. Implicit in addressing such a construction is Greenaway's lesson: the 'nativity' and foetus as inscribed and encoded presences, arguably – to use Greenaway's term – propaganda. This discussion is intended both as an illustration of the complex investment of reproduction and the foetus and as a 'complementary piece of the jigsaw'[32] of factors that mediate women's access to abortion services.

The Abortion Act: 'Tired Housewives' and 'Tarts'

> When issues which we habitually conceptualize in terms of women's bodies are reconsidered in the light of ... history, it is possible to see that they in fact involve questions concerning women's roles. (Reva Siegel, 'Reasoning from the Body: A Historical Perspective on Abortion Regulation and Questions of Equal Protection' *Stanford Law Review*, **44**, (1992), 261 at 265)

> The living unborn deserve better than obscene and macabre games. (Elizabeth Peacock, H.C. Deb. vol. 125, col. 1292, 1988 (18 October))

The campaign to criminalize abortion in the nineteenth century was, as has been illustrated, in part a campaign to reaffirm and enforce women's traditional roles. The adoption of anti-abortion legislation was seen by many as a means of securing the challenged public/private gender divide. In many ways, the debate surrounding the decriminalization of abortion in the twentieth century replayed this earlier campaign.

As in *The Baby of Macon*, the abortion debate of the mid-twentieth century was predicated upon two divergent constructs of Woman. These constructs were spun out of stereotype, individual experience, and prejudice. The parliamentarians' discourse 'crisscrosse[d] the realm of 'fact' (the real) and 'interpretation' (the ideal) ... transect[ing] the splits between objective and subjective, empirical and normative, value free and biased'.[33] The images, a melding of the real and the ideal, constructed by the parliamentarians became generalized and normalized to the exclusion of the experiences of *real* women. Through the parliamentary interplay of these two women the debate was largely played out.

In recognizing the existence of two predominant constructs within the framework noted above, it is not intended to imply that these images (or 'stories') were exclusive, or in their telling unified. There did, however, exist two dominant paradigms within the parliamentary discourse. Within this discourse the female subject bifurcated, emerging (predominantly) as *Angel* or *Witch, Wearied Mother* or *Feckless Girl, Tired Housewife* or *Tart*.[34] These projections are also evident in other discourses, infecting, and infected by, the parliamentarians' own discourse. Thus these constructions may be understood intertextually. Woman exists as the embodiment of a miasma, a web, of interwoven and reciprocating discourses and representations. As Roland Barthes recognized, the 'text' (or 'story') is 'a multi-dimensional space in which a variety of writings, none of them original, blend and clash. The text is a tissue of quotations drawn from innumerable centres of culture.'[35] Similarly, J. Hillis Miller has observed the literary work as 'inhabited ... by a long chain of parasitical presences, echoes, allusions, guests [and] ghosts of previous texts'.[36] The 'text' of the parliamentarians cannot, therefore, be withdrawn from the discourses/texts which are narrated in other 'centres of culture'. It is intended here, to a limited extent, to place the texts generated within the abortion debate within this intertextual analysis. To do so illuminates more clearly the nature of the female subjects that resides within the legal imagination. It also suggests, perhaps informing feminist engagement with the law, the complexity of cultural factors nourishing the beliefs that predicate these parliamentary constructions of Woman.

The duality within the legal/extralegal discourse, the positing of women seeking abortions as 'tired housewives or tarts', reflected (approximately) the divide between proponent and opponent. Although it must be recognized that what could be called parliamentary pragmatism would have limited the reformers' campaign strategy options, proponents of David Steel's bill saw women who sought abortions as primarily victims. Such women were emotionally and physically exhausted. Importantly, abortions were sought by women who were pushed to their limit, having already fulfilled their maternal roles. She was Angel, Wearied Mother and Tired Housewife. Conversely, opponents of the Medical Termination of Pregnancy Bill (as it was in its passage through Parliament) cast the woman who may have sought to terminate her pregnancy as indulgent, selfish and immoral. Again the family was central, opponents believing such women to be eschewing their maternal and familial obligations. Such a woman was Witch, Feckless Girl and Tart. The discourse of opponent and proponent shared the commonality of a presumption of motherhood as the primary role for women. Their conflict was whether abortion would affirm or weaken this relationship. The question of abortion and women's rights did not enter the discourse until after the enactment of the 1967 provisions.[37] It is the campaign of the proponents that will be examined in this chapter. Chapter 4 will address the Witch, Feckless Girl and Tart of the opponents' discourse. Importantly, within these constructs there resonate several of the themes prominent in the nineteenth-century discourse.

The Tired Housewife

The story most often told by the proponents of David Steel's bill was that of the 'distracted multi-child mother'.[38] Typically, she was 'a working class woman [with] six or seven children',[39] a 'woman in total misery'.[40] Many in Parliament rationalized their support for the bill on the basis of these 'poor, unfortunate women, driven to desperation'[41] by their 'overlarge families'.[42] Dr John Dunwoody, for example, stated: 'I am thinking particularly of mothers with large families and the burdens of large families very often with low incomes.'[43] Not only was this parliamentarian Woman 'at the mercy of her fertility',[44] but she was also invariably the victim of an inappropriate and ruinous husband. Repeatedly, he was described as 'unsupport[ing]',[45] 'errant',[46] 'a chronic drunkard'.[47] He may even have 'fecklessly hounded her from pregnancy to pregnancy'.[48] If the husband was not otherwise inappropriate, he was sometimes charged with forcing or pressurizing the woman to visit the abortionist: 'In some cases which have come to my attention in my constituencies abortions have been occasioned by pressure from the husband upon the wife when it has been discovered that an additional child is to be born into the family.'[49]

It is interesting to note the presence of the husband within this discourse. The parliamentarians appear to provide a normative assessment as to appropriate male heterosexual behaviour. This supports the assertion made by Beverly Brown that the private realm, which was once free from the penetrating gaze of the state, is now collapsing.[50] Although she is referring to the issue of indecency laws, Brown's observation is pertinent. Perhaps more pertinent, however, is her recognition of the home as a focus for surveillance, a surveillance born out of the fear of 'an inherently dangerous, unpredictable, latent and punitive sexuality, a degenerate sexuality capable of extinguishing future generations'.[51]

Returning to the image of the wearied mother/suffering wife, it is worth noting that this was not restricted to Parliament. Alice Jenkins, the first secretary of the Abortion Law Reform Association (ALRA),[52] the organization probably instrumental in having abortion debated before Parliament,[53] wrote of 'poverty-stricken women in the lower income groups'.[54] Other extraparliamentary campaigners utilized this image, as well as the brutal and priapic image of the husband. Madeleine Simms, for example, another member of the ALRA, was to explain several years after the enactment of the Bill: 'It was chiefly for the worn out mother of many children with an ill or illiterate or feckless or brutal or drunken or otherwise inadequate husband that we were fighting.'[55]

Within this discourse, the stories and images that are told and evoked, Woman and Mother become indistinguishable. The 'Woman of Law' is a legal fiction, a product/envelopment of male imaginings.[56] Here the 'Woman of Law' appears as Mother, as Alison Young has observed: 'Women as individuals have been blurred into the amorphous mass of the Mother, the Incubator, the Ecosystem which exists only to sustain the bud, the germ within.'[57] Motherhood is portrayed as natural, almost inevitable. Dame Joan Vickers, for example, at one point attested: 'I think that most women desire motherhood. It is natural for a woman to want to have children.'[58] As a corollary it must then be unnatural not to want to have a child. Woman as mother is natural, women beyond the home, without children are unnatural, abberations. As a consequence it can be seen that within the parliamentarians' discourse a model of female sexuality is clearly prescribed, defined and delimited.[59] Female sexuality is tied to husband, home and procreation. Recognizing the productive nature of discourse, it can be seen that proponents of the bill constructed a role for women to play, a role similar to that of *True Womanhood* recognized in Chapter 2. As Luce Irigaray has observed, the role or 'path ... historically assigned to the feminine [is] that of mimicry'.[60] The proceedings and report of the Birkett Committee (a ministerially appointed interdepartmental committee which reported on abortion in 1939)[61] further illustrate the role to be *mimicked* which is constructed within the abortion debates. It was clearly motherhood, and not women themselves, that became the primary focus for the committee and those giving evidence before it.[62] Many of the secular female groups proposing reform before the committee, for example, sought liberalization of the law and yet discouraged contraception until the woman had a child, or sometimes two.[63] Female sexuality was therefore clearly located within a heterosexual procreative framework. Even where procreation was eschewed, female sexuality was fixed firmly within the heterosexual.[64]

While constructing or affirming a female role and a model of female sexuality, Parliament also constructed a *figure* needing and justifying protection. Providing a further continuity with the nineteenth century, not only was motherhood seen as a natural role but the female subject was also seen as determined by her reproductive organs and their physiological processes. It is this I want to turn to next.

Returning to Biopower

The previous section outlined the way in which parliamentary and other proponents of reform constructed the aborting Woman. The present section and the one that follows return to Foucault's concept of biopower. This is done with the aim of highlighting the broader regulatory framework within which the proponents' discourse may be understood.

As in the nineteenth century, medico-legal discourse can be located within the complex series of power networks that invest and inscribe the body, sexuality, the family, and so on.[65] Again 'hysterization' facilitated the drawing in of reproduction, and particularly women's bodies, into a more visible social arena.[66] Made more visible, reproduction and women's bodies became a means of regulation. This continuing process of *investment*, of hysterization, was evidenced verbally in the House of Commons by Dr David Owen: 'The whole reproductive cycle of woman is intimately tied to her psyche. We know that a woman is susceptible to depression at times of pregnancy, at times of menopause and at times of menstruation.'[67] Interfering with the woman's uterus-centred internal economy therefore ran great risks, as Owen further explained: 'Interfering with a natural course of pregnancy is something which a doctor does only with great care, knowing full well that he is doing something which could have adverse effects.'[68] Woman, therefore, appears a hostage to her physiology 'by reason of a pathology intrinsic to it'.[69] Her natural procreative role, frailty and emotion combine to justify paternalistic legislation. She is brought within the social body through the biomedical construction of her reproductive system. As Zillah Eisenstein reminds us, 'The soul is male, and the follies of the body are female.'[70] Pathologized within the abortion debates, this Woman of Law becomes a part of the historical and overworked motif of the passive, suffering and resigned female.[71] Woman within reproductive/political discourse appears to merge effortlessly with the projections of the cultural imagination, an imagination that both invests and is invested by this discourse. She appears, as Barthes has written, 'woven entirely with citations'.[72] It becomes impossible to disentangle her from the popular images of motherhood, and particularly the metaphors of illness that are accommodated within these images. Woman comes to inhabit what Susan Sontag has called 'the night-side of life, a more onerous citizenship'.[73] Woman becomes 'other' both to man and to health. Where man may exist within the kingdom of the well, woman, holding this 'onerous citizenship', must reside in the kingdom of the sick. She becomes indistinguishable from the many popular images of female/maternal suffering. This *passive victim* is the many emaciated, languid and funereal figures of nineteenth-century literature, the hollow-eyed and haunted tubercular women of Edvard Munch, the tragic consumptive figures of opera. In her beatific suffering and innocence she is the tubercular Little Eva in Harriet Beecher Stowe's *Uncle Tom's Cabin*, Milly Theale in Henry James' *The Wings of the Dove*, the long-suffering and pious Madame Grandet in Balzac's *Eugénie Grandet*.

Biopower and the Family

Remembering that Foucault's concept of biopower recognizes a bifurcation (its discourses and practices centring around both the 'anatomopolitics of the human body' and a more general regulatory concern for the population[74]), it is interesting to note how the female reproductive system becomes a point of confluence, an axis at which these two poles converge. Within the parliamentary discourses there is an obvious convergence: a regulatory interest in the (re)production of the population. A woman's reproductive health, the health of the family and therefore that of the population become indivisible. Within the parliamentary imagination, Woman becomes the figure whose health must be secure 'to enable her to carry out her responsibilities to others',[75] this responsibility obviously extending to the state. This nexus between female reproductive health and the health of the population, as well as the associated and more general locating of the woman within the family, is seen in attempts to explain the necessity of what was labelled the 'Social Clause', which legitimated the termination of a pregnancy where 'the pregnant woman's capacity as a mother [would be] severely overstrained by the care of a child or of an other child'.[76] Dr John Dunwoody, for example, stated: 'It means the ability to be the person who brings the family together, who knits the various children and the mother and father together, so that the mother can play the part she ought to play in building and maintaining the family unit.'[77] Dunwoody further explains that the provision is intended to protect the woman from a situation where it is 'impossible for her to fulfil her real function, her worthwhile function as mother, of holding together the family unit, so that all too often the family breaks apart, and it is for this reason that we have too many problem families in many parts of the country'.[78] Also referring to the social clause, Home Secretary Roy Jenkins was to argue that, in the absence of such a provision, 'many women who are far from anxious to escape the responsibilities of motherhood, but rather wish to discharge their existing ones more effectively, would be denied relief'.[79] Beyond the 'Social Clause', reform of the abortion law generally was justified on similar grounds. Discussing the 'distracted multi-child mother', David Owen also demonstrated how abortion law reform was needed for the sake of the family:

Such a woman is in total misery, and could be precipitated into a depression deep and lasting. What happens to the woman when she gets depressed? She is incapable of looking after those children, so she retires into a shell of herself and loses all feeling, all her drive and affection. Members of my profession in the House have seen people who are depressed and the total lack of energy and drive.[80]

Again the legal imagination appears invested with a complex series of cultural representations. Woman becomes a figure exhausted, mentally and physically, by her sacrifice to the family. In this she is almost a female *Ecce Homo* (*Ecce Femina*?), a figure of pain, anguish and sacrifice. She becomes submerged in both sacred and secular iconography. This tissue of different texts perpetuates the mythology of Woman, as Nina Auerbach writes: 'The myth of womanhood flourishes not in the carefully wrought prescriptions of sages, but in the half-life of popular literature and art, forms which distil the essence of a culture.'[81] Importantly, such intertextuality fails to be innocuous: 'Myth transmits and transforms the ideology of sexism and renders it invisible.'[82] The ideology subverted and made invisible here is the presumption of a maternal/familial role for women.

Rationalizing abortion on the basis of familial responsibility, centring Woman within the home, was also evident in parliamentary debates that occurred subsequent to the 1967 Act. These later discourses also appear shaped by the many cultural and religious representations of maternal sacrifice and pain. Discussing David Alton's Private Member's Bill, which attempted to place an 18-week upper time limit on abortion, Jo Richardson, opposing the bill observed: 'Whatever the reason for an unintended pregnancy, it affects the mental and physical health of a woman in terms of her children or other family responsibilities, adding further strains to an already over-strained household income.'[83] Theresa Gorman, another opponent of David Alton's bill, while eschewing the imagery of maternal sacrifice and suffering, clearly locates Woman within the home. Gorman very clearly stated her belief that women had a 'right' to abortion: 'It is a matter of civil rights. It is a matter of a woman's right to decide her own future and her own fertility.'[84] Yet, for Gorman, this right only appeared to manifest itself 'after consulting her family, her doctors and, where appropriate, her religious adviser'.[85] In these terms, abortion appears a highly qualified 'civil right'. It is a right that cedes to the woman only if she is married, and in this it is similar to the historic denial of the 'civil right' to vote to all but married women.[86] There appears a clear association between marriage, judgment and stability. Marriage is normal and normalizes.

The benefits for the family to accrue from less restrictive abortion provisions were also stressed in earlier discourses. Such provisions were held to guarantee greater marital happiness, family stability and security.[87] Alice Jenkins, in her influential book *Law for the Rich*, placed much emphasis upon the need for access to abortion services for continued family happiness. She described the 'late' child (again evoking the image of the wearied mother who had fulfilled her child-rearing role) as a 'family catastrophe',[88] and warned that 'when an unplanned pregnancy occurs it will jeopardise the happiness and well being of the family'.[89] More fully, Jenkins was to go on to warn against 'the unhappy marital atmosphere caused by a failure of contraception, especially the bad psychological effect on the mother concerned'.[90] More prosaically perhaps, Sir Dugald Baird was to advocate termination followed by sterilization for the pregnant 'multi-child mother'. Baird concurred with the assertion of others that freer access to abortion was needed, perhaps mostly for family stability. He told of his findings in Aberdeen:

> In older women who do not want more children and are sustained to breaking-point by the occurrence of another pregnancy, the results of termination plus tubal ligation are most satisfactory. There is a striking improvement in the woman's physical and mental health and in the well-being of the whole family, with a more congenial home atmosphere and better marital relations. In short, removal of the constant threat of pregnancy allows the woman to be a better wife and mother.[91]

Woman as wife/mother was also used to justify the provision of legal abortion with the fear that the burdens imposed by an unwanted pregnancy, and an 'overlarge family', would drive a woman to suicide.[92] In this the discourse of the proponents plunders and 'crisscrosses' with some of the most tragic representations of tortured selfless motherhood. The discourse consumes images of maternal death, not just the suicidal but also the sacrificial. Perhaps more tellingly, there are evoked distant cultural resonances of maternal death in childbirth – the greatest sacrifice of Mother: Dicken's saintly Clara Copperfield, Tolstoy's Princess Bolkonskaya, Prue in Virginia Woolf's *To the Lighthouse*. Lord Strange in the House of Lords, for example, revealing these assumptions as to gender (sacrifice, innocence, suffering, frailty), claimed that 'nearly every woman in this condition [facing an unwanted pregnancy] would be in a state bordering on suicide'.[93] Thus the overworked and/or anxious woman is believed invariably to be suicidal. She is seen as unable to cope, frail, dependent, irrational, even pathological – in need of normalizing (male) medical care. Alice Jenkins discussed several cases where women had indeed committed suicide having faced such circumstances. She conflates the imagery of *Woman as Mother* and *Woman as Victim* who must be 'preserved for the sake of her children':

Several suicides have taken place in recent years when mothers have feared an addition to the family. In a large city in Yorkshire a mother of five in the lowest income group gassed herself and all her children rather than face the birth of another. In the same city a mother in similar plight found the same way out; leaving her five children motherless. A County Durham mother of five sons gassed herself, and her husband said at the inquest that she was 'very disturbed at the prospect of another child'.[94]

While the death of the pregnant woman was figured rather differently by others, it was nonethless contextualized and used comparably. Dr Joan Malleson, a veteran campaigner for abortion reform, for example, called for the liberalization of the law on the basis that illegal abortion threatened the continuity of the family owing to the risks of mortality. Writing in *The Lancet*, Malleson warned:

Countless women undergo the dangers of unprofessional abortion when no pregnancy exists and without having received any medical opinion whatever. Yet it happens that with invalidation or death of the mothers the family disintegrates, for around their health and their capacity to tend the children the whole house revolves and, therefore, these mothers are the very last to be permitted to jeopardise their well-being.[95]

Malleson's description of the *invalidation* of the woman appears almost deliberately ambiguous. Woman may be physically invalided through the act of abortion, yet such an act may also leave her socially and morally *invalid*, no longer a True Woman. This use of the family as a justification for abortion reform was strengthened by the portrayal of abortion decisions as primarily motivated by selfless consideration of the family, with 'no fear of death or thought of self preservation'.[96] This strengthened both the call for reform and the iconography of Woman/Mother. Abortion became justified, not only on the grounds of paternalism, but also on the basis that it was *natural* for women to rationalize and structure their (reproductive) lives around their families. As Dame Joan Vickers observed, 'I do not think that women are selfish. In general they are very law-abiding. They rarely seek an abortion for its own sake, but for the sake of the family and the unborn child.'[97] Almost identically, Diane Munday was to assert, before the Family Planning Association conference in the University of London Union in 1966, that 'Women were not selfish: they rarely sought abortions for their own sake but rather for the sake of their families and the child to be born.'[98] Munday was to go so far as to suggest an almost *genetic* drive towards abortion in certain circumstances: 'In women whose personal population problem was too much for them, there was an instinctive drive to abortion. It was no good legislating against a feeling as strong as this.'[99] These sentiments were also seen in a memorandum predating the 1966 debates which was presented before the Birkett Interdepartmental Committee on Abortion by the ALRA:

> It is our experience that ... the reason most often given for desiring abortion is the maintenance of an adequate standard of life for the family as a whole, whether this be judged financially, or in terms of health, houseroom, ambition in education or general well being. We find it rare for the mothers to think of their own health alone, however obvious this reason may appear to others. The demand for abortion is frequent amongst those parents who loyally serve the best interests of the family, as they see them.[100]

Returning to the 1967 debates, two Members of Parliament offered *case studies* from their constituencies supporting both the image of Woman as mother/victim and the need for abortion if family life was to be maintained. Lena Jeger (Member for Holborn and St Pancras, South) offered a study of a depressed and 'honest young woman',[101] a mother of five expecting her sixth, who had been refused an abortion:

> This young woman had her sixth baby, by which time her mental depression had become so bad, after a few desperate sad weeks, in a fit of complete despair she threw the baby which she had not wanted and could not bear having on the floor and killed it. The result of that refusal to terminate was that the mother has been in Holloway, the baby is dead and the other children are in care.[102]

Dr Winstanley provided, from his own practice, a case study of 'a mother who had already two children',[103] but who had suffered German Measles early in her third pregnancy. After being persuaded against a termination, she carried the foetus to term:

> The child was born blind, deaf, mentally defective, and with spastic paralysis. This woman had a nervous breakdown and was later admitted to hospital and was under care for some time ... it was necessary for the other two children to go for some time into the care of the local authority. This family was virtually destroyed by [this] event.[104]

This section has illustrated how the proponents of abortion law reform justified their position on the basis of securing women's position within the home. The liberalization of access to abortion services was seen as essential in maintaining appropriate gender roles. Presented in these terms, the decriminalization of abortion may be understood as a technology of gender. Associated with this, the complex biopolitical interest in women's reproductive bodies was clearly visible. The final section of this chapter pursues briefly the eugenic arguments that were seen in the parliamentary speeches and which are suggested by Winstanley's case study noted above.

Regulation, the Population and Eugenics

The preceding section ended with a case study presented by Dr Winstanley. He argued for the provision of abortion services on the grounds of foetal disability. This was justified by reference to the effects giving birth to a disabled child would have on the subsequent procreative role of the woman. Evidencing a convergence of regulatory concerns regarding appropriate gender behaviour and the (re)production of the *normal* population, the implicit 'moral' of Winstanley's case study was subsequently used to justify the eugenic provisions of the 1967 bill. Clause 1(1)(b) provided that an abortion may be performed if 'there is a substantial risk that if the child were born it would suffer from such physical or mental abnormalities as to be seriously handicapped'. Although perhaps the most controversial of the bill's provisions, it was justified on the same grounds as the rest of the bill, namely, that women should be encouraged in their primary role as mother. Forcing a woman to give birth to a disabled child would impair the fulfilment of her proper role:

> It is my experience, and that of other doctors, that a woman who has been persuaded against her will to continue a pregnancy and then bears an abnormal deformed child seldom becomes pregnant again. The experience may be such that she will not under any circumstances become pregnant again. It is my experience that with the woman who does have a termination of pregnancy the first thing she wants to do afterwards is to become pregnant again and have a family. I have seen families born which would never have been born had relief not been allowed under this clause.[105]

This rationale became much more evident in subsequent debates. Eugenic considerations formed the basis for some of the strong opposition to the Alton Bill, for instance. Many claimed that the proposed 18-week upper limit would fetter recourse to abortion after tests revealed abnormalities. Opposition again focused on the effect of this upon the family. It was argued that such a restriction would deny parents 'normal' children where they were unwilling to take the risk that a child might be disabled. David Steel, for example, read a letter written to him by a constituent who had terminated her pregnancy after she was told the foetus would not have lived:

> I know I personally would not have coped with a full term baby being born like this. I have had a healthy daughter since this tragic event but I am sure that I

would never have had the courage to become pregnant again if I knew that I would have to go nine months and not be offered a late termination had the baby had the same abnormalities.[106]

These arguments arose again in connection with the amendments made to the Abortion Act by section 37 of the Human Fertilization and Embryology Act 1990. Possibly the most vocal of those who used these arguments was the Earl of Erroll, who asked:

How many lives and how many families might be wrecked ... as a result of the trauma and mental pressure? In setting a time limit one puts pressure on normal families ... I disagree with anything that would produce that sort of pressure. For abnormal situations there should be no time limit. The family is more important.[107]

Conclusions

For the proponents of abortion reform, a woman's reproductive options were being formulated on the basis of her perceived role as Mother, and on the basis of this role within the family. The source of origin for the (legitimate) population, the woman within the home becomes the focus for a number of interrelated regulatory discourses. As in *The Baby of Macon* and the narratives spun around the miraculous child, the foetus emerges as interpolated within a number of these discourses. Returning momentarily to the analysis provided in Chapter 2, the parallels with the criminalization campaign in the nineteenth century are unmistakeable. Interpreted in this way, proponents of the Private Member's Bill were seeking liberalization of the law not as a *permissive* measure but as a move towards securing traditional gender roles and the stability of the family.[108] To an extent, such uniformity is illusory: many of the reformers, most notably within the ALRA, tempered their views on the need for greater access to abortion services in order to promote their cause within the prevailing political climate. The ALRA, for example, did not campaign for abortion on demand, on the basis that it would have been politically inexpedient.[109] Yet, viewing the campaign as a whole, the provisions suggested by the reformers appear far from permissive. The Bill may be interpreted as, if anything, reactionary. It appears plausible to argue that the Bill's only liberalizing intent (as distinct from effect) was the limitation of burden. Abortion is constructed as not only a means of securing womanhood, but also almost as a *reward* for maintaining the family. Women who fulfil their 'real function'[110] can be expected to perform their duty only up to a point. Whilst this may appear liberalizing it can, of course, be understood as merely another means whereby woman/motherhood is secured. This interpretation of motive, reasoning and the Bill is further supported by the moves made by some of those who once supported the Bill to see its restriction after it had become law. Such apparent changes of heart show little but a continuity of intent, a desire to secure motherhood, as Jeffrey Weeks illustrates:

> many women were seizing the opportunity provided by the 1967 Act to deliberately control their fertility. It was this area of 'choice' which disturbed some supporters of reform, and during the 1970s they combined with the traditionalist opponents of reform to try to amend the law in a more restrictive manner.[111]

This chapter has provided a particular reading of the campaign waged by those who favoured the relaxation of the laws relating to abortion through David Steel's Private Member's Bill. As has been stressed, other readings are possible, or rather, necessary to understand the complexity of factors influencing women's fertility options. The next chapter presents the reverse side of the analysis presented above. That is to say, it will examine the discourses of the opponents of David Steel's Bill. More specifically, it will highlight the figure constructed within the opponents' discourse and assess the nature of the commonalities that existed between these apparently conflicting discourses.

Notes

1   'Peter Greenaway and the Sound of Clouds', *International Herald Tribune* (24 November 1992).
2   M. Raymond, 'Something Else', *Screen International* (24 April 1992), 9, at 10.
3   Ibid.
4   P. Greenaway, *The Baby of Macon – Synopsis* (London, 1993), 3.
5   Ibid., at 1.
6   Greenaway, cited in Raymond, *supra*, at 10.
7   Greenaway, *supra*, at 3.
8   L. Nilsson, 'Drama of Life Before Birth', *Life* (30 April 1965).
9   Campbell-Savours, HC Deb. vol. 125, col. 1281, 1988 (22 January).
10   Nilsson's photographs are discussed by A. Young, 'Decapitation or Feticide: The Fetal Laws of the Universal Subject', *Women: A Cultural Review*, 4, (1993), 288, at 291; C. Stabile, 'Shooting the Mother: Fetal Photography and the Politics of Disappearance', *Camera Obscura*, **28**, (1992), 179; E. Ann Kaplan, *Motherhood and Representation: The Mother in Popular Culture* (London: Routledge & Kegan Paul, 1992), 180–219; V. Hartouni, 'Containing Women: Reproductive Discourses in the 1980s', in C. Penley and A. Ross (eds), *Technoculture* (Oxford: University of Minnesota Press, 1991), 27. For a similar analysis of distortion in foetal representation, see Rosalind Petchesky's analysis of the successful anti-choice propaganda film, *The Silent Scream*: R. Petchesky, 'Foetal Images: The Power of Visual Culture in the

Politics of Reproduction', in M. Stanworth (ed.), *Reproductive Technologies: Gender, Motherhood and Medicine* (Cambridge: Polity, 1987), also R. Braidotti, *Nomadic Subjects: Embodiment and Sexual Difference in Contemporary Feminist Theory* (New York: Columbia University Press, 1994), Ch. Two.

11   While I have conflated foetus and child at a number of points, I do this solely for heuristic purposes to emphasise the nature of the investment of the foetus and of the foetal–maternal economy.

12   Greenaway, *supra*, at 1.

13   See R. Barthes, *Image, Music, Text* (London: Fontana, 1977), 19.

14   K. O'Donovan, 'Marriage: A Sacred or Profane Love Machine?', *Feminist Legal Studies*, **1**, (1993), 75, at 90.

15   See Chapter 2, also M. Thomson, 'Woman, Medicine and Abortion in the Nineteenth Century', *Feminist Legal Studies*, **3**, (1995), 159.

16   See Chapter 1.

17   410 US 113 (1973), 35 L Ed 2d 147, at 174-5.

18   Wells, HC Deb. vol. 732, vol. 1087, 1966 (22 July).

19   H. Storer, *Is It I? A Book for Every Man* (Boston: Lee and Shephard, 1867), 89–90.

20   A. Howe, '"Social Injury" Revisited: Towards a Feminist Theory of Social Justice', *International Journal of the Sociology of Law*, **15**, (1987), 423.

21   See, generally, R. Graycar and J. Morgan, *The Hidden Gender of Law* (Annandale: The Federation Press, 1990).

22   N. Naffine, *Law and the Sexes* (London: Unwin & Hyman, 1990).

23   See, for example, K. O'Donovan, 'Defence for Battered Women Who Kill', *Journal of Law and Society* (1991), 219, which challenges the neutrality of defences to murder, asserting that 'law's claim to universality are under indictment because of a failure to incorporate the experiences of abused women' (at 236). Such laws reflect and legitimate predominantly male behavioural responses. See also O'Donovan, 'Law's Knowledge: The Judge, The Expert, The Battered Woman, and Her Syndrome', *Journal of Law and Society*, **20**, (1993), 427; S. Bandalli, 'Battered Wives and Provocation', *New Law Journal*, (14 February 1992), 212. For a consideration of this defence in the United States, see Schneider and Jordan, who assert that 'Standards of justifiable homicide have been based on male models and expectation' (E. Schneider and P. Jordan, 'Women's Self-Defence', *Women's Rights Law Reporter*, **4**, (1978), 150, at 153). For a discussion of the gendered nature of rape provisions, and why the 'ideal of the male sexual subject has been retained within English and Australian rape law', see N. Naffine, 'Possession: Erotic Love in the Law of Rape', *Modern Law Review*, (1994), 10.

24   S. Sheldon, '"Who is the Mother to Make the Judgment?": The Constructions of Woman in English Abortion Law', *Feminist Legal Studies*, **1**, (1993), 3, at 4.

25   Ibid.

26   In writing Woman in this way, I am intending to make the same distinction as made in Chapter 2. See, p. 38.

27   J. Conaghan and W. Mansell, *The Wrongs of Tort* (London: Pluto Press, 1993), 65.

28   Z. Eisenstein, *The Female Body and the Law* (London: University of California Press, 1988), 11.

29   R. Petchesky, *Abortion and Woman's Choice: The State, Sexuality and Reproductive Freedom* (London: Verso, 1986), 72.

30   J. Keown, *Abortion, Doctors and the Law* (Cambridge: Cambridge University Press, 1988), 84–109. For the influence of the medical profession in the United States, see J. Mohr, *Abortion in America: The Origins and Evolution of National Policy* (New

York: Cambridge University Press, 1978); K. Luker, *Abortion and the Politics of Motherhood* (Berkeley: University of California Press, 1984).

31   O'Donovan, 'Marriage: A Sacred or Profane Love Machine?', *supra*, at 90.

32   Conaghan and Mansell, *supra*.

33   Eisenstein, *supra*, at 10.

34   P. Ferris, *The Nameless: Abortion in Britain Today* (London: Hutchinson and Co., 1966), 10–11. For a discussion and critique of this duality from a predominantly American cultural viewpoint, see Kaplan, *supra*. For a discussion of the construction of the female subject within legal responses to violence, again within an American context, see K. Bumiller, 'Fallen Angels: The Representation of Violence Against Women in Legal Culture' in M.A. Fineman and N.S. Thomadsen (eds), *At the Boundaries of Law: Feminism and Legal Theory* (London: Routledge & Kegan Paul, 1991), 95.

35   R. Barthes, 'The Death of the Author', in *Image, Music, Text, supra*, 142, at 146.

36   J. Hillis Miller, 'The Limits of Pluralism III: The Critic as Host', *Critical Inquiry*, 3, (Spring 1977), 446.

37   As far as the debates in the House of Commons are concerned, the possible liberating effect of freer availability of abortion appears not to have been on the proponents' agenda. It is not until almost the conclusion of the amendment debates that any possible liberating effect is alluded to. Christopher Price, Member of Parliament for Perry Bar, remarked: 'When I have mixed with people both inside and outside of the House who want the Bill, it has often occurred to me that it is not about abortion at all; it is part of the process of the emancipation of women which has been going on gradually over a very long period' (Price, HC Deb. vol. 750, col. 1372, 1967 (13 July)). The question of 'freedom' is also dealt with, though with rather more acerbity, by the Member for Stafford and Stone, Hugh Fraser, who questioned the record of the administration: 'It is a sad commentary – sad perhaps, but accurate – that after 1,000 days of this Government there has been no extension of freedom save to the bugger and the abortioner' (Fraser, HC Deb. vol. 750, col. 1362, 1967 (13 July)). Given the apparent influence of campaigners in shaping the debate, it is important to note that early campaigners were not unaware of these issues. The ALRA led a pragmatic campaign which attempted, as far as possible, not to alienate potential support. Such pragmatism obscured the more 'extreme' views held by individuals within the association. See B. Brookes, *Abortion in England 1900–1967* (London: Croom Helm, 1988), 154.

38   Lyons, HC Deb. vol. 732, col. 1089, 1966 (22 July).

39   Abse, HC Deb. vol. 732, col. 1150, 1966 (22 July).

40   Ibid., at col. 1115.

41   Braine, HC Deb. vol. 747, col. 496, 1967 (2 June).

42   Dunwoody, HC Deb. vol. 732, col. 1098, 1966 (22 July).

43   Ibid., at col. 1096. The construction of Woman as victim was still clearly being utilized by the proponents of the 1967 Act when the Act was challenged by David Alton's Abortion (Amendment) Bill. See, for example, Moonie, HC Deb. vol. 125, col. 1247, 1988 (22 January).

44   D. Thurtle, *Minority Report of the Birkett Government Abortion Committee 1939*, cited in A. Jenkins, *Law for the Rich* (London: Gollanz, 1960), at 62. All references to Jenkins are to this text, unless otherwise stated.

45   Jeger, HC Deb. vol. 749, col. 978, 1967 (29 June).

46   Ibid.

47   'The doctor may enter a house of squalor, filth and dirt where the husband is a chronic drunkard' (Galpern, HC Deb. vol. 749, col. 943, 1967 (29 June)).

48 Lyons, HC Deb. vol. 732, col. 1089, 1966 (22 July).

49 Gurden, HC Deb. vol. 749, col. 1034, 1967 (29 June).

50 B. Brown, 'Troubled Vision: Legal Understandings of Obscenity', *New Formations*, **19**, (1993), 29.

51 Ibid., at 40.

52 For an early history of the ALRA, see A. Jenkins, 'The History, Aims, and Composition of the Abortion Law Reform Association', ALRA Archives, Fo. 2/3/36, CMAC.

53 As Barbara Brookes observes 'The 1967 reform of the abortion law was a victory won by the ALRA, with important input from the BMA, in the face of opposition from many obstetricians and gynaecologists' (Brookes, *supra,* at 154).

54 Jenkins, *supra,* at 29.

55 V. Greenwood and J. Young, *Abortion in Demand* (London: Pluto Press, 1976), 81. Similarly, see M. Woodside, 'The Woman Abortionist', in *Abortion in Britain: Proceedings of a Conference Held by the Family Planning Association at the University of London Union on 22 April 1966* (London: Pitman, 1966), 35, at 37.

56 J. Grbich, 'The Body in Legal Theory', in M.A. Fineman and N.S. Thomadsen (eds), *At the Boundaries of Law: Feminism and Legal Theory* (London: Routledge & Kegan Paul, 1991), 61, at 67–9.

57 Young, *supra,* at 293.

58 Vickers, HC Deb. vol. 732, col. 1108, 1966 (22 July).

59 As Foucault writes, 'Sexuality must not be thought of as a kind of natural given which power tries to hold in check, or as an obscure domain which knowledge tries to uncover. It is the name that can be given to a historical construct' (M. Foucault, *The History of Sexuality, Volume One* (London: Penguin, 1990), 152).

60 L. Irigaray, *The Sex Which Is Not One,* trans. C. Porter (Ithaca: Cornell University Press, 1985), 84.

61 *Report of the Inter-departmental Committee on Abortion* (London: HMSO, 1939).

62 Brookes, *supra,* at 98.

63 See, for example, the position assumed by the North Kensington Women's Welfare Centre, reported in *BMJ* (12 January 1929), 76.

64 Brookes, *supra,* at 97.

65 M. Foucault, 'Truth and Power', in C. Gordon (ed.), *Michel Foucault: Power/Knowledge. Selected Interviews and Other Writings, 1972–1977* (Hemel Hempstead: Harvester Press, 1980), 122.

66 Foucault, *The History of Sexuality, supra,* at 104.

67 Owen, HC Deb. vol. 732, col. 1113, 1966 (22 July).

68 Ibid.

69 Foucault, *The History of Sexuality, supra,* at 104.

70 Eisenstein, *supra,* at 28–9.

71 L. Hall, *Hygienia's Handmaid: Women, Health and Healing* (London: Wellcome Institute, 1988), 55.

72 Barthes, 'The Death of the Author', *supra,* at 146.

73 S. Sontag, *Illness as Metaphor* (London: Penguin, 1991), 3.

74 P. Rabinow, 'Artificiality and Enlightenment: From Sociology to Biosociality', *Incorporations, Zone,* **6**, (1992), 234.

75 Ibid.

76 Steel, HC Deb. vol. 732, col. 1073, 1966 (22 July).

77 Dunwoody, HC Deb. vol. 732, col. 1098, 1966 (22 July).

78 Ibid., at cols 1098–99.

79 Jenkins, HC Deb. vol. 732, col. 1144, 1966 (22 July).

80   Owen, HC Deb. vol. 732, col. 1115, 1966 (22 July).
81   N. Auerbach, *Woman and the Demon: The Life of a Victorian Myth* (London: Harvard University Press, 1982), 10.
82   C. Johnston, 'Myths of Women in Cinema', in K. Kay and G. Peary (eds), *Women and the Cinema: A Critical Anthology* (New York: Dutton, 1977), 409.
83   Richardson, HC Deb. vol. 125, col. 1273, 1988 (22 January).
84   Gorman, HC Deb. vol. 125, col. 1289, 1988 (22 January).
85   Ibid., at col. 1288.
86   Interestingly, Brenda Hogget and Susan Atkins observe that 'The Victorian concepts of family and morality and the biologically based notions of gender and competence which shaped the law in relation to family law, work and taxation, for instance, also governed the reintroduction of citizenship rights for women' (B. Hogget and S. Atkins, *Women and the Law* (Oxford: Blackwell, 1984), 181). For a discussion of the gradual enfranchisement of women, see ibid., at 180–83.
87   Similar arguments had been used earlier in the twentieth century in the campaign for freer access to contraceptives. Marie Stopes, for example, in her inter-war crusade for birth control clinics, had aimed at obviating 'the health-destroying, home-wrecking work of *fear* of pregnancy' (M. Stopes, *Contraception (Birth Control): Its Theory, History and Practice* (London: John Bale, Sons and Danielsson, 1926), 186). As Barbara Brookes has observed, 'It was sex reform within the home, rather than without … that publicity campaigns addressed' (Brookes, *supra*, at 11).
88   Jenkins, *supra*, at 35.
89   Ibid., at 36.
90   Ibid., at 54.
91   D. Baird, 'The Experience of Aberdeen', in *Abortion in Britain*, *supra*, 15, at 20. See also J. Douglas Dant, 'Concern for the Woman', in *Abortion in Britain*, *supra*, 96 at 97–8, also R.A. Schwartz, 'Abortion on Request: The Psychiatric Implications', in D.F. Walbert and J.D. Butler (eds), *Abortion, Society and the Law* (Cleveland: Case Western Reserve, 1973).
92   Suicide and a resultant breakdown in the family were also used by the opponents of reform. The alleged 'psychosis' that arose from interfering with the 'natural order' could result in the 'suicide of the mother and the breakdown of the family' (R. Tredgold, 'The Psychiatrist's View', in *Abortion in Britain*, *supra*, 10, at 12).
93   Strange, HC Deb. vol. 277, col. 1235, 1966 (23 October).
94   Jenkins, *supra*, at 76–7.
95   Cited by Vickers, HC Deb. vol. 732, cols 1109–10, 1966 (22 July), see also Jenkins, *supra*, at 69.
96   Letter from W.H.F. Oxley to the Birkett Committee, 10 October 1937, Ministry of Health 71/21, Public Records Office, Kew.
97   Vickers, HC Deb. vol. 732, cols 1108–9, 1966 (22 July).
98   D. Munday, 'Discussion and Resolutions', in *Abortion in Britain*, *supra*, 105, at 106.
99   Ibid.
100 Jenkins, *supra,* 89 at 91.
101 Jeger, HC Deb. vol. 747, col. 977, 1967 (2 June).
102 Ibid., at cols 977–8.
103 Winstanley, HC Deb. vol. 747, col. 1056, 1967 (2 June).
104 Ibid., at cols 1056–7.
105 Winstanley, HC Deb. vol. 747, col. 1059, 1967 (2 June). Dr Winstanley saw this provision as not only a way of encouraging maternal and familial obligations, but also as *necessary* for the profession: 'But I ask the House to understand that it is necessary

to have this provision in the Bill ... for the protection of the medical profession, who are at present doing this in good faith because they believe it necessary' (ibid., at col. 1058).

106 Steel, HC Deb. vol. 125, col. 1241, 1988 (22 January). Jo Richardson made a similar point, retelling her experience of the testimonials of women who had abortions on the basis of foetal abnormality: 'We heard from mothers who had since had or who are going to have perfect babies. They said that if, because of the law, they had been forced to carry on with their earlier pregnancy and were now against their will trying to cope with handicapped children, they would never have risked having another child. They ... are all glad that the back-up screening and our present humane and compassionate laws gave them the opportunity to make their individual choice and to go on with confidence to have more children' (Richardson, HC Deb. vol. 125, col. 1275, 1988 (22 January)). See also Gordon, ibid., at col. 1285; MacKay, ibid., at cols 1236–7.

107 The Earl of Erroll, HC Deb. vol. 522, col. 1072, 1990 (18 October). See also Lord Rea, ibid., at col. 1076.

108 For a persuasive challenge to the projection of the 1967 Act as permissive, see S. Sheldon, *Beyond Control: Medical Power and Abortion Law* (London: Pluto, 1997); also, S. Sheldon, *The British Abortion Act (1967): A Permissive Reform?* European University Institute Working Paper Law No. 94/2 (San Domenico: European University Institute, 1994).

109 See M. Simms and K. Hindell, *Abortion Law Reform* (London: Owen, 1971), 25.

110 Dunwoody, HC Deb. vol. 732, col. 1098, 1966 (22 July).

111 J. Weeks, *Sex, Politics and Society* (London: Longmans, 1989), 275.

4   The Abortion Act 1967: Opposing Narratives

Ever since Eve invented costume, and, coached by the Serpent, enacted that little comedy by which she persuaded Adam that the bitter apple of knowledge was sweet and comforting, there has been something satanic in the very nature of the theatre. (Rosamond Gilder, *Enter the Actress* (New York and Boston: Houghton Mifflin, 1931), 8)

Introduction

The preceding chapter examined the discourse of those who supported the Bill which was to become the Abortion Act 1967. More specifically, it examined the construction of the woman it was claimed would benefit from reform of the law. Providing a continuity with the discourses of the nineteenth century, this woman of the parliamentarian imagination – selfless, wearied, at the centre of the family – was clearly located within a traditional narrative of gender. In this chapter, completing this particular history, I examine the woman emerging from the opponents' discourse. Although the *aborting* woman formulated here proves dramatically different, it is important to see that she exists within the same framework – indeed, within the same narrative. As in the previous chapter, the degree to which these narratives are played out in abortion discourses both before and subsequent to the enactment of the Abortion Act will be illustrated. Bringing these two chapters together, the final section will highlight how this traditional framework extends to the final provisions of the Act – more precisely, how the woman within the proponents' and opponents' discourse is enshrined within and validated by the Act. Before addressing these issues, it is worth briefly outlining the political and social context of the Bill.

Responding to the 1960s

David Steel's Bill was introduced as part of a broad sweep of social reforms. The 1960s saw reform of the law regarding suicide,[1] a lowering of the voting age to 18,[2] reform of the divorce law,[3] an almost complete abolition of the death penalty,[4] increased access to contraception,[5] the liberalization of play censorship[6] and the partial decriminalization of gay sex.[7] Reform of the abortion law was an integral part of the reform process. Although, like many of the other reforms, the Medical Termination of Pregnancy Bill was introduced to Parliament as a Private Member's Bill, it was only enacted through the assistance of the government, which had provided drafting assistance and, most critically, parliamentary time. All preceding[8] and, until 1990, all subsequent[9] attempts to reform the law have failed to gain government sponsorship or assistance. In 1990 the government supported reform of the law under section 37 of the Human Fertilisation and Embryology Act. This is considered briefly below.

The broad reforming legislation of the 1960s has been contextualized in a number of ways. It has been construed as a response to a new affluence, and as 'long overdue and humanising reforms of archaic laws, a necessary part of … "modernisation"'.[10] Yet such legislation may also be seen as having a further, perhaps greater, significance. The legislative changes may be seen as heralding a division between state and Church, and a concomitant re-alignment in decision making. Referring to the Suicide Act, 1961, Professor Hart observed: 'It is the first Act of Parliament for at least a century to remove altogether the penalties of the criminal law from a practice both clearly condemned by conventional Christian morality and punishable by law.'[11] For some the perception of a general move away from Christian morality, the belief that 'there must remain a realm of private morality and immorality which is … not the law's business',[12] marked a decline in public morals and values. Within this the 1967 legislation was, for many, a high point in what was seen to be a wave of permissive reforms. For these opponents of reform, the Bill represented a natural conclusion, or progression, for a society that had lost its way morally and ethically. Illustrating this general belief in declining morals, Professor Carstairs, in the Reith Lectures in 1962, noted that 'popular morality is now a wasteland, littered with the debris of broken convictions … . The confusion is perhaps greatest over sexual morality.'[13] This sentiment was reiterated later in the decade as a correspondent of Mary Whitehouse was to write after the 1967 reforms: 'the last session of Parliament has subjected us to the progressive moral disarmament of the nation BY LAW and there's worse to come'.[14]

The responses of many to the Bill therefore became responses not only to the object of the Bill itself, but also to the reforms of which it was very much a part. Opposition became a challenge to a perceived redefinition of society and, particularly, a redefinition of gender roles and the family. As with the campaign of the proponents, and as in the nineteenth-century criminalization campaign, the definition of the aborting woman was central to the campaign of the opponents. Revealing many points of similarity with the proponents' discourse, there was, within this figuring of the aborting Woman, a privileging of the maternal as natural and inevitable, physiological justification for this, and an intense regard for the social importance of the family. In assessing the Woman of the opponents' discourse each of these will be considered in turn.

Tarts

As was noted in the previous chapter, the woman of the parliamentary imagination was alternatively cast as a tired housewife or a tart.[15] Whilst proponents of reform spoke of the wearied, abused mother of many, opponents of the Bill had in mind the feckless, whimsical and selfish. Invariably, such a woman had entered into sex, this 'sacrament in love',[16] without due consideration. She had acted 'lightly, wantonly and inadvisedly'.[17] She was perhaps a 'promiscuous juvenile ... who indulges in sexual intercourse at a very early age'.[18] As John Peel noted in 1966, 'the common stereotype of the woman seeking abortion is that of the promiscuous girl student'.[19] By the time of the Alton Bill, this figure, almost a spectre, had become an emblem of a 'disposable generation'.[20] By the mid-1990s, she was associated with 'selfishness ... sexual promiscuity, and distorted notions of the family'.[21] Where the proponents had relied largely upon a cast of middle-aged women, those opposing the Bill provided a chorus line of the young and intemperate.[22]

The characterization of both the aborting woman and of the nature of abortion itself was detailed. Where the woman seeking an abortion was invariably a 'wanton' and 'promiscuous juvenile', the abortion was concomitantly constructed as 'a sleazy comfort',[23] encouraging such promiscuity. Women who sought such *comfort* were mentally and morally immature, with little awareness or regard for responsibility or commitment. Tied to this and to the idea of abortion encouraging promiscuity, the possibility of a feckless woman receiving an abortion on her request, 'according to her wishes or whims',[24] was a scenario that was pursued and manipulated throughout the debates. This manipulation occurred regardless of the images constructed by the Bill's proponents and the professed intent of the sponsor not to allow *abortion on demand*.[25] Considering Clause 1(c) (which involved the provision of abortion where the woman's 'capacity as a mother' was seriously impaired), Jill Knight raised the question of abortion on demand and the feckless immature woman:

> I should say that I have never supported abortion on demand. Although I have been sympathetic to this Bill, I could never go all the way with the suggestion that there should be abortion on demand, which, of course, is what subsection 1(c) actually means. This subsection is so wide and so loose that any woman who felt that her coming baby would be an inconvenience would be able to get rid of it. There is something very wrong indeed about this. Babies are not like bad teeth to be jerked out because they cause suffering.[26]

The decision to terminate a pregnancy is therefore reduced to a casual consideration, a decision taken without adequate thought, a situation that could have been pre-empted.[27] With abortion contained within these parameters, it becomes possible for the proponents to question whether such a flippant and unconsidered approach be allowed: 'surely as a healthy, living baby it has a right not to be killed simply because it may be inconvenient for a year or so to its mother'.[28] Similarly, discussing the case of a pregnant minor, Knight states: 'here is the case of a perfectly healthy baby being sacrificed for the mother's convenience ... is it morally right to destroy one child to help another?'[29] Knight goes to further extremes, suggesting a woman may terminate a pregnancy 'so that a planned holiday is not postponed or other arrangements interfered with'.[30] To terminate a pregnancy is therefore repeatedly characterized as an easy decision, a casual response. The *immorality* of such action is compounded by the pain Knight claims the foetus will suffer: 'We must recognise that, if an abortion is carried out merely because the child is inconvenient, then considerable pain is inflicted on the child for that reason ... to do it merely because the child is not wanted is, to my mind, a dreadful thing to do.'[31] A failure to consider fully the implications of a termination persisted as a motif resurfacing within consideration of the Alton Bill. Sir Bernard Braine introduced this motif to the predominantly eugenically based debate:

> in our compassion for all who are likely to suffer from some handicap, we should not allow ourselves to forget that the overwhelming majority of babies being aborted at eighteen weeks or after would, if born and not destroyed because they are momentarily inconvenient, be perfectly normal healthy children.[32]

The decision to terminate is therefore generally characterized as an expression of the woman's immaturity and immorality. It is a decision denied its problematic nature, its complexity and the possibility of pain. Even on a purely fiscal level, the proponents appear not to comprehend the nature of people's lives – abortion's social context. This again suggests theatre, with Parliament defining its own boundaries, constructing the subject it wishes to regulate.[33] Jill Knight, for example, suggested: 'if the difficulty is financial, then there are plenty of ways in which the financial difficulties of the woman who is pregnant can be resolved'.[34] Knight denies knowledge of the persistent nature of poverty and social deprivation. As she concludes: 'frequently the difficulty resolves itself because it is of a purely temporary nature'.[35] Out of this equation of immaturity, immorality, youth, the sanctity of life and that 'most innocent of all things, an unborn baby',[36] denial and paternalism emerge.

To return to Sheldon's assertion that law creates its own fiction of the subject it wishes to regulate,[37] where the proponents constructed a martyr and beatified the wearied mother to allow abortion as respite and reward (encouraging motherhood and fecundity), so opponents constructed a figure demanding more direct regulation. Law in this instance is imagined as an educator, instilling an understanding of values and a sense of responsibility. Regulation becomes more visibly a question of the assertion of appropriate gender roles. Again, Jill Knight is characteristically vocal, asserting: 'people must be helped to be responsible, not encouraged to be irresponsible'.[38] Knight pursues this role of law with the example of the minor who becomes pregnant; she asks: 'does anyone think that the problem of the 15-year-old mother can be solved by taking the easy way out?'[39]

This educative and responsibilizing function of law is probably most graphically presented by the Member for Stratford-on-Avon, Angus Maude, who gave 'qualified support to the Bill'[40] and yet professed: 'I am not at all sure that I believe that we should remove what is in a sense a useful sanction. I know that perhaps sounds a heartless thing to say, but one needs to think twice before one removes all the consequences of folly from people.'[41] The retributive function envisaged here is laconically noted by Stuart Carne: 'to some, pregnancy is regarded as a divine retribution; a nine month sentence with hard labour at the end'.[42] Yet pregnancy and childbirth were not merely retributive. Child bearing was alternatively a natural role which was both rewarded and protected. The mother–child relationship provided strength and support, even for the *feckless girl*, as Kevin McNamara observed: 'Fecklessness, a bad background, being a bad manager – these are handicaps, but they are nothing to do with love, that indefinable bond, no matter how bad the social conditions, no matter how strange or difficult the circumstances, which links a mother to her child and makes her cherish it.'[43] Motherhood was, therefore, seen as natural, as a source of strength. In the discourse of Kevin McNamara and other opponents, the feckless girl should be denied an abortion because her maternalism (manifesting itself upon the birth of her unwanted child) would override other anxieties, problems and

obstacles. Pregnancy and motherhood are imagined as calming, as benefi-
cial for the troublesome, as normalizing. The feckless girl is brought to heel
by the responsibilities of motherhood. It is a popular image: the prodigal
daughter returning mature with her child.

Maternalism is therefore constructed as part of the natural order and, as
such, inevitable. This construct compounded the portrayal of the woman
who sought abortion as immature, fickle and erratic. Pregnancy as natural
and inevitable defined a wish to eschew child bearing, or a specific pregnancy, as a confusion, a failure of reason – often temporary: 'All too often, a
woman who does not want a child for purely social reasons at one stage
subsequently wants one desperately.'[44] This transient quality is suggested by
Stuart Carne, who refers to 'back street' or self induced attempts to terminate: 'In the vast majority of cases, all they get for their money is pain in
their stomach. Almost always, in fact, the pregnancy continues; usually
happily and often to the relief of the mother.'[45]

The proponents of abortion reform did not, however, concern themselves
exclusively with the feckless girl. As with the proponents, and as is clear
from what has just been noted, there was a clear conflating of woman and
mother, and a privileging of this role. Within the imagination of the opponents, the role of woman clearly parallels the framework of the nineteenth-
century 'Cult of True Womanhood'.[46] Consequently, for the opponents woman
was primarily bearer and rearer of children. This was her *real* and *worthwhile* function and role, one 'she ought to play'.[47] Discussing those women
who sought abortions 'according to [their] wishes or whims',[48] Peter Mahon,
Member for Preston South, reminded the House of woman's proper role:
'She is the first and greatest guardian of her child's safety and rights. It has
always been the glory of the mother to defend her child, in the womb or
outside it, against any aggression.'[49] This role encouraged Mahon to an
almost fevered religious conclusion: 'It is indeed our sacred duty to maintain the dignity and rights of mothers.'[50] Jill Knight also made clear this
belief in motherhood as a woman's proper role, at one point asserting that,
'if it comes to a choice between the mother's life or the baby's, the mother is
very much more important'.[51] This importance, however, was not derived
from any inherent worth, rather it was contingent. She was more important
because 'She has ties and responsibilities to her husband and other children.'[52]

Motherhood, as the primary role for women, therefore becomes an indi-
cator of worth. As if to underline this, Kevin McNamara asked: 'How can a
woman's capacity to be a mother be measured before she has a child?'[53]
Given the presumption of motherhood, the synonymity of woman and mother,
McNamara may be seen as equating success at child bearing and rearing as
the only measure of a women's worth. In retracing these earlier narratives,

the proponents perpetuate and propound the nineteenth-century idea of separate spheres of action, particularly a woman's 'appointed sphere'.[54] This illustrates the continuing fetishization of motherhood and the family. Where the last century saw Woman/Wife/Mother deified as, in part, a counter-revolutionary force – 'the main bulwark against revolution'[55] – the 1960s saw her as central to the family and home, providing cohesion and the protection of mores and values. In this the opponents, like the proponents, beatified the married mother. Simon Mahon, for example, posited the feckless girl against the icon of married mother, of True Womanhood:

> Who is to have ... priority treatment? Is it the *feckless girl* who has an unwanted pregnancy from time to time; or the *decent married woman* who is awaiting investigation, or treatment for sterility, or the woman with a positive cervical smear or symptoms that suggest a possible early cancer? I think that the House would give a very quick answer.[56]

In his question, Mahon juxtaposes the two dominant paradigms evident within the discourse. Mahon's sympathies clearly lie with the *decent married woman*, the *tired housewife*: for her the act of termination is not an evasion of her role as mother. She has attained a respectability through her marital status and her fulfilment of child bearing duties,[57] her commitment to the latter possibly injuring her health, a selfless sacrifice to husband and children. The *feckless girl*, the *tart*, however, does not manage this mantle of respectability that affords the married woman licence. The *feckless girl* is the counterpoint of the wearied mother. Where the wearied mother rationalized a liberalization of the abortion laws as a way of securing and rewarding motherhood, the feckless girl is portrayed as an argument against such liberalization. She eschews the responsibilities of maternity, motherhood and the family. She becomes an almost totemic figure warning of the collapse of values, family and society.

Mechanisms of Knowledge and Power Centring on Sex[58]

The issue of motherhood as natural, desirable and inevitable therefore provides a strong point of similarity in the apparently oppositional positions adopted by the parliamentarians. Intimately tied to this, and providing a further similarity, the opponents also employed physiological arguments to support their claims. A belief in the primacy of child bearing and rearing, and opposition to abortion, were validated (and regulation therefore legitimated) through the construction of abortion as in some way injurious to health. Motherhood was constructed, as it has been historically, as essential to a woman's well-being. As Berkwith Whitehouse was to inform the Birkett Committee, 'we seem to be living in an age where the best interests of the individual woman seem to be subordinated to her desires'.[59] Eschewing what was in her *best interests* necessarily led to ill health. The nexus constructed between an attempt by a woman to eschew her maternal role and disease extends Susan Sontag's assertion that disease imagery is used to express concern for social order.[60] In the deployment of this technology the discourse appears, crisscross[ing] the realm of 'fact' (the real) and 'interpretation' (the ideal),[61] to play with the classic image of disease resulting from stifled passion, a passion physical or spiritual.[62] Passion appears transformed to disease when denied, as with Michel in André Gide's *The Immoralist*; Gustav von Aschenbach in Mann's *Death in Venice*; or the cancer that afflicts the celibate Miss Gee in W.H. Auden's poem from 1937:

> Childless women get it,
> And men when they retire;
> It's as if there had to be some outlet
> For their foiled creative fire.[63]

While, reiterating Auden's warning, childlessness through celibacy or contraception was constructed as a danger to health, this paled in comparison to the dangers posed by abortion. Opposing abortion on this basis again placed the belief in 'natural maternalism' upon a scientific/objective basis. Relying on *medical* contraindications, the beliefs of the opponents became grounded in the perceived objectivity of physiology and bioscience. In utilizing this form of validation, the parliamentarians clearly illustrate the enduring hysterization of the female body, their discourse enveloping many of the images and metaphors of illness that animate this process. Within this discourse, abortion becomes an obstacle to a woman's fulfilment of her natural role, and therefore antithetical to *natural law*. As in the nineteenth century, breaches of the natural law become manifest in physical and mental ills. As in ancient myth and fable, disease is a supernatural punishment, a reward for an infringement of divine law.[64] It is also revealing: 'show[ing] the true face of the beautiful liar – a most involuntary revelation'.[65] Discussing the 'alarmingly high' incidence of post-operative 'psychoses' that may arise after a termination, Kevin McNamara illustrated this with a familiar image: 'These psychoses are, unfortunately, very difficult to treat, because they often arise from a feeling of guilt which all too clearly has a factual basis, being based on the denial of the maternal instinct and the natural law.'[66]

This bioscientific validation was also evident in the discourse around David Alton's Private Member's Bill. Although bioscientific discourse was employed, there was an important difference. Much, although not all, of the scientific discourse concerned foetal status. This may be located within a more global shift in emphasis to an increasingly explicit foetal presence within reproductive and non-reproductive discourses. As will be argued in the remaining chapters of this volume, this foetal presence is inscribed with the same narratives as have so far been unpacked in earlier reproductive discourses. That is to say, *foetal narratives* recode discourses which previously had either explicitly referred to maternal obligations or coded these within the language of female physiology. Introducing the degree to which biomedical arguments were to be deployed, Alton contextualized his Bill as necessitated by 'the gigantic strides in medicine and technology'[67] that had occurred since the passage of the Abortion Act. This technological context has been understood as 'perhaps what most distinguished ... the debate about the Alton Act [*sic*] from that in which other proposed amendments to the 1967 Abortion Act had been considered'.[68] This shift/recoding has also been mapped in the United States by Rosalind Petchesky: 'Increasingly, in response to accusations of religious bias and violations of church–state separations, the evidence marshalled by the anti-abortionists to affirm the personhood of the foetus is not its alleged possession of a soul, but its possession of a human body and geno type.'[69]

Supporters of the Alton Bill therefore attempted to negate opposition to their restrictive proposals by appearing motivated purely by neutral scientific advances. This was seen both with the emergence of a scientific foetal identity and in more traditional ways. In terms of these more traditional ways, it is possible to argue that the discourse constructed around Alton's Bill is almost emblematic in its fulfilment of Siegel's assertion that social and physiological discourses have converged as 'two distinct but compatible ways of reasoning about women's obligations as Mothers'.[70] Giving warning of this, Alton, in his introduction to the second reading of the bill, claimed: 'Where medical knowledge has increased in leaps and bounds, it is incumbent on any civilised or ordered society to review its public policy and strike a proper balance between claimed rights and responsibilities.'[71] One of the clearest deployments of this strategy – both within Parliament and outside – has been seen in the emergence of post-abortion 'psychosis' or 'trauma'.[72] Within Parliament this allowed the opponents to work within a scientifically justified, clinical, apparently judgment-free framework: 'We have learnt much in twenty years ... . Since 1967... we have revolutionised our awareness ... we have learnt a lot about the consequences of abortion, both for the mother and the child. [We have learnt] of the potential physical and psychological consequences.'[73]

This section has suggested the degree to which the female and foetal bodies were employed in opposition to the 1967 Act. Such opposition was descernible in its original passage through Parliament and in more recent attempts to restrict the provision of abortion services. Most notable in these later debates has been the shift in emphasis from the woman's body to the foetal body. As noted earlier, I shall return to this in Part III. In the following section, I return to the relationship constructed within the parliamentary debates between abortion and the family.

Returning to the Family

Having constructed the immediate point of regulation – the woman – the discourse of the opponents touched upon broader, less immediate, regulatory desires. Here abortion was seen as not only a threat through creating 'an added temptation to loose and immoral conduct',[74] or leading to dangerous 'psychosis', but also as a danger to the family, and therefore society, through infertility. Although there was a pretence of scientific objectivity, the (bio)arguments of the opponents became pregnant with the weight of both religious and cultural representations. As with the claims of 'psychosis', infertility was seen almost as retribution. A denial of natural law was rewarded with barrenness, a *blighted womb*. Infertility, a 'disease' of difficult pathology, becomes invested with a complex series of meanings, as Sontag writes: 'An important disease whose causality is murky, and for which treatment is ineffectual, tends to be awash in significance.'[75]

Whilst the immediate effect of the abortion – infertility – was located in the woman, this, animating Sontag's assertion, clearly had wider significance. Norman St.John Stevas, in the last stages of the bill's passage, characterized this aspect of the debates: 'We have to look around in the Bill whenever we can to find means of safeguarding not only the moral values but the health of the nation.'[76] St.John Stevas suggests two important and enduring binary relationships: that between moral conduct and physical health, and that between women's health and that of the nation. More specifically and prosaically, but no less invested with these broader narratives, Leo Abse, before the House of Commons, related the injurious dangers of abortion to the security of the family and home: 'There are dangers of sterility ... the personal tragedy of the premarital abortion which eventually means that when a girl marries she is unable to have children.'[77] This sterility becomes the cause of divorce, as Abse continued, telling of the many 'well-documented case histories of abortion within the divorce papers, where an abortion taken too trivially and too lightly in the early years of a marriage has led unfortunately to sterility and the subsequent mutual recriminations that almost inevitably follow'.[78]

Providing a valuable concluding focus, vocal opponent Bernard Braine, Member for Essex South-East, gave further clear warning of the dangers and significance of infertility. Braine warned that such procedures 'may adversely affect the woman's future reproductive life and hopes of marital happiness'.[79] Braine in fact prioritized the long-term effects of abortion on a woman's fertility status, and the effects of this upon the marital home, above the termination itself. To Braine this appears as perhaps the primary consideration to be weighed in the provision of abortion: 'Essentially, ... what we are concerned with here is two crucial decisions – first, whether a pregnancy should be terminated for the sake of the woman herself, with all that means for her child-bearing capacity and marital happiness; and, secondly whether a potential life should be ended'.[80] Braine's assertion is revealing. He discloses for us the essential nature of the reproductive rights debate. Assuming primacy within his account of the decision making is the need to regard 'the woman herself'. Yet, within regard for the woman, emphasis is placed upon the imperative of considering 'all that [a termination] means for her child-bearing capacity and marital happiness'. The woman's health is paramount, but only in so far as her child bearing and marital roles define and validate her.

The campaign of those against reform of the abortion laws was therefore a campaign based upon both the *feckless girl* and the *decent married mother*, 'tarts as well as ... tired housewives.'[81] The feckless girl was assessed in terms of her failure to meet the beatific glory of the married mother. The feckless girl was a symbol of moral decay, of social decline. More specifically, she was a threat to Woman. For the proponents, the threat to Woman was a failure to ease her burden, a failure to allow her limited control of her fertility. Yet such control was located within a married, heterosexual, procreative framework. Opponents and proponents expressed the common desire for a stable consensual society underpinned by Woman as Wife and Mother, the centre of the family. While reform came and the opposition was 'defeated', these commonalities became legitimated and validated by the final, fought-over, provisions of the Act.

Beyond the Act

Although this chapter has mentioned abortion discourses beyond those concerning the 1967 Act, it is worth re-emphasizing the continuity of narrative across these discourses before moving on to consider the provisions of the Act. A re-emphasis is particularly of value given the earlier contextualization of the primary discourses within a general reponse to the broader legal reforms of the 1960s. The issue of continuity is perhaps most visibly evident with the example of the narrative of the family which has just been considered. Such concern for the family, with its implicit narrative of gender roles, may be clearly seen, for example, in the evidence to, and report of, the Birkett Committee which considerably predated the *permissive* 1960s. The preoccupations of the committee testify to the regulatory nature of reproductive laws. As Barbara Brookes has observed, the committee was preoccupied with the same questions that shaped responses to abortion in the nineteenth century: 'Underpinning all aspects of the debate was apprehension regarding the declining birth rate and anxiety over the threat to marriage and the family posed by birth control. The separation of sex from reproduction threatened to undermine parental responsibility and hence the family.'[82] Illustrating Brookes' assertion, the Birkett Committee concluded that to liberalize access to family planning provisions was to challenge perhaps the most important 'unit of family life [and] one of the great sources of happiness to the individual'.[83] More censoriously, Norman Birkett was to warn the ALRA that to provide abortion for the unmarried as well as the married would 'give licence to all sorts of undisciplined and uncontrolled behaviour'.[84]

These concerns were also evident within consideration of the Human Fertilisation and Embryology Act. Section 37 of the Act ultimately made a series of amendments to the law regulating abortion. The most significant for the purposes of this chapter were the fixing of the upper time limit at 24 weeks, with the waiving of this limit where the pregnant woman's health or life was seriously threatened, or when the foetus was seriously disabled. The arguments employed both for and against these amendments duplicated in many respects the earlier abortion debates. Baroness Elles, for example, speaking in the House of Lords, reiterated earlier concern for the family:

> in a few weeks' time this country will have a law which will allow abortion freely up to term. ... That is a prospect which I and many of my colleagues do not view with equanimity. It does not accord with our view of the standing of family life in this country or our respect for the sanctity of human life.[85]

More directly, Baroness Elles concluded that: 'this Bill is a disaster for the moral standing of the country ... it is not conducive to upholding the family and the value of human life'.[86] Building upon the assertion that both proponents and opponents of abortion have historically privileged traditional gender roles and the family, government support for section 37 may be understood within the radical conservatism of Thatcherite politics. As in the 1960's liberalization of access to abortion services was seen, by proponents of reform, as a means of securing the maternal role. This was also a necessary part of Thatcherism. As Philip Thomas has noted, the economic and social restructuring envisioned by Thatcher was predicated on 'common sense and traditional values' whose 'ideological bedrock' was the nuclear family.[87]

The radical anti-statism of Thatcherism was facilitated by a reassertion of traditional interpretations of Woman and the family. As Thomas continues, 'The campaign to put the "Great" back into Britain indicated the rejuvenation of the nation that is promised by this ideology. Such a process begins with women and mothers who are guardians of the family.'[88] The family formed an integral part of the Thatcherite vision of the state, centring responsibilities and stability within the home:

> There is no such thing as society. There are individual men and women and there are families. And no government can do anything except through people, and people must look to themselves first. A nation of free people will only continue to be great if family life continues and the structure of the nation is a family one.[89]

Thus, as in the nineteenth century, the twentieth century saw the question of abortion become enmeshed in the politics not only of gender but also of economics and the nature of governance. The discourses of reproductive rights and responsibilities remain a coded lexicon through which constructs of gender can be asserted. This phenomenon was noted by Claire Short in her response to the Alton Bill. Short recognized the coding of gender anxieties within reproductive discourses. Noting the New Right's campaign against abortion in the United States, Short observed: 'The growing New Right in Britain is saying that women should stay at home and bear children and care for elderly and disabled people ... they want to push women back into a traditional role and deprive them of the freedom to control their lives.'[90]

The manipulation of the abortion issue in this context has also been noted by the American anthropologist Faye Ginsburg. Writing of the pro-life campaign in the United States, she has recognized both the manipulation and the historical continuity, a feature not noted by Short. As Ginsburg states: 'the right-to-life movement resembles other campaigns in American history to reconstruct culturally constituted female domains against what are seen as opposing forces'.[91] Pertinently, she recognizes the fragility of opposition. Her anthropological work in Fargo, North Dakota, focuses on the commonalities in the pro-life/pro-choice movements. For Ginsburg there exists shared concern for a culture and economy that does not allow a pregnancy to be wanted. Ginsburg's subjects share a desire for, *inter alia*, economic support and male responsibility:

> Both sides voice a critique of a society that increasingly stresses materialism and self enhancement while denying the cultural value of dependants and those who care for them. Although their solutions differ, each group desires, in its own way, to alleviate the unequal conditions faced by women in American culture.[92]

For Ginsburg, her research offered 'empirical evidence that the pro-life and pro-choice stances, like all genuine dialectical oppositions, have a number of elements in common'.[93] While Ginsburg is writing of the United States in the 1980s, this assertion is true of the United Kingdom in the 1960s. In the 1960s, the commonalities were anxieties regarding *permissiveness*, gender roles and female sexuality. For the opponents of abortion, these anxieties were reduced and recoded within the specifics of the abortion debate to the character of the permissive feckless female. This fiction, created by the opponents of David Steel's Bill, is diametrically opposed to that created by the proponents. Yet both fictions, both creations, exist within the same narrative and aim to provide the same lesson or *moral*. Both proponents and opponents share a common, though in no way exclusive, social objective: the security of motherhood as the primary role for women, and the legally validated family as the primary social grouping. It is also clear from the debates around the amendments made by the Human Fertilisation and Embryology Act that these common social objectives remain.

From Construction to Legislation

Having initiated this discussion of the 1967 Act with a recognition of the importance of stories to law, our legal landscape and imagination, I wish now to consider how these stories have become realized *within* the law. It will be argued that the characters that played so persistently throughout the debates have become embodied within the legislation. There appears value in returning momentarily to Peter Greenaway, *The Baby of Macon* and, specifically, to Greenaway's desire to resolve 'Intriguing and damning questions about ... symbols, reality, history... ways, methods, and techniques of telling a story.'[94] The Abortion Act accepts and employs many of the tales and judgments that are explicit and implicit within the discourses of both proponent and opponent. It corporealizes, and in so doing it becomes part of the fiction: a new 'technique' of telling the story. It emerges as involved in the 'confusion as to what is real, [and] what is theatrical'.[95] The law validates a number of stories and narratives and yet in itself it may be seen as again a piece of narrative, of theatre.

In tracing the persistence of these stories to the final form of the Act, it is not intended to suggest that the Act directly embodies the parliamentary participants' debate. To suggest as much would be to deny the complexity of the parliamentary process, most notably the role of sometimes very visible and vocal non-governmental groups. Tracing the persistence, and acceptance, of the fictions within the parliamentary narratives does, however, illustrate the engagement of stories and law, the way illusions and imaginings may predicate the laws that govern our lives. In tracing this persistence, the power of discourse/'texts', not merely the legal but also the cultural which infects and is infected by the legal, is revealed. In looking at the continuity between story and legislation, I intend first to consider the broad medicalized system that structures the Act, before considering its internal provisions.

A Medical Model

After providing a history of abortion, a history of death and inequality that was held to justify reform, David Steel, in introducing the second reading of his Bill, turned to 'specifics': 'The first point to make is that my bill demands that an operation for the medical termination of pregnancy can be carried out only on the opinion of two registered medical practitioners.'[96] This prioritization illustrates how the debate, and indeed the Act, is clearly predicated on abortion existing as a medical matter, this in turn illustrating the success of the medical campaign considered in Chapter 2. It is arguable that reform of the law would have been unimaginable outside a clinical framework. Steel's location of termination within a rigid medical model may, in these terms, be seen as an issue of pragmatism, possibly a necessity. This clinical framework may also be construed as a reflection of successful parliamentary lobbying by the medical profession to ensure that they were not reduced to 'mere technicians'.[97] Both considerations were undoubtedly influential, but it is necessary to appreciate the construction of medicine, and specifically *the doctor*, within the reasoning of Parliament. This parliamentarian doctor is entangled with the images of Woman employed throughout the debates. Within this rhetoric there persists the traditional construction of female hysteria and the normalizing tradition of (male) medicine. It is this configuration that is relied upon to affirm the gender roles that were central to the campaign on both sides.

Within the stories told by Parliament, the doctor appears the most constant of all projections. Largely without the duplicity evident in the imagining of Woman, the doctor is static, unblemished, unreproached.[98] It is not without considerable irony that this figure is the product, in part, of the nineteenth-century campaign to criminalize abortion. The doctor is, almost without exception, a male figure.[99] Within the context of the 1966–7 debates, the possibility that the doctor may be a woman is only once alluded to.[100] Doctors were typically referred to as 'professional men',[101] 'professional medical gentlemen',[102] men who belonged to a 'high and proud profession'.[103] Being members of such a profession, they practised with 'skill, judgement and knowledge'.[104]

Constructed as reliable, as constant, the doctor became a stabilizing and normalizing figure. He became a point of security for both the *wearied mother* and the *feckless girl*. For the wearied mother, he appeared tender and supportive, 'sensitive [and] sympathetic'.[105] He is imagined as perhaps a substitute husband. He offers to the dependent figure a constancy that is denied by the inappropriate husband. To the feckless girl, he exists more as the authoritarian, the father, a corrective figure. Where the Woman of the narratives may have at times become etherealized, indistinguishable from the saintly invalids of literary and visual representation, the doctor becomes constituted out of less pained and ethereal images. He becomes a romantic figure: Tertius Lydgate in Eliot's *Middlemarch*; the Nihilist Bazarov in Turgenev's *Fathers and Children*; Fitzpiers in Hardy's *The Woodlanders*. Yet although romantic he is also a point and object of enforcement. He is the patriarchal and patrician Sir William Bradshaw in Virginia Woolf's *Mrs Dalloway*; the noble and moral Thomas Stockmann in Ibsen's *An Enemy of the People*.

Within the medical model of reform, the doctor became as much a figure of security as a provider of surgical skills. Ensuring that women could only seek abortions through *medical men* constructs the doctor as a surrogate or substitute decision maker. His skill is social as well as surgical. This was essential to many calling for reform. *The Economist*, for example, in 1959 stated its support for reform within this context: 'The legal barriers should be removed and the matters left absolutely at the doctor's discretion, although except where there are strong therapeutic reasons for the operation, efforts should be made to dissuade the mother from it.'[106]

The question of dissuasion, however, is seen as almost unnecessary, given the dominant construct of the doctor. He is seen as naturally a figure of moral authority: 'Father and Judge, Family and Law'.[107] David Steel, for example, illustrated the almost intangible, effortless quality which would mean that, given a greater access to the doctor, a greater ease to discuss pregnancy, the woman would 'in some way be reassured and feel that she had been offered some guidance, and no abortion will take place at all'.[108] David Owen reiterated this belief later in the same debate:

> If we allow abortion to become lawful under certain conditions, a woman will go to her doctor and discuss with him the problems which arise ... he may well be able to offer that support which is necessary for her to continue to full term and successfully to have a child.[109]

Under the normalizing 'gaze' of the doctor, the woman fulfils her role, 'her sexuality is "read off" her female body through male [medical] eyes'.[110] Her role 'read' properly, she is normalized, no longer a hysteric, and is duly 'grateful to the doctor for enabling [her] to ... reach full term'.[111] Later in the debates, presenting the bill for its third reading, David Steel was to offer a *case study* of a woman who was able to talk to the doctor in this way:

He talked to the girl and put her in touch with people who could help her. Her pregnancy is now going through in the normal way. It does not follow that because women desire termination it will automatically be carried out. If we can manage to get a girl such as that into the hands of the medical profession, the Bill is succeeding in its objective.[112]

The desirability of drawing women 'into the hands of the medical profession' was also recognized by Bernard Braine, a vocal opponent of the Bill. Braine, adopting elements of the proponents' characterization, remarked upon the benefits of 'some poor, unfortunate woman, driven to desperation [being] brought within the framework of legality'.[113] The doctor may therefore be seen not only as an arbiter of appropriate female behaviour, and point at which the stability of the family is secured, but also as a challenge to female criminality.[114] Indeed Simon Mahon, recognizing this considerable role, was at one point to offer the salute: 'it would be as well if we applauded the work of some of these men to keep our homes and families and country right'.[115] The doctor emerges as both an almost mystical affirming presence and a 'parallel judge': 'officially accorded the power to judge the woman and then decide whether she should have the possibility of an abortion, or whether she should be denied relief and made to face the "punishment" of being forced to continue with an unwanted pregnancy'.[116]

Thus, the medical model for abortion reform, while providing limited access to legal abortion services, may nonetheless be understood as replaying important elements of the criminalization campaign of the previous century. As Brookes has noted, 'Over the decades from 1900–1967 abortion was transformed from an important female-centred form of fertility control into a medical event closely monitored by the State.'[117] Yet, while Brookes highlights the medicalization of abortion and the intervention of state surveillance, she fails to note the degree to which the Act was structured to affirm Motherhood.[118] This affirming role was provided both by the presence of the 'parallel judges' and by further provisions of the Act.

The Provisions

The Abortion Act 1967 is located not only within a medical model but also within a presumption of criminality.[119] Section 58 of the Offences Against the Person Act 1861 asserts the illegality of abortion. Within this framework, the Abortion (Amendment) Act 1967 provides that 'a person shall not be guilty of an offence under the law when a pregnancy is terminated by a registered medical practitioner' acting in accordance with the provisions of the Act.[120] The Act may therefore be understood structurally as an adjunct (but not, as will be discussed, necessarily an exception) to a criminal law presumption of maternity. Abortion is assumed illegal, unless sanctioned otherwise by two doctors. As Sheldon writes:

> The decision to abort is therefore never seen as an intrinsically acceptable one, the possibility of which any woman could face at some time during her life. ... Conceptually then, abortion stands as the exception to the norm of maternity. No woman can reject motherhood: the only women who are allowed to terminate are those who can do so without rejecting maternity/familial norms per se.[121]

The provisions of the Act, particularly the circumstances in which two registered medical practitioners may sanction a termination, clearly embody the presumption of motherhood that was a commonality in the discourse of the proponents and opponents. Most importantly, they provide statutory *relief* for women from the situations which were conceptualized as threatening to the *role* of motherhood. In this the provisions evidence, and extend into legislative enactment, Carol Smart's assertions as to the nature of women's engagement with law:

> Where women resort to law, their status is already imbued with specific meaning arising out of their gender. They go to law as mothers, wives, sexual objects, pregnant women, deserted mothers, single mothers and so on. They are not simply women (in distinction to men) and they are most definitely not ungendered persons.[122]

The female subject narrated within the Abortion Act is quite clearly 'not an ungendered person'. In many ways she is the 'Angel', 'Wearied Mother', 'Tired Housewife' of the proponents of reform. This is particularly clear in the provisions of ss. 1(1)(*a*), (*b*), and (*d*).

Section 1(1)(*a*) of the Act provides, *inter alia*, that a pregnancy may be terminated where 'the continuance of the pregnancy would involve risk, greater than if the pregnancy were terminated, of injury to the physical or mental health of ... any existing children of her family'. This provision appears to reflect the considerable concern of the proponents that excessive child bearing and rearing responsibilities would lead to maternal ill health (or possibly death) and a consequential disintegration of the family. The provision appears to borrow from the tales and images of the 'wearied mother', the adopting within the discourse of sacred and secular images of maternal suffering and the effects of this on the children. Women are therefore allowed access to abortion services on the basis that it will facilitate the fulfilment of their existing responsibilities. Importantly, the woman helped by the provision may be seen as rejecting, not Motherhood, but an isolated, individual pregnancy, and this in fact is done for Motherhood.

Abortion services are also afforded to the pregnant woman, under s.1(1)(*b*), where it is believed that 'the termination is necessary to prevent grave permanent injury to the physical or mental health of the pregnant woman'. The woman's health may again be seen as protected for her familial responsibilities, for the 'ties and responsibilities to ... husband and other children'.[123] This provision helps to ensure that she may 'fulfil her real function, her worthwhile function as mother, of holding together the family unit'.[124] Again, her request for a termination is acceptable where she is not eschewing her duty as wife and mother. This construction, however, is perhaps most clearly seen in the provision of s. 1(1)(*d*). This section provides for the termination of a pregnancy where there is a 'substantial risk that if the child were born it would suffer from such physical or mental abnormalities as to be seriously handicapped'. While it is undoubtedly predicated, in part, upon eugenic considerations, the section may be interpreted as clearly transposing from the discourse into legislation the proponents' construction of Woman the female subject. A woman is permitted to terminate her pregnancy on the basis that the birth of a handicapped child may 'virtually destroy' the family,[125] and dissuade her from further child bearing. As Sheldon recognizes, this construct is also predicated upon a particular understanding of female sexuality: 'This clause ... serves to provide "get-out clauses" for good women who want to become pregnant (and thus do not commit the sin of making the fatal distinction between sex and procreation), but through no fault of their own happen to be carrying a foetus "of the wrong sort".'[126]

In each of these provisions there is a clear image of the Woman desired by the parliamentarians. An arguably more complex story, however, is narrated in s. 4(1) of the Act. This section provides that 'no person shall be under any duty ... to participate in any treatment authorised by this Act to which he has a conscientious objection'. The provision internalizes some of the problems and contradictions of the Act. Throughout the passage of the bill, abortion is clearly conceptualized as 'primarily a medical matter',[127] a 'matter for skilled medical judgement',[128] 'always a medical decision'.[129] Abortion is centred within the purview of the medical profession, an obviously clinical issue. Yet s. 4 asserts abortion as a predominantly moral issue. It appears difficult to conceptualize a tolerance, particularly an institutional tolerance, elsewhere for a conscientious objection to 'treatment'. Would supporters of s. 4 support similar provisions enabling medical staff to refuse to treat gay or prostitute HIV/AIDS sufferers, (licit and illicit) drug users, contraceptive users or smokers? There exist doctors with strong moral/religious objections to each of these. Indeed, David Owen, supporting the clause, nonetheless found it alien to traditional medical ethics: 'It is quite wrong for any doctor to put his ethical reasons before the consideration of his patient, but I suppose that this would be the only case in which we would refuse an operation on those grounds.'[130] The conscientious objection clause both belies the formulation of abortion as an intrinsically medical matter (which is also suggested by the social history of women's use of abortion) and touches upon the regulatory nature of the Act. The presumption of maternity/ motherhood, as elsewhere in the Act, is entrenched within s. 4. This provision may be interpreted as reasserting the belief in abortion as never 'intrinsically acceptable'.[131] Abortion (and – as a corollary within the medico-legal imagination – the possible rejection of motherhood) is left morally ambiguous. This interpretation is further evidenced by the fact that the doctor, although unable to refuse where 'treatment ... is necessary to save the life or prevent grave permanent injury to the physical or mental health of a pregnant woman',[132] is under no explicit obligation to refer the woman to another doctor.[133] The *moral* status of abortion/'rejected' motherhood is therefore conceived of as such that a woman may seek an abortion and yet should not be surprised if the doctor refuses to perform one in all but life-threatening circumstances. In this the woman who seeks to eschew child bearing is tainted with moral uncertainty. The 'conscientious objection' clause is also indicative of the construction of the doctor within the debates and the Act. The failure of the Act to require an objecting doctor to refer his patient to another doctor further entrenches the unblemished and unshakable image of the doctor. It constructs the doctor's judgment (moral as well as medical) as infallible; it assumes it unnecessary to seek a second opinion.

The professed desire to draw women 'into the hands of the medical profession'[134] is secured not merely by the medical model within which the Act functions, but also by the requirements of notification. The Act provides, by virtue of s. 2, that the Minister of Health (or Secretary of State for Scotland) will ensure that any practitioner acting within the ambit of the provisions shall provide the Minister of Health (or the Scottish Home and Health Department) with 'such notice of termination and such other information relating to the termination as may be prescribed'. Within the course of the debates the importance of this provision was emphasized. The requirement of notification was understood as a means of further drawing in and regulating abortion and women. The Bill's sponsor, referring to the notification provision, informed the House that 'the result of the passing of the Bill will be to provide us with more concrete information about the whole subject of abortion – because of the regulations for notification – than we have had up to the moment'.[135] The desire for 'more' information may be located within the regulatory intent of the Bill's supporters, an intent which is amply illustrated by Hugh Rossi:

> the country is faced at the moment with large numbers of illegal abortions annually, and ... the best way to cope with this situation is to bring it into the

open by permitting abortion in circumstances in which they can be controlled and supervised by the state under the National Health Service.[136]

Again, the desire to regulate appears predominantly concerned with the regulation of the *type* of woman who is allowed access to abortion services. David Steel envisaged the notification involving, along with general details, details of the 'age of the woman, how many children she has ... whether her husband agreed to the abortion [and] how soon ... the woman [became] pregnant again after the abortion'.[137] These provisions appear to reflect a desire to secure abortion for *specific* women: the middle-aged, multi-child Mother, the woman pregnant with a 'damaged' foetus. While the Abortion Regulations[138] do not include information as to the 'husband''s consent or post-termination pregnancies, they do require information as to the reasons for performing them, the woman's marital status and how many children (if any) she has already. The concern that abortion should primarily be available to those not eschewing their maternalism, safeguarding a 'woman's proper role', is clearly embedded within the requirement of notification and the specifics of that requirement.

Conclusions: *The Baby of Macon* – a Different Reading

In the final scenes of *The Baby of Macon*, the pestilence that had been banished by the birth of the miraculous child–saint returns. Famine, disease and death once again befall the people of Macon upon the death of their magical child. Viewed differently, edited skilfully, perhaps reworked in places, *The Baby of Macon* could be a different film. Greenaway's work would shift, resettle and find comfort with a new narrative. Like the autopsied embryos of Lennart Nilsson's 'Drama of Life Before Birth', the ultrasound images in *The Silent Scream*, the film could become that which it is now not. Greenaway's debate as to the nature of abuse and manipulation could easily become recoded as an allegory for the abuse of 'traditional' values. It could become a piece of pro-life/'traditionalist' propaganda. Greenaway could become a victim of his own fascination with the nature of story telling. As Nilsson presents death as life, so Greenaway's parable, a commentary on corruption and manipulation, could become a part of that manipulation.

Tales may therefore become revised, reinterpreted and assume a new 'reality'. The Abortion Act and its enacting discourse is such a tale. It has been widely and differently interpreted and reinterpreted. It has been conceived of as a relatively positive measure: a liberal mediation between competing 'rights', a landmark achievement for those campaigning for the emancipation of women, an example of innocuous medical and governmental paternalism. It has also been interpreted negatively: as a further challenge to public morality, an encouragement to permissiveness, a further entrenchment of a medicalized culture. Yet while it is recognized that there may be truths within these differing readings, a consideration of the discourse around the emergence of the Act suggests a quite different narrative thread.

This narrative retells a much simpler, much older story, one that 'retains a powerful hold ... affect[ing] the creation of law and its application'.[139] It is a story of roles and of Woman. It has been argued within this and the preceding chapter that the Abortion Act was predicated upon, and ultimately restates, a belief in child bearing and rearing as the primary role for women. Reading both sides of the debates, this is revealed as a commonality shared by those traditionally believed to have assumed antithetical ideologies. There also exists a commonality in the desire to protect this role, signifying, as it does, the maintenance of traditional values, most notably the sanctity of the family, that 'viable, working and happy unit'.[140] The desire to secure appropriate gender roles through the parameters we erect delimiting reproductive choices exhibits a remarkable persistence. Gendered arguments justifying the denial of abortion services to women in the nineteenth century are evident in the discourses around the 1967 Act. The female body, particularly her generative organs and the 'Other' that may develop within, remains vested with the power to define.

The remaining chapters of this volume consider the degree to which this still remains true. Since the enactment of the Abortion Act, has social change been such that female physiology and the foetus have been divested of their many swaddling narratives, stories and connotations? Has 'power [loosened] its grip on bodies and their materiality, their forces, energies, sensations and pleasures'?[141] One explicit change in the nature of the discourse that has already been noted is the degree to which discourses have become much more *foetus-centred*. Not only are discourses located around the foetal body, but knowledge of the foetus has become scientific and medical. Religious and moral arguments have been replaced by 'objective' scientific fact. Yet this form of discourse may be subject to the same analysis utilized so far. The following chapter will consider industrial foetal protection policies and the (scientific) discourses which argue their legitimacy. Examining the experience of both the United States and the United Kingdom, I will suggest that foetal protection discourses involve the same narratives of gender as the other reproductive discourses already considered. Thus foetal protection policies may be understood as a technology of gender, part of the complex political technology which creates and recreates this social relationship.[142]

Notes

1 Suicide Act 1961.
2 Representation of the People Act 1969.
3 Divorce Reform Act 1969.
4 Murder (Abolition of the Death Penalty) Act 1965.
5 National Health Service (Family Planning) Act 1967.
6 Theatres Act 1968.
7 Sexual Offences Act 1967.
8 Attempts to reform the law had been introduced prior to the enactment of the Abortion Act by Joseph Reeves (House of Commons, 1952), Lord Amulree (House of Lords, 1954), Kenneth Robinson (House of Commons, 1961), Renee Short (House of Commons, 1965) and Lord Silkin (House of Lords, 1965).
9 Attempts to restrict the provisions of the 1967 Act have included Private Member's Bills by Norman St.John-Stevas (House of Commons, 1969), Godman Irvine (House of Commons, 1970), Michael Grylls (House of Commons, 1973 and 1974), James White (House of Commons, 1975), William Benyon (House of Commons, 1977), Sir Bernard Braine (House of Lords, 1978), John Corrie (House of Commons, 1979) and David Alton (House of Commons, 1980 and 1987).
10 J. Weeks, *Sex, Politics and Society* (London: Longmans, 1989), 251. For an alternative contextualization of the nature of the abortion reforms, see S. Sheldon, *Beyond Control: Medical Power and Abortion Law* (London: Pluto Press, 1997). Sheldon argues that the Abortion Act may be understood as 'modernization', not in terms of the 'humanizing', but in terms of changes in the modalities of power.
11 H.L.A. Hart, *Law, Liberty and Morality* (London: Oxford University Press, 1963), Preface.
12 Wolfenden Report, *Report of the Committee on Homosexual Offences and Prostitution*, Cmnd 247 (London: HMSO, 1957), para. 257.
13 G.M. Carstairs, *This Island Now: The BBC Reith Lectures 1962* (London: Hogarth Press, 1962), 55.
14 M. Tracy and D. Morrison, *Whitehouse* (London: Macmillan, 1979), 67.
15 P. Ferris, *The Nameless: Abortion in Britain Today* (London: Hutchinson and Co., 1966), 10–11.
16 Deedes, HC Deb. vol. 732, col. 1092, 1966 (22 July).
17 Maude, HC Deb. vol. 732, col. 1121, 1966 (22 July).
18 Knight, HC Deb. vol. 749, col. 1184, 1967 (29 June).
19 J. Peel, 'Attitudes in Britain', in *Abortion in Britain: Proceedings of a Conference Held by the Family Planning Association at the University of London Union on 22 April 1966* (London: Pitman, 1966), 67. This was also noted by Barbara Brookes: 'When it did come to public attention it was in the form of stereotypes of slovenly avaricious back street operators providing services for promiscuous single women' (B. Brookes, *Abortion in England 1900–1967* (London: Croom Helm, 1988), 163).
20 Smyth, HC Deb. vol. 125, col. 1252, 1988 (22 January).
21 This characterization appeared in the papal response to the proposed agenda for the United Nations Population and Development Conference held in Cairo in September 1994 (*Observer*, 14 August 1994). The planned final document of the conference was expected to advocate artificial contraception and the right of women to safe and legal abortion in its efforts to control, or at least stabilize, global population growth. See *The Guardian*, 3 June 1994; *Independent*, 16 June 1994.
22 Obviously, such a dichotomy based upon age was not rigid. The case of Alec Bourne

was undoubtedly successful, in part, because of the *nature* of Bourne's patient. Although the girl was 14 years old, Bourne convinced the court (the judge was later to adopt the doctor's remarks) that she was 'decent', not a 'mental defective' or of the 'prostitute type'. See *R* v. *Bourne* [1939] 1 K.B. 687. See also *BMJ* (23 July 1938), 202, where much of Bourne's testimony is printed.

23   Knight, HC Deb, vol. 732, col. 1102, 1966 (22 July).
24   Mahon, HC Deb. vol. 750, col. 1356, 1967 (13 July).
25   David Steele, for example, made the intended scope of reform clear: 'the difficulty of drafting a Bill of this kind is to decide how and where to draw the line. We want to stamp out back-street abortions but it is not the intention of the promoters of the Bill to leave a wide open door for abortion on request' (Steel, HC Deb. vol. 732, col. 1075, 1966 (22 July)).
26   Knight, HC Deb. vol. 732, col. 1100, 1966 (22 July).
27   With the availability of contraceptives, opponents were able to assert that 'the mother could have appreciated the situation before the event took place' (Glover, HC Deb. vol. 749, col. 972, 1967 (29 June)).
28   Ibid.
29   Knight, ibid., at col. 1103.
30   Knight, ibid., at col. 926, 1967 (29 June).
31   Knight, ibid., at col. 928, 1967 (29 June). Knight further claimed that the foetus, which is 'perfectly recognisable as an infant', 'does feel pain' and that it 'takes a considerable time for it to die' (ibid., at cols 927–9).
32   Braine, HC Deb. vol. 125, col. 1247, 1988 (22 January).
33   See Chapter 3, pp. 66–7.
34   Knight, HC Deb. vol. 749, col. 1032, 1967 (29 June).
35   Ibid. Yet see Simon Mahon, who retorted: 'In my experience, I have never found that, when people are in great social need, help of the right kind in proportion to the need is available' (*ibid.,* at col. 1043).
36   Knight, HC Deb. vol. 732, col. 1101, 1996 (22 July). The 'innocence' of the foetus was/is a recurring motif; see, for example, Knight, HC Deb. vol. 732, col. 1105, 1966 (22 July); St.John Stevas, ibid., at 1156; P. Mahon, vol. 750, col. 1357, 1967 (13 July).
37   S. Sheldon, '"Who is the Mother to Make the Judgment?": The Constructions of Woman in English Abortion Law', *Feminist Legal Studies* (1993), 3, at 4.
38   Knight, HC Deb. vol. 749, col. 1032, 1967 (29 June).
39   Knight, HC Deb. vol. 732, col. 1102, 1966 (22 July).
40   Maude, HC Deb. vol. 732, col. 1117, 1966 (22 July).
41   Ibid., at col. 1121.
42   S. Carne, 'The General Practitioner', in *Abortion in Britain, supra,* 75, at 78.
43   McNamara, HC Deb. vol. 732, col. 1129, 1966 (22 July).
44   Knight, HC Deb. vol. 749, col. 931, 1967 (29 June).
45   Carne, supra, at 77. See also Jill Knight, who claimed the period of 'rejection' is short-lived, and recounts instances of women 'express[ing] their gratitude ... for [a] refusal to terminate' Knight, HC Deb. vol. 732, col. 1102, 1966 (22 July)).
46   See B. Welter, 'The Cult of True Womanhood: 1820–1860', *American Quarterly*, **18**, (1966), 151.
47   Dunwoody, HC Deb. vol. 732, col. 1098, 1966 (22 July).
48   Mahon, HC Deb. vol. 750, col. 1356, 1967 (13 July).
49   Ibid.
50   Ibid., at col. 1357.

51   Knight, HC Deb. vol. 732, col. 1104, 1966 (22 July).
52   Ibid. The corollary of Knight's position here must then be that, where the woman's life is in danger, and yet she has no husband or existing children (and therefore no vicarious value), the woman and foetus are of equal 'worth'.
53   McNamara, HC Deb. vol. 732, col. 1129, 1966 (22 July).
54   C. Beecher, 'The Peculiar Responsibilities of American Women', in N.F. Cott (ed.), *Root of Bitterness* (New York: Dutton, 1974), 173–4.
55   S. Alexander, 'Women's Work in Nineteenth-Century London: A Study of the Years 1820–1850', in E. Whitelegg *et al.* (eds), *The Changing Experience of Women* (Milton Keynes: Open University Press, 1982), 30, at 32.
56   Mahon, HC Deb. vol. 747, col. 1046, 1967 (2 June), emphasis added.
57   This appears similar to the nineteenth-century belief in marriage providing moral security for women, marriage construed as 'the true preserver of women's dignity' (H. McCormack, *Moral–Sanitary Economy* (London: 1853), 7).
58   M. Foucault, *The History of Sexuality, Volume 1* (London: Penguin, 1990), 103.
59   Evidence of the College of Obstetrics and Gynaecology before the Interdepartmental Committee on Abortion, Ministry of Health 71/23, Public Records Office, Kew. Child bearing and rearing was in the best interests not only of the woman herself but also of her family. The Catholic Women's League, for example, called for 'propaganda to encourage women to live happy normal lives in their own, their children's, and their husband's interests' (Memorandum from Dr Genevieve Rewcastle on behalf of the Catholic Women's League, Ministry of Health 71/24, Public Records Office, Kew).
60   S. Sontag, *Illness as Metaphor* (London: Penguin, 1991), 73.
61   Z. Eisenstein, *The Female Body and the Law* (London: University of California Press, 1988), 10.
62   See Sontag, *supra*, at 21–6.
63   W.H. Auden, *Selected Poems*, ed. E. Mendelson (London: Faber, 1987), 55, at 58.
64   For example, in the *Iliad* and the *Odyssey*; see Sontag, *supra,* at 44.
65   Sontag, *supra,* at 44.
66   McNamara, HC Deb, vol. 732, col. 1126, 1966 (22 July). See also Abse, HC Deb. vol. 732, col. 1149, 1966 (22 July); St.John Stevas, HC Deb. vol. 732, col. 1153, 1966 (22 July). Renee Short, however, suggests 'the attitude of society' as the cause for such 'psychological disturbance', (HC Deb. vol. 732, col. 1162, 1966 (22 July)).
67   Alton, HC Deb. vol. 125, col. 1228, 1988 (22 January).
68   M. McNeil, 'Putting the Alton Bill in Context', in S. Franklin, C. Lury and J. Stacey (eds), *Off-Centre: Feminism and Cultural Studies* (London: Harper Collins Academic, 1991), 149, at 155.
69   R.P. Petchesky, *Abortion and Woman's Choice: The State, Sexuality and Reproductive Freedom* (London: Verso, 1986), 334.
70   R. Siegel, 'Reasoning from the Body: A Historical Perspective on Abortion Regulation and Questions of Equal Protection', *Stanford Law Review*, **44**, (1992), 261, at 265.
71   Alton, HC Deb. vol. 125, col. 1228, 1988 (22 January). It is interesting to note how this discourse differs from that used within Alton's book, *What Kind of Country?* (London: Marshall Pickering, 1988). Alton's call for reform in the book is much more explicitly moral and religious in nature. This suggests the pragmatic adoption of a discourse more acceptable within the political process.
72   Alton, HC Deb. vol. 125, col. 1231, 1988 (22 January).
73   Ibid., at cols 1230–31, 1988 (22 January).

74 *Report of the Inter-departmental Committee on Abortion* (London: HMSO, 1939), 84–5.

75 Sontag, *supra*, at 60.

76 St.John Stevas, HC Deb. vol. 750, col. 1277, 1967 (13 July).

77 Abse, HC Deb. vol. 732, col. 1149, 1966 (22 July).

78 Ibid.

79 Braine, HC Deb. vol. 747, col. 459, 1967 (2 June).

80 Ibid. See also Sir Hobson, who warned that 'some of the complications [are] very serious, not only the physical condition of the mother, her sexual future and her reproductive capacity, but also on many occasions her morbidity and mental and nervous reaction.' (ibid., at 474).

81 Ferris *supra*, at 11.

82 Brookes, *supra*, at 106.

83 *Report of the Inter-departmental Committee on Abortion, supra*, at 124.

84 Comment by N. Birkett, Evidence of the ALRA, Ministry of Health 71/21, Public Records Office, Kew.

85 Baroness Elles, HL Deb. vol. 522, col. 1102, 1990 (18 October).

86 Ibid., at col. 1109.

87 P.A. Thomas, 'The Nuclear Family, Ideology and AIDS in the Thatcher Years', *Feminist Legal Studies*, **1**, (1993), 23, at 27.

88 Ibid., at 28.

89 *Woman's Own* (31 October 1987), 10.

90 Short, HC Deb. vol. 125, col. 1262, 1988 (18 October). Interestingly, the Minister of Health, Tony Newton, replying to Short, asserted that such intention was not important, or at least it should not bear upon consideration of the provisions of the bill: 'I would say to the honourable Member... that the honourable Gentleman is at least entitled to seek the judgement of the House on the proposal that he has put before it, rather than on what is in his mind but which he has not brought before the House' (Ibid., at col. 1264).

91 F.D. Ginsburg, *Contested Lives* (Berkeley: University of California Press, 1989), 215.

92 Ibid., at 225–6.

93 Ibid., at 225.

94 M. Raymond, 'Something Else', *Screen International* (24 April 1992), 9.

95 Ibid., at 10.

96 Steel, HC Deb. vol. 732, col. 1073, 1966 (22 July).

97 The image of the doctor as technician was evident within a consultation document produced by the Royal Medico-Psychological Association, see J. Keown, *Abortion, Doctors and the Law* (Cambridge: Cambridge University Press, 1988), 89. It was adopted within Parliament by Kevin McNamara, who also asked: 'where does the medical profession stand if women in certain instances can claim abortion of right, as they could under the Bill?' (McNamara, HC Deb. vol. 732, col. 1127, 1966 (22 July)). See also Norman St.John Stevas, who refers to the undesirability of reducing doctors to a 'purely mechanical position' (HC Deb. vol. 751, col. 1738, 1967 (25 October)).

98 Whilst there does exist a striking constancy, there was a fear expressed that *unscrupulous* doctors may see the provisions as a licence to *trade* in abortion. See Hogg, HC Deb. vol. 747, cols 469–70, 1967 (2 June); Hobson, ibid., at col. 479; Galpern, ibid., at col. 485; Turton, ibid., at col. 488; Hogg, HC Deb. vol. 749. col. 946, 1967 (29 June); Cooke, ibid., at col. 985; Hogg, HC Deb. vol. 750, col. 1178, 1967 (13 July).

99 For example, see Wells, HC Deb. vol. 732, col. 1084, 1966 (22 July); Owen, ibid., at

1111; Maude, ibid., at 1122; McNamara, ibid., at 1131; St.John Stevas, HC Deb. vol. 749, col. 914, 1967 (29 June).

100 It was not until the final stages of the debate that David Steel alluded to a 'body of professional men and women' (HC Deb. vol. 750, col. 1346, 1967 (13 July)).

101 Jenkins, HC Deb. vol. 749, col. 967, 1967 (29 June).

102 Hobson, HC Deb. vol. 747, col. 531, 1967 (2 June).

103 Lyons, HC Deb, vol. 732, col. 1090, 1966 (22 July).

104 Hobson, HC Deb. vol. 747, col. 531, 1967 (2 June).

105 Raglan, HL Deb. vol. 274, col. 591, 1966 (10 May).

106 *The Economist* (February 1959).

107 M. Foucault, *Madness and Civilisation: A History of Insanity in the Age of Reason* (London: Tavistock, 1989), 272.

108 Steel, HC Deb. vol. 732, col. 1076, 1966 (22 July).

109 Owen, HC Deb. vol. 732, col. 1116, 1966 (22 July).

110 J. Grbich, 'The Body in Legal Theory', in M.A. Fineman and N.S. Thomadsen (eds), *At the Boundaries of Law: Feminism and Legal Theory* (London: Routledge, 1991), 61, at 74.

111 Owen, HC Deb. vol. 732, col. 1116, 1966 (22 July).

112 Steel, HC Deb. vol. 750, col. 1349, 1967 (13 July). David Steel makes use of the same argument within the debates around the Human Fertilisation and Embryology Act. He asserts that the 1967 legislation had created a legal climate where doctors may see women before they abort and persuade them otherwise; see Steel, HC Deb. vol. 171, col. 210, 1990 (24 April).

113 Braine, HC Deb. vol. 747, col. 496, 1967 (2 June).

114 Sally Sheldon has understood the Abortion Act as having facilitated a '"dark mass" of unknowable female criminality [being] brought into the open and isolated in the bodies of individual women. The problem of abortion is changed from one of widespread and unquantifiable *deviance*, to one of isolated and identifiable *deviants'* (S. Sheldon, *The British Abortion Act (1967) A Permissive Reform?*, EUI Working Paper LAW No. 94/2 (San Domenico: European University Institute, 1994), 28. For a fuller account, see Sheldon, *Beyond Control, supra.*)

115 Mahon, HC Deb. vol. 747, col. 501, 1967 (2 June).

116 Sheldon, *The British Abortion Act, supra,* at 29.

117 Brookes, *supra,* at 163.

118 Indeed, Brookes appears to 'avoid' her knowledge of the medical and state interest in abortion when she states: 'The expansion of the legal protection given to the foetus in the nineteenth century, which took place at the expense of women, has been restricted in recognition of women's need for abortion' (ibid., at 164).

119 References to the Abortion Act are references to the Act as amended by the provisions of section 37 of the Human Fertilisation and Embryology Act 1990, on the basis that these provisions appear largely cosmetic and do not substantially affect the construction of Woman within the Act. For a discussion of the nature of the operative changes made by the 1990 Act, see J. Murphy, 'Cosmetics, Eugenics and Ambivalence: The Revision of the Abortion Act 1967', *Journal of Social Welfare and Family Law* (1991), 375.

120 Section 1(1) Abortion Act 1967.

121 Sheldon, 'Who is the Mother?', *supra,* at 15.

122 C. Smart, 'Law's Truth: Women's Experience', in R. Graycar (ed.), *Dissenting Opinions: Feminist Explorations in Law and Society* (Sydney: Allen & Unwin, 1990), 7.

123 Knight, HC Deb. vol. 732, col. 1104, 1966 (22 July).

124   Dunwoody, HC Deb. vol. 732, cols 1098–9, 1966 (22 July).
125   Winstanley, HC Deb. vol. 747, cols 1056–7, 1967 (2 June).
126   Sheldon, 'Who is the Mother?', *supra*, at 19.
127   Turton, HC Deb. vol. 747, col. 487, 1967 (2 June).
128   St.John Stevas, HC Deb. vol. 749, col. 913, 1967 (29 June).
129   Deedes, HC Deb. vol. 732, col. 1092, 1966 (22 July). See also Wells, ibid., at col. 1083; Abse, ibid., at col. 1148; Hobson, HC Deb. vol. 747, cols 472–3, 1967 (2 June); Deedes, HC Deb. vol. 749, col. 914, 1967 (29 June); Steel, HC Deb. vol. 750, col. 1165, 1967 (13 July).
130   Owen, HC Deb. vol. 732, col. 1111, 1966 (22 July).
131   Sheldon, 'Who is the Mother?', *supra*, at 15.
132   Section 4(2).
133   The Act contains no explicit obligation, but it has been argued that a legal obligation does nonetheless exist in certain circumstances. See I. Kennedy and A. Grubb, *Medical Law: Text with Materials* (London: Butterworths, 1994), 892–6.
134   Steel, HC Deb. vol. 750, col. 1349, 1967 (13 July).
135   Steel, HC Deb. vol. 747, col. 498, 1967 (2 June).
136   Rossi, HL Deb. vol. 747, col. 510, 1967 (2 June).
137   Steel, HC Deb. vol. 747, col. 499, 1967 (2 June).
138   Originally Statutory Instrument 1968 no. 390, currently Statutory Instrument 1991 no. 499.
139   K. O'Donovan, 'Marriage: A Sacred or Profane Love Machine?', *Feminist Legal Studies*, **1**, (1993), 75, at 90.
140   Steel, HC Deb. vol. 749. col. 965, 1967 (29 June).
141   Foucault, *The History of Sexuality, supra,* at 155.
142   T. de Lauretis, *Technologies of Gender: Essays on Theory, Film and Fiction* (London: Macmillan, 1987), 3–5.

PART III

5   Employing the Body and Industrial Foetal Protection

The functional biological differences between the sexes with respect to human reproduction is still openly adduced to support a wide ranging set of assumptions about social roles which have nothing demonstrable to do with biology. (C. MacKinnon, *Sexual Harrassment of Working Women* (New Haven and London: Yale University Press, 1979), 40)

Proponents of [foetal protection policies] almost universally defend them as a strictly scientific, value neutral approach to protecting women and their children from reproductive harm. In reality, however, foetal exclusion practices – much like prenatal diagnosis, abortion, or sterilization – are not purely technical or scientific matters. (E. Draper, 'Fetal Exclusion Policies and Gendered Constructions of Suitable Work', *Social Problems*, **40**, (1993), 90)

Introduction: More Stories

Articulacy of fingers, the language of the deaf and dumb, signing on the body body longing. Who taught you to write in blood on my back? Who taught you to use branding irons? You scored your name into my shoulders, referencing me with your mark. The pads of your fingers have become printing blocks you tap your message onto my skin, tap meaning into my body.... Written on the body is a secret code only visible in certain lights; the accumulation of a life time gather there. In places the palimpsest is so heavily worked that the letters feel like braille. I like to keep my body rolled away from prying eyes. Never unfold too much, tell the whole story. I didn't know that Louise would have reading hands. She has translated me into her own book.[1]

The ambiguously sexed Lothario is corporally deciphered and decoded by the Leukaemic Louise. In reading Lothario's body, she offers a new inscription, leaves her own story. Lothario in exile locates his/her love in turn in Louise's physiology:

> If I could not put Louise out of my mind I would drown myself in her. Within the clinical language, through the dispassionate view of the sucking, sweating, greedy, defecating self, I found a love poem to Louise. I would go on knowing her, more intimately than the skin, hair and voice that I craved.[2]

The bodies of lovers become inscribed, mapped and redrawn. A lover's discourse informs and imprints the physical, the corporal. We read and inscribe, fetishizing, as Barthes may claim, the corpse.[3] Reading, searching the other's body, we aim to understand our desire.[4] Yet, as previous chapters have suggested, the palimpsest that is the body is not solely the repository for the discourses of lovers. The body lodges and reveals other texts. These texts/discourses reveal a different desire.

In Kafka's *In the Penal Colony* (*In der Strafkolonie*, 1916) a voyager observes the colony's system of capital punishment, *the Harrow*.[5] Without opportunity for defence and unknowing of his sentence, the condemned has the commandment which he has transgressed transcribed upon his body. The transgressor comes to know his sentence by his flesh. The harrow, over a period of 12 hours, tattoos the sentence upon his body. The needles that write upon the body are mounted in glass, 'And now everyone can observe through the glass how the inscription on the body takes place.'[6] The script is not simple, indeed it is almost indecipherably complex: 'the actual lettering has to be surrounded with many, many decorations; the text itself forms only a narrow band running round the body; the rest of the body is set aside for embellishments'.[7] Unknowing of his sentence, the transgressor learns of it only in the sixth hour. He deciphers not with his eyes but with his wounds. On the twelfth hour the Harrow impales him completely and throws him into a pit.[8]

Located upon the body, therefore, are numerous discourses, among them the erotic discourse of lovers, the disciplinary discourse of captors. While bodies are written upon, they are also, partly through this writing, disciplined and constructed. The body is *harrowed*: mapped, landscaped, structured, defined. Located within a political field, invested with meaning, the body is rendered productive and docile – politically and economically useful.[9] There is an 'optimization of its capabilities, the extortion of its forces, the parallel increase in its usefulness and its docility'.[10] The body may thus be understood as a made rather than a given, the product of prevailing norms and discourses.[11]

It is from within this understanding of the body that the analysis of abortion discourses and practices has so far, in part, proceeded. As the analysis in Part I illustrated, the nineteenth-century (female) body was clearly defined by, and contained within, the gender framework which underscored, and in many respects determined, the abortion discourses. Similarly, Part II illustrated the endurance of this framework, or at least dominant elements of it, within more recent abortion discourses. In both the nineteenth and mid-twentieth centuries, the body of the aborting woman was constructed so as to legitimate regulation, ensuring political and economic usefulness. Continuing within this framework, this part moves beyond abortion to look at two contemporary reproductive issues, those of industrial foetal protection and the emergence of the new reproductive technologies.

The present chapter considers the first of these contemporary issues. Analysing industrial foetal protection policies within the framework adopted so far, it illustrates how they rely on dominant/prevailing discourses which construct the female body in such a way as to exclude participation in certain areas of the labour market. The body is written upon, constructed by, and in turn validates, traditional discourses and practices which define appropriate and acceptable forms of female employment. Recognizing this, these employment discourses may be understood as one of the dispersed technologies which construct gender. Following this, I shall move on to argue that these policies emerge as socially harmful in terms of the prioritizing of types of harm and methods of toxic exposure. Finally, it will be suggested that foetal protection policies are part of a broader discursive pattern which has seen the removal of the woman from reproductive discourses. This removal appears an integral element of the shift to a more *foetocentric* reproductive discourse.

In order to contextualize and locate our response to the employed body in the late twentieth century, I shall first consider discursive responses to the employed female body at the beginning of the century. Biomedical responses to this body were considered in Chapter 2, but it is of value to briefly consider here medico-legal discourses. An interesting case study is provided by a series of employment cases which came before the United States Supreme Court at the beginning of the twentieth century.

Employing the Body as the Century Begins

Lochner v. *New York*, heard before the United States Supreme Court in 1905, held unconstitutional a state statute which limited the number of hours that either sex could work in a number of specified occupations.[12] Three years later the Supreme Court was asked to consider the legitimacy of a similar provision in the case of *Muller* v. *Oregon*.[13] The Oregon statute under consideration prohibited the employment of any woman for more than 10 hours a day 'in any mechanical establishment, or factory or laundry in th[e] State'.[14] With the exception of their sex-specific nature, the provisions were similar to those considered unconstitutional in *Lochner*. Yet the court found the Oregon statute constitutionally unobjectionable. Brewer CJ explained the decision of the court, stating that 'healthy mothers are essential to vigorous offspring', and as such 'the physical well-being of woman becomes an object of public interest and care in order to preserve the strength and vigour of the race'.[15] Pre-empting the logic of the American courts of the 1980s, the statute was defended as not solely for the benefit of the woman but 'also largely for the benefit of us all'.[16] The *Lochner* decision was distinguished by the court on the basis that women were *naturally dependent* upon men. The court believed that, even if 'she stood, so far as statutes are concerned, upon an absolutely equal plain with him, it would still be true that she is so constituted that she will rest upon him and look to him for protection'.[17] Again, a body constructed as fragile, and here quite explicitly dependent, legitimates regulation. Not only did dependence warrant differential treatment, but so too did the inherent differences between the sexes: 'Many words cannot make this plainer. The two sexes differ in structure of body, in the function performed by each … . This difference justifies a difference in legislation.'[18]

In 1915, the United States judiciary were again asked to consider the legitimacy of sex-specific protectionist legislation. In the New York case of *People* v. *Charles Schweinler Press*, a challenge was brought to a New York statute that prohibited the employment of women for night shift work in factories and laundries.[19] The accompanying brief, written by Louis Brandeis and Josephine Goldmark, detailed the reasons for excluding women from such employment.[20] In common with contemporary exclusionary policies, the brief detailed problems of female employment that were in no way sex-specific. For instance, the report detailed the problems associated with the deprivation of sunlight and sleep.[21] Similarly, the brief warned of the higher than average incidence of morbidity and mortality among night workers,[22] and the dangers encountered travelling home at night.[23] As in the United Kingdom, the morality of allowing men and women to work closely together also caused alarm.[24] Night work was believed to lead to undue sexual temptation through exhaustion, drinking and the unhealthy proximity of the sexes. In addition to this, in justifying the exclusion of women the brief used data concerning male workers: more specifically, the detrimental effects of such shift work on their families and their reproductive health.[25] The bias in this application of data suggests the social logic determining the policies challenged by these cases, as Mary Becker states:

> At bottom, the argument for the limitation was based, not on empirical evidence of special hazards for women and their families, but on general assertions that factory and laundry work was difficult, that night shift work was especially taxing, that women were weaker than men, and that the strength of women should be protected for the future of the race.[26]

Whilst these beliefs may still appear to inform employment structures, it is the last that is of interest here. This belief relies upon the construction of women as determined by their reproductive organs: 'primarily biological actors'.[27] Again the female reproductive system emerges as the most defining part of her physiology: 'In places the palimpsest is so heavily worked that the letters feel like braille.'[28] As in the biomedical discourse of the period, a woman's generative organs were the controlling organs of her body,[29] they gave her all her characteristics of body and mind.[30] To recap: 'Instincts connected with ovulation made her by nature gentle, affectionate, and nurturant. Weaker in body, confined by menstruation and pregnancy, she was both physically and economically dependent upon the stronger and more forceful male, to whom she necessarily looked up to with admiration and devotion.'[31] Duplicating biomedical discourse, the determinative powers of the reproductive organs were increased in their pathologizing. As earlier chapters have noted, constructed as inherently weak or diseased, problematized, this 'hysterization' facilitated the drawing in of women's (reproductive) bodies, into a more visible social arena.[32] Following this, women's behaviour could be regulated as areas of experience could be labelled unphysiological. This was perhaps most clearly seen in the *Muller* case.

This chapter questions the degree to which contemporary sex-specific employment policies are predicated on the same gendered assumptions which determined these earlier cases. More particularly, it asks: to what extent is the female body still employed in the construction of gender appropriate employment? Integral to this, and following earlier chapters, is an assessment of the gendered subject who is constructed by this *employed* body.

Employing the Twentieth-Century Body

Foetal protection policies have arisen, on both sides of the Atlantic, primarily in the last two decades. These policies typically exclude women from the toxic workplace on the basis of potential exposure to foetus-damaging substances. Perceived foetal vulnerability has been met by both legislative and employer-led policies. Before considering the nature of the (gendered) body within these policies, it is necessary to outline the nature of occupational reproductive hazards and the legal responses to perceived foetal vulnerability.

The Science

Reproductive health may be damaged as a result of occupational conditions in a number of ways. Animal studies, for example, have indicated that gonadal function may be disrupted by exposure to a considerable range of chemicals. In male animals these have included antimetabolites, diuretics, psychopharmocological agents, heavy metals, herbicides, fungicides and solvents.[33] For female animals the list has proved shorter but has contained many of those affecting male animals.[34] Information concerning human sensitivity is largely based on animal studies. Sensitivity to chemical exposure may cause harm ranging from diminished libido to impotency and infertility. Exposure of either parent to chemical or other toxins may also affect the foetus, causing spontaneous abortion, foetal death or other adverse pregnancy outcomes.[35]

Foetally toxic agents may be classified according to the way in which they adversely affect foetal health. There are four classifications. Foetotoxins, the first of these, are chemicals that affect the foetus in the same way as they would a child or adult. A clear example of this is carbon monoxide, which through the same process will cause brain damage in the pregnant woman and the foetus.[36] Teratogens are substances that produce physical defects in the foetus without necessarily affecting parental health.[37] Transplacental carcinogens form a third, very limited, class of foetally toxic substances. These toxins cause cancer in the offspring of women exposed to them during pregnancy. The drug diethylstilboestrol (DES), a synthetic oestrogen which was prescribed to women to prevent spontaneous abortion, was found to cause cancer by crossing the placental barrier. The drug led to vaginal cancer in pubescent female children to whose mothers it had been prescribed.[38] DES remains the only known human transplacental carcinogen, although laboratory studies have indicated that other substances may also cause cancer in this way.[39] Mutagens form a fourth group of toxins which may adversely affect a pregnancy. Mutagens cause mutation in the genetic material of cells. The mutations may result in cell death, cancerous cell division, or altered cell function. Mutagens interrupt normal reproduction by altering the genetic structure of either the sperm cells (spermatogenesis) or the ova (oogenesis). They may otherwise leave no noticeable defect or injury in the health of the adult. Mutagens may cause spontaneous abortion or physical and mental abnormalities. If mutations are carried on into the offspring they may cause injury or death in successive generations.[40]

The Law

The United States   Undoubtedly the result of vigorous lobbying, health and safety provisions in the United States regulating workplace exposure to known reproductive hazards set a single standard for both sexes.[41] Until recently, however, lobbyists have been less successful in terms of challenging employers who have sought to go beyond the required levels of safety and exclude women from the toxic workplace. American employers who have sought to exclude women from the workplace on the basis of foetal health include Olin, American Cyanamid, Allied Chemicals, B.F. Goodrich, Monsanto, Sun Oil, Gulf Oil, Union Carbide, General Motors, Delco-Remy, St. Joe's Minerals, Bunker Hill, ASARCO, Eastman Kodak, St. Joseph Zinc and Firestone Tire and Rubber. These policies have affected approximately 100 000 American women[42] and threatened the jobs of 20 million others.[43]

Although a number of cases have been settled out of court,[44] the issue of industrial foetal protection, and specifically the legality of such policies under federal anti-discrimination provisions, has been challenged within the courts on a number of occasions. Foetal protection policies have been considered by three Courts of Appeals and, most recently, by the Supreme Court.[45] While there is a rich history of litigation, my immediate focus is on this most recent challenge. Although the broader discrimination issue is important, the material is again used here primarily to illustrate the *use* of the reproductive body. Consequently, subsequent analysis will be just as concerned with the case 'facts' as with the legal decisions. In considering the experience of the United States, it is worth bearing in mind that it may be seen as suggestive of what may be a British experience not yet revealed through a paucity of litigation.

In *UAW* v. *Johnson Controls*, the United States Supreme Court declared foetal protection policies impermissible under Title VII, the anti-discrimination provision of the 1964 Civil Rights Act.[46] After 10 years of Federal Appeal Court decisions to the contrary, the Supreme Court recognized foetal protection policies as sex-based discrimination. Blackmun J, who had delivered the principal opinion in *Roe* v. *Wade*, stated that to interpret them otherwise was simply *incorrect*.[47] The court defended the right of women to choose 'whether they wish[ed] to risk their reproductive health for a particular job'.[48] The majority concluded: 'It is no more appropriate for the courts than it is for individual employers to decide whether a woman's reproductive role is more important to herself and her family than her economic role. Congress has left this choice to the woman as hers to make.'[49]

The *Johnson Controls* decision is, however, at a number of levels, problematic. At a functional level, the Supreme Court's ruling appears not to have removed foetal protection policies from American industry. One year after the decision, a number of companies in the United States still had foetal protection policies in existence.[50] Also, in the case of *Boureslan* v. *Arabian American Oil Company et al.*,[51] the Supreme Court refused to recognize the legitimacy of Title VII, and therefore the *Johnson Controls* decision, to American companies operating abroad. This means that American companies operating outside the United States, for example in the United Kingdom, may exclude fertile women without fear of a legal challenge under Title VII. On a further practical level, in the light of the litigatory history of *Roe* v. *Wade*,[52] the *Johnson* decision may also not be the *final word*, as Alison Grossman notes:

> Because fetal protection policies implicate both these issues – the ideas that a woman's primary role is as child bearer at home and not at work and that society must be concerned with and act to protect fetal health – it is easy to imagine that the majority position will not be the final word on fetal protection policies.[53]

The Supreme Court's decision is also problematic at a more pervasive level. The decision of the court was premised on a familiar 'right to choose' argument. Whilst the ultimate decision is to be welcomed, this position failed to address the biomedical and earlier medico-legal manipulation of the female reproductive body. This will be expanded upon below, following an outline of the legal position in the United Kingdom.

The United Kingdom   Contrary to the experience of the United States, in the United Kingdom sex-specific foetal protection policies have received and retained judicial and governmental validation. The Factories Act, 1961, the Control of Lead at Work Regulations 1980 and the Ionizing Radiation Regulation 1985 all discriminate against women of reproductive capacity. While these provisions provide a basic level of exposure, fertile women are treated differentially, subject to a lower exposure limit. In the case of the Factories Act, for example, and the various ancillary pieces of legislation still in force,[54] all women (defined as any woman over the age of 18,[55]) are excluded from prescribed areas of employment where lead is in use, regardless of their reproductive status.

Whilst the United States saw a considerable number of legal challenges to corporate policy in the 1980s,[56] the United Kingdom has only seen one such action. *Page* v. *Freight Hire (Tank Haulage Co.) Ltd*[57] involved a challenge to a policy held by ICI which prevented women working in contact with the organic solvent dimethylformamide (DMF). ICI justified this exclusion on the basis of possible adverse reproductive outcome. The Employment Appeals Tribunal (EAT) upheld the legality of the policy, relying on s. 51 of the Sex Discrimination Act 1975. The section provides that 'Nothing in [the

Act] shall render unlawful any act done by a person if it was necessary for him to do it in order to comply with a requirement ... of an Act passed before this Act.' This includes statutory instruments brought into effect through powers conferred in Acts predating 1975. The EAT turned to the Health and Safety at Work Act 1974, and the general duty created there on employers to provide a safe workplace.

The decisions of the courts to have considered the question of foetal protection policies, and many of the commentaries, have questioned the legitimacy of such policies within the liberal rhetoric of choice and the clinical legal framework of discrimination. Addressed in these terms, the body is ignored. The role of the inscribed body in constructing gender and prescribing appropriate employment is left unconsidered. The analysis adopted here locates *the body* within legal discourse, highlighting the disciplinary relationship between legal (particularly medico-legal) discourses and the body. Within this analysis, the literary body enables us to understand the legal body. The persistence of the manner in which the (female) body is constructed to fit within certain social structures (including gender structures) is suggested here in the gendered interpretation and selective implementation of reproductive science. An examination of this reconfigures the debate, reanimating the legal provisions outlined above.

Gendered Interpretation

Margaret Atwood's novel, *The Handmaid's Tale*, offers a chillingly Orwellian vision of the future.[58] In a post-apocalyptic world of information control and war, most women are left barren. Fertile women outside the ruling elite are 'reprogrammed' by the state, assigned new lives as the handmaids of the powerful. The fertile, re-educated to celebrate their own fecundity, are subject to ritualized intercourse. Positioned between husband and wife, they are covered and denied, solemnly accepting and receiving. They provide a brutal and macabre surrogacy. Atwood's narrative may easily be coopted as a fable warning of the present-day objectification of women as reproducers, as 'two-legged wombs ... sacred vessels, ambulatory chalices'.[59] Yet Atwood's tale is also illustrative in more specific ways. She locates her parable in a devastated post-apocalyptic landscape. In a heavily toxic environment, the primary damage appears to be to female reproductive health. Little mention is made by the state of male infertility and little is made of other bodily processes. Industrial foetal protection policies, like the state of Atwood's dystopia, employ a similarly focused concern for health. These policies ignore the hazards that exist to male reproductive health and to non-reproductive health generally.

Notwithstanding this focus on female reproductive health, it is important to note that, metabolically and physiologically, the differences between the sexes are relatively minor. Testes and the ovaries have the same embryonic origin and therefore a similar biochemistry.[60] Consequently, 'Men and women are more alike than different in terms of biomedical and physiological processes.'[61] As a result, it is very rare that a toxin will affect women only.[62] More often it will have a range of effects adverse to women, men and foetuses.[63] In many instances of exclusion there appears little or no evidence that exposure to the substance in question is of greater risk to the foetus via the woman than it is via the man.[64] This assertion appears very much contrary to our traditional association between adverse pregnancy outcomes and maternal responsibility, and needs to be explained further.

Male exposure to certain substances may affect reproductive health, specifically foetal health, in a number of ways. Many substances have been shown to affect sperm morphology. Teratospermia (malformed sperm), asthenospermia (decreased motility) and hypospermia (decreased sperm count) may all result from exposure to toxins and may all adversely affect pregnancy outcome. Increases in sperm abnormalities may also be transmitted to subsequent generations.[65] Male exposure to toxins in the workplace may also affect foetal health through directly affecting female reproductive health. Women may be exposed to workplace hazards through the transportation of toxins from work to home on work clothes, and the skin or hair of male workers. This has been evident with exposure to lead, asbestos and beryllium.[66] Such transportation has also affected children in the home. In one instance, the synthetic oestrogen diethylstilbestrol (DES), a known transplacental carcinogen, caused pre-pubertal children to develop secondary sex characteristics.[67] The pregnant woman, and therefore the foetus, may also be exposed to potential hazards through transmission in the seminal fluid of contaminated male workers.[68] In these circumstances it becomes exceptionally difficult to know which parent, and which process, is the *cause* of an adverse pregnancy outcome. Added to this is the confusion of ascertaining whether the adverse outcome is the result of an occupational exposure, some non-work related exposure, or for that matter an unfortunate product of chance.[69]

If the toxin does affect both sexes, it may often be the case that it will pose a greater risk to male reproductive health than to female reproductive health. Because the testes are (after puberty) constantly producing sperm, they are by nature metabolically very active. The ovaries, on the other hand, are not, women being born with all the ova they will ever produce. This makes the possibility of chemical damage stronger for men as the quantity of contaminated blood passing through the tissue will be greater.[70] Men may also be at greater risk if the reproductive hazard is a mutagen. Mutagens are more likely to damage developing cells than non-developing cells, therefore creating a greater risk of damage to sperm than ova. It is also important to note that with mutagens, because they alter the structure of the genetic material, they may cause injury and fatality into future generations.

The perceived greater susceptibility of women to reproductive hazards on the basis of biological difference is therefore largely without merit. Yet such 'hysterization' continues, as in the nineteenth century, to legitimate regulation and exclusion. What little evidence does exist indicates that, in the preconception period at the very least, paternal exposure is as harmful to the foetus as maternal exposure. As Eula Bingham noted, as Director of the United States Occupational Safety and Health Administration, 'Concern for female reproductive capacity and the foetus is praiseworthy, but experience is demonstrating that any given substance may be equally damaging to the male reproductive system and through the male to the foetus.'[71] The problems of this bias are illustrated very clearly with the example of lead (which has most often been the subject of exclusion) and ionizing radiation.

Lead and lead compounds are used in approximately 120 occupations.[72] The Health and Safety Executive has estimated that approximately 10 000 people in Great Britain are significantly exposed occupationally to lead.[73] In the United States, approximately 835 000 workers are exposed to lead in the workplace.[74] Several companies in the United States have barred women from the lead-exposed workplace. The Lead Regulations in the United Kingdom provide for the removal of fertile women from the workplace where blood levels may exceed 40 µg/100 ml, as compared to a maximum male level of 80 µg/100 ml. Yet exposure to lead at these levels has been associated with a number of male reproductive problems. Lead has been associated with decreased sperm count and motility,[75] and abnormal sperm.[76] It has also been associated with mutagenic dysfunction, spontaneous abortion in unexposed partners,[77] and Wilm's tumour (a cancer of the kidney) in offspring. More generally, lead affects male reproductive health by causing difficulties in erection and ejaculation, a reduction in orgasm and a decreased libido.[78] Despite this, the Court of Appeals for the Seventh Circuit in the *Johnson* case described the evidential link between male exposure to lead and adverse effects on pregnancy outcome as 'at best speculative and unconvincing'.[79]

Ionizing radiation regulations in the United Kingdom also treat women of reproductive capacity differentially. Fertile women are prohibited from areas of employment with potential exposure levels much lower than those affecting men. Ionizing radiation is a mutagenic hazard and has been found to carry a greater risk of leading to an adverse pregnancy outcome through male exposure than through female exposure.[80]

Other chemicals that have justified excluding women from the workplace include benzene,[81] vinyl chloride,[82] carbon disulphide,[83] hexafluoroacetone[84] and glycol ethers.[85] Each of these poses substantial risks to male reproductive health and pregnancy outcome through paternal exposure. No company has yet proposed excluding fertile men from workplaces where exposure to any of these chemicals is a risk. In the *Page* case, no evidence was put before the EAT as to the effects of DMF on male reproduction. Neither did the EAT exercise the power vested in it and order an industrial tribunal to seek new facts. Rather, the court based its decision on a document produced by ICI itself. The document considerably overplayed the risks to female reproductive health, played down the general health risks and ignored the dangers to male reproductive health. The only two studies to have associated DMF with an increased incidence of miscarriage among exposed workers have been of questionable methodology.[86] These studies also make no mention of the foetal damage claimed by ICI. In contrast to this, two studies have highlighted the increased risk associated with DMF of developing testicular cancer.[87]

Selective Implementation

The female body, and particularly female reproductive health, has therefore been erroneously constructed as hypersensitive to occupational toxins. The hypersensitive body has legitimized exclusion, yet this hypersensitivity has been selective. Women have only been cast as threatened by reproductive hazards in industries which have historically been seen as *male,* in industries that have a history of discrimination. As Diane Hoadley writes:

> When women move into jobs not previously held, their presence becomes a problem and different health risks become an issue. This pattern holds both for male-intensive industries as a whole and for specific jobs traditionally held by men. Even after the courts have restricted employment policies targeting women workers and scientific articles have pointed to male reproductive hazards overlooked by fetal exclusion policies, employers still associate reproductive hazards with women in male-dominated jobs.[88]

Like the sex-specific protectionist legislation of the turn of the century, foetal protection policies limit women's access to areas of employment deemed *inappropriate.* Concern for foetal well-being has only been manifest in relatively well paid, traditionally male industries – most frequently, the car, steel and petrochemical industries. Equally potentially damaging areas of employment have been left unregulated. These areas have typically been within the 'pink-collar ghetto', areas of employment that rely predominantly on underpaid female labour. Women working in health care occupations, for example, face potential reproductive harm from biological agents, the anaesthetic gases halothane and nitrous oxide,[89] and laboratory chemicals such as benzene. Women constitute approximately 80 per cent of the workforce in these occupations.[90] No hospital has excluded women from these areas on the basis of potential foetal damage. In the United States, women are seldom employed in nuclear power plants, yet at the same time women X-ray technicians are exposed to comparable reproductive hazards from radiation exposure.[91] The same is true of other female-intensive occupations where there exist potential hazards, such as electronic assembly work,[92] laundries, dry cleaners, textile and clothing industries, and child care/education occupations, where biological risks such as rubella and cytomegalovirus pose obvious dangers.

Similar problems of implementation are evident in the breadth of these policies. Typically, foetal protection policies act to exclude women for all of their reproductive lives. In the United Kingdom, the Approved Codes of Practice of the Control of Lead at Work Regulations provide for the exclusion of women of 'reproductive capability' from certain workplaces.[93] As noted above, the provisions of the Factories Act are broader, making no reference to reproductive capability, excluding all women (over the age of 18) from industries falling within its ambit.[94] In the *American Cyanamid* case, the company's policy excluded all women of child-bearing age, defined as those between the ages of 15 and 55.[95] In *Wright* v. *Olin*, the policy adopted by the company excluded all women between the ages of five and 63.[96] Most other policies have excluded those who may be deemed 'fertile' or of 'child-bearing capability'.[97] In one illuminating instance, General Motors excluded *all* women, regardless of reproductive status, from workplaces where lead exposure was a risk.[98]

In the light of the professed intent of these companies to safeguard foetal health, and the requirement recognized by the Courts of Appeals in *Olin*,[99] *Hayes*[100] and *Johnson Controls*[101] that companies must act in the least discriminatory manner, the broad ambit of these policies appears inappropriate. These policies pay no heed to the question of whether the woman is *likely* to become pregnant. They ignore questions of reproductive intent, sexual activity, the gender and fertility of any partner, and contraceptive use. Even setting aside choice and difference, these policies ignore the fact that the overwhelming majority of women in the developed world have finished their child bearing by the age of 39. For blue- or pink-collar women over the age of 30, the birth rate is generally less than 2 per cent.[102] For women in England and Wales between the ages of 40 and 44, there are only 4.5 births per thousand women.[103] For women over 45 who are employed outside the home, the birth rate per thousand women is only 0.4.[104] Of all the births in the United States in 1987, only 1 per cent were to women over the age of 40.[105]

Foetal protection policies thus appear to offer a means of maintaining the marginal character of female workers in areas of industry that have traditionally been perceived as male. This rationale explains the acceptance of a gendered reading of reproductive science – the failure to note male reproductive (and more general) hazards. Yet the risk posed to foetal health through male toxic exposure is not the only way in which these gendered policies contradict the (professed) intent of those who introduce them. In many areas these industries provide the only means of an income allowing an existence above the poverty line. The association between poverty, with its effects on nutrition, housing, pollution exposure, illness and disease, and foetal and neonatal health is very clear.[106] This is particularly the case in the United States, where higher paid areas of employment normally involve greater access to health care and other benefits.[107] The correlation between income and a healthy pregnancy and birth may often mean that a woman and her family, present and future, will benefit more from her employment in the toxic workplace than from employment outside. Such employment outside, in lower paid feminized or pink-collar industries, may in addition to this prove to be just as toxic as the industry from which the woman has been *protected*. The following section considers further the nature of the harm that is caused by these policies.

Harm and Gender

The preceding sections have detailed how foetal protection policies exclude women from certain sectors of the labour market. Such exclusion causes direct economic harm. Yet foetal protection policies do not only harm those women who attempt to enter industries where such policies are in use. The existence of these policies ultimately harms all workers regardless of their sex and all women regardless of the nature of their engagement with the labour market.

Foetal protective policies prioritize types of harm and sources of exposure. By the focusing of attention on female reproductive health, the workplace remains a potentially damaging environment. By perpetuating the belief that only female exposure to occupational hazards may cause an adverse pregnancy outcome, companies and legislatures continue to put the health of workers' families at risk. Tackling reproductive hazards in this way creates a false belief that male workers, those not excluded, are safe. Similarly, concentrating on the hazards that are posed by traditionally male occupations means that little attention is paid to the considerable risks that women working in female-intensive industries are exposed to. Removing the female worker rather than removing the hazard also fails to combat other health dangers that the toxins may pose. The spectre of general toxicity is reduced to the specifics of possible damage to female reproductive health within industry. Removing women from the workplace also detracts from an employer's duty to those who live in the vicinity of the plant. Employers may profess concern for foetal health, but several of the companies to have introduced these policies have faced lawsuits for the pollution of neighbouring residential areas with the chemicals that have provided the basis for exclusion.[108] In the light of the effects of prioritizing sources of exposure and types of harm, current sex-specific policies need to be replaced by policies which protect not only women's reproductive health but also male reproductive health and health generally. This should be the case both for those within the workplace and for those who may be affected in the community.

Furthermore, the harm caused by these policies is not solely economic or physical. They arguably manifest a broader, less tangible, social harm. The *selective* physiological construction of women as hypersensitive to reproductive hazards again embeds within the female generative organs social attitudes to women. As Chapter 2 detailed, the nineteenth century saw female physiology embody societal perceptions of the role of women. Now, as then, areas of acceptable female employment have become determined by gendered health concerns. The nineteenth century saw women instructed to eschew higher education and employment for the health of herself and of her children. The twentieth century in turn prohibits the employment of women in traditionally *male* industries on the basis of safeguarding foetal health.

Beyond defining areas of appropriate employment, foetal protective policies act to define a role for women, to write a role upon the body. The indiscriminate nature of the policies constructs all women as potentially pregnant, as primarily bearers and rearers of children, first and foremost 'biological actors'. A woman's reproductive role is seen as considerably more important than her economic role, regardless of the impact of unemployment on herself, her pregnancy or her existing children. When women are defined by their generative organs, as primarily breeders, they become homogenized. Foetal protection policies ignore individuality and the existence of autonomous interests beyond the traditional family group. The possibility that women may choose not to have children, or may plan when to have them, is not recognized. Women may only participate in the public/ economic sphere within the terms of heterosexuality and traditional views of womanhood.

This traditional view asserts, not only physical and fiscal, but also intellectual, dependence. Women are constructed as unable to function as competent autonomous decision makers. More culpably, they are 'irresponsible, untrustworthy and uneducated'.[109] They are seen in the same light as they were at the turn of the century – unable to appreciate the risks of employ-ment, as Louis Brandeis' brief noted: 'Ignorant women can scarcely be expected to realise the dangers not only to their own health but to that of the next generation from such inhuman usage.'[110] Women are thus clearly por-trayed as lacking the competence to reach informed decisions as to their own reproductive health. As Siegel notes, this 'denigrates women's compe-tence to make reproductive decisions that reconcile responsibilities to them-selves and other family members, existing or potential'.[111] In many ways, this silencing, a denial of competence, may be understood as part of the contemporary abstracted or removed image of the pregnant woman. The discourses and practices of industrial foetal protection policies mirror a broader denial of the woman in reproductive discourses. This is evident within the generality of the denial of competence and the more specific *science* of exclusion, and it is to this that I now turn.

Removing the Woman

Recent critiques of the representation of women within reproductive dis-courses have highlighted her *disappearance*.[112] Foetal imaging techniques,[113] representations within popular culture,[114] Pro-Life rhetoric[115] and the dis-courses of law[116] and science are removing the presence of the woman. Pregnancy moves towards becoming a state which is no longer, the woman's body growing superfluous. The language of reproduction denies the woman; she is 'stripped away',[117] made 'transparent'.[118] Professional dominance and maternal exclusion are 'now enshrined within language; the role of the mother has been written out of the birth process which is now projected as an interaction between doctor and foetus'.[119] The shift to a *foetocentric* discourse and the privileged hegemonic status of the visual in late capitalist culture (and indeed in the western scientific tradition[120]) has moved to locate the mother beyond our popular knowledge of birthing. The discourses of foetal protection may be located within this general shift.

Jacobus *et al.* have written that 'The politics of the (feminine) body … are the politics of a social body either denied or disciplined, ideologically encoded or fantastically constructed (any or all at once).'[121] Where other discourses see denial, the discourses of foetal protection see both denial and distortion. Whilst the foetus retains a centrality, subordinating and denying the woman – the privileging of the visual impoverishing the whole[122] – the woman is also fantastically constructed. Discourses intersect at the fecund or potentially fecund uterus, enlarging and distorting the generative organs. This is perhaps most clearly illustrated with the regulations governing expo-sure to ionizing radiation.

Ionizing radiation regulations in the United Kingdom provide a standard maximum level of whole body occupational exposure to ionizing radiation of 50 mSv (millisieverts) in a calendar year. Women of reproductive capacity, however, are subject to a lower level of exposure. This disparity exists notwithstanding the abundant evidence that ionizing radiation poses greater risk to male reproductive health than to female reproductive health. This lower level of exposure, however, is not measured as whole body exposure but as *abdominal* exposure. A woman's abdomen, so long as it is fertile, is subject to a greater degree of protection than the entirety of her body and her health. For the purposes of radiation exposure, she appears almost as though viewed through a *camera obscura*: her generative organs distended, the rest of her physical self diminished, wizened, impoverished. The instruments of radiological protection, the ionizing chambers, Geiger-Müller tubes, scintillation chambers, proportion counters and thermoluminescent dosimeters diminish the *trappings* of the reproductive organs in ensuring the health of the fecund or potentially fecund uterus.

Conclusions

In James Hogg's nineteenth-century novel, *The Confessions and Memoirs of a Justified Sinner*, the young protagonist, on considering religious dogma, celebrates: 'How delightful to think that a justified person can do no wrong.' To claim to protect foetal health in the late twentieth century may leave a person *justified*, incapable of wrong. In the *Johnson Controls* case in the Seventh Circuit, the Court of Appeals held that to justify an exclusionary policy on the basis of protecting foetal health 'effectively distinguishes' the policy from 'the myths or purely habitual assumptions that employers sometimes attempt to impermissibly utilize to support the exclusion of women from employment opportunities'.[123] Yet calls to protect the foetus obscure stereotypes, assumptions and intentions impermissible under anti-discrimination provisions on both sides of the Atlantic. Such justification also obscures how contemporary foetal identity may be readily located within an understanding of the inscribed and constructed feminine body. Foetal identity has challenged the female reproductive organs as the primary repository for gender desires. This is evident not only within foetal protection policies but also, as was shown to a limited extent in the previous chapter, within the abortion debate. The body – particularly the reproductive body and the possible foetal body within – remains written upon, *harrowed*. Very much a part of this, the female reproductive organs are still constructed as having an inherent pathology. The foetal body is now endangered. The employed female body is disciplined, its pathology -and the possible endangered foetus within – defining its sphere of action.[124]

As has already been noted, the (female) body becomes understandable only when we understand what a society such as ours requires.[125] Within this position there is a clear recognition of the mutability of the body. The body is in flux, contingent in its structure upon its place in history, it is 'always subject to historic change, shifting in accordance with the differing ways in which the body is articulated and located within the intersecting and competing discourses of each era'.[126] Where the nineteenth century saw a complex investment in the female body, contemporary embodiment has empowered the foetus. In the process where the body is mythologized, enwombing and constituting social realities, the foetus has become encysted. The foetus has become a more focused repository for contemporary lore, myth and tale. As Chapter 2 illustrated, the nineteenth century saw women advised and encouraged to eschew higher education and employment on the basis of possible injurious effects to their fragile internal economy and their children. At the end of the twentieth century, *appropriate* female behaviour is delimited by new physical realities, by concern for the health and life of the foetus. Where Alison Young has described the foetus as biologically 'both a helpless dependant, and a voracious vampiric parasite',[127] so the foetus appears culturally vampiric, sustained by the stories, meaning and *truths* that invest its body. The body, and now the foetus within, remains 'the temporal site ... at which meaning about sexuality, labour and identity are constituted'.[128]

Notes

1   J. Winterson, *Written on the Body* (London: Vintage, 1993), 89.
2   Ibid., at 111.
3   R. Barthes, *A Lover's Discourse* (London: Penguin, 1990), 71.
4   Ibid., at 72.
5   F. Kafka, *In the Penal Colony*, in *The Transformation and Other Stories* (London: Penguin, 1992), 127. I would like to thank Katherine O'Donovan for highlighting the applicability of this tale to legal analysis; see K. O'Donovan, 'Genes or Jean's: Who Am I?' (unpublished paper, 1994).
6   Kafka, *supra*, at 134.
7   Ibid., at 135–6.
8   The form of inscription suggested in Kafka's fable may be illustrated by other narratives. The Marquise de Merteuil's smallpox in Choderlos de Laclos' *Les Liaisons Dangereuses*, and Cresseid's leprosy in Henryson's *The Testament of Cresseid* mark upon the body an inscription telling of deceit and manipulation. As Alexander Dumas' melodrama, *La Tour de Nesle*, comes to its conclusion, Buridan draws back the sleeve of the dying Gaultier d'Aulnay to reveal to Marguerite de Bourgogne the cross cut into his shoulder as an infant before he was abandoned on the steps of Notre Dame

Cathedral. The cross provides the final revelation that Gaultier is the child of Buridan and Marguerite, and that she has committed both incest and infanticide. In this instance the individual learns of her *transgression* through the inscription of another's body.

9   B. Smart, *Michel Foucault* (London: Tavistock, 1985), 75.

10   M. Foucault, *The History of Sexuality, Volume One* (London: Penguin, 1990), 139.

11   R. Diprose, *The Bodies of Women: Ethics, Embodiment and Sexual Difference* (London: Routledge & Kegan Paul, 1994), 25.Yet this investment and transformation of the body is in no way universally homogenous: women and men face different forms of investment, different divisions and transformations. See Z. Eisenstein, *The Female Body and the Law* (London: University of California Press, 1988), 10–11, R. Braidotti, *Nomadic Subjects: Embodiment and Sexual Difference in Contemporary Feminist Thinking* (New York: Columbia, 1994), 61. Within this difference the construction of the female body is itself not homogenous. The investment of the female body is determined not only by sexual difference but also by class and racial difference. See D.E. Roberts, 'Punishing Drug Addicts Who Have Babies: Women of Colour, Equality, and the Right of Privacy', *Harvard Law Review*, **104**, (1991), 1419. In this chapter I will be dealing with the construction of the female body within medico-legal and employment discourses, but, recognizing that the bodies of white women and women of colour are figured differently within these discourses, the assertions made will be applicable only to white women. This stance is particularly necessitated by my focus on reproductive discourses where white women and women of colour have historically been constructed almost oppositionally. It is hoped to show that white women are constructed within the dominant discourse as primarily biological actors, as bearers and rearers of children. On the other hand, women of colour have historically been constructed as unfit for motherhood – an integral part of oppression, as Roberts writes: 'The systematic, institutionalized denial of reproductive freedom has uniquely marked Black women's history in America. An important part of this denial has been the devaluation of Black women as mothers. A popular mythology that degrades Black women and portrays them as less deserving of motherhood reinforces this subordination. This mythology is one aspect of a complex set of images that deny Black humanity in order to rationalize the oppression of the Blacks' (ibid., at 1436–7).

12   198 US 45 (1905).

13   208 US 412 (1908).

14   Ibid., at 416–17.

15   Ibid., at 421.

16   Ibid., at 422.

17   Ibid.

18   Ibid., at 422–3.

19   214 NY 395, 108 NE 639 (1915).

20   'A Summary of "Facts of Knowledge" Submitted on Behalf of the People in Support of its Brief', *People of New York* v. *Charles Schweinler Press.*

21   Ibid., at 54–96 and 97–111.

22   Ibid., at 111–55.

23   Ibid., at 252–60.

24   See 'Hygiene of Female Workers', *BMJ* (26 September 1884), 578. For a different emphasis, see, S. Atkins and B. Hoggett, *Women and the Law* (Oxford: Blackwell, 1984), 12–13.

25   M.E. Becker, 'From *Muller* v. *Oregon* to Fetal Vulnerability Policies', *University of Chicago Law Review*, **53**, (1986), 1219 at 1223, nn.25–7.

26   Ibid., at 1224.

27   G.J. Annas, 'Fetal Protection and Employment Discrimination – The Johnson Controls Case', *New England Journal of Medicine*, **325**, (1991), 740, at 742.

28   Winterson, *supra*, at 89.

29   See, for example, F. Hollick, *The Diseases of Women, Their Cause and Cure Familiarly Explained* (New York: T.W. Strong, 1848), 42.

30   See, for example, G.L. Austin, cited in B. Ehrenreich and D. English, *For Her Own Good: 150 Years of the Experts' Advice to Women* (London: Pluto Press, 1979), 108.

31   C. Smith-Rosenberg and C. Rosenberg, 'The Female Animal: Medical and Biological Views of Woman and Her Role in Nineteenth-Century America', *Journal of American History*, **60**, (1973), 332, at 337–8.

32   Foucault, *supra*, at 104.

33   J. Harrington and F.S. Gill, *Occupational Health* (Oxford: Blackstone Scientific, 1992), 108–9.

34   Ibid.

35   Possible pregnancy outcomes may include low birth weight; perinatal death (death occurring between the twenty-eighth week of pregnancy and one week of life); mental retardation; altered growth patterns (pre-and post-natal growth); abnormal adaptation to the birth process; teratogenesis; carcinogen; impaired sexual organs and reproductive capacity; haematological abnormality; and metabolic abnormalities. See J. Barnard-Radford, 'Women and Chemicals', *Occupational Health* (October 1987), 316, at 321.

36   A. Hricko, *Working for Your Life: A Woman's Guide to Job Health Hazards* (Berkeley: Health Research Group, 1976), c-37–8.

37   Possibly the most notorious cause of teratogenesis is the prescription drug thalidomide.

38   DES was also found to affect the reproductive tract of male offspring. The drug caused lesions on the male genital tract and the production of abnormal semen. More generally, oestrogens have been associated with birth defects and adult cancer. See W. Williams, 'Firing the Woman to Protect the Foetus: The Reconciliation of Fetus Protection With Employment Opportunity Goals Under Title VII', *Georgia Law Journal*, **69**, (1981), 641, at 658.

39   Vinyl chloride is an example of a toxin that animal experiments have highlighted may act as a transplacental carcinogen in humans. Pregnant rats exposed to vinyl chloride have given birth to offspring that have later developed liver cancer. See J. Wagoner, P. Infante and D. Brown, 'Genetic Effects Associated With Industrial Chemicals', in E. Bingham (ed.), *Society for Occupational and Environmental Health Proceedings: Conference on Women and the Workplace* (28–9 June 1976), 100 (hereinafter cited as *SOEH Proceedings*). The foetus appears generally more sensitive to carcinogens than adults; see S.M. Barlow and F.M. Sullivan, *Reproductive Hazards of Industrial Chemicals* (London: Academic Press, 1982).

40   Hricko, *supra*, at b-5–6.

41   The Occupational Safety and Health Administration's (OSHA) Standard of Exposure to Lead prohibits workplace exposure over 50 micrograms per cubic metre airborne and 50 micrograms per 100 gram blood level for all employees: 22 CFR 1910.1025 (c)(1) and (k)(1)(i)(D). The United States Nuclear Regulatory Commission's policy is that women should be notified of the dangers of ionizing radiation and should be allowed to decide whether or not to become pregnant while working in an environ-

ment where they may be exposed to ionizing radiation: U.S. Nuclear Regulatory Commission, Nuclear Regulatory guide, 8.13 (1975).

42 *Washington Post*, 3 November 1979, A3, col. 4.

43 Bureau of National Affairs, *Pregnancy and Employment* (1987), 57.

44 For example, *Benson v. Environmental Protection and Aeration Sys., Inc.*, No. 79–2610 (W.D. Tenn., filed 5 September 1979), a case involving a welder who alleged that she had been discriminated against on an assigned job site on the basis of exposure to lead; *EEOC v. General Motors Corp.* No. 76–583–E (SD Ind., filed 22 September 1976), a challenge by a non-fertile woman to General Motors' policy of excluding all women from workplaces where lead exposure is a risk; and *Read v. St. Joe's Mineral Corp.*, (WD Pa. filed 13 November 1975), a class action challenging St. Joe's policy of excluding fertile women from jobs involving a risk of exposure to lead.

45 The Courts of Appeals cases were *Wright* v. *Olin* 697 F.2d 1182; *Hayes* v. *Shelby Memorial Hospital* 726 F.2d 1543 (11th Cir. 1984); *UAW* v. *Johnson Controls Inc.*, 886 F.2d 871 (7th Cir. 1989). *Johnson Controls* was later heard in the Supreme Court, 59 USLW 4209 (1991).

46 59 USLW 4209 (1991).

47 Ibid., at 4211.

48 Ibid.

49 Ibid., at 4215.

50 E. Draper, 'Fetal Exclusion Policies and Gendered Constructions of Suitable Work', *Social Problems*, **40**, (1993), 90, at 94.

51 111 S.Ct. 1227.

52 410 US 113 (1973), USSC.

53 A.E. Grossman, 'Striking Down Fetal Protection Policies: A Feminist Victory?', *Virginia Law Review*, **77**, (1991), 1607, at 1635.

54 For example, Yarn (Dyed by Lead Compounds) Heading Regulations 1907, Regulation 2; Tinning of Metal Hollow-ware, Iron Drums, and Harness Furniture Regulations 1909, Regulation 2; Electric Accumulator Regulations 1922, Regulation 1; and the Pottery (Health and Welfare) Special Regulations 1950, Regulation 6.

55 Section 176(1).

56 For a review of the cases, see Becker, *supra*; Williams, *supra*; E.A. Philips, 'The Status of Sex-Specific Fetal Protection Policies', *Missouri Law Review*, **57**, (1992), 979.

57 (1981) IRLR 13.

58 M. Atwood, *The Handmaid's Tale* (London: Virago, 1991).

59 See M. Thomson, 'After *Re S*', *Medical Law Review*, **2**, [1994], 127, at 148.

60 G.Z. Nothstein and J.P. Ayres, 'Sex-Based Considerations of Differential Treatment in the Workplace: Exploring the Biomedical Interface Between OSHA and Title VII', *Villanova Law Review*, **26**, (1991), 239, at 244.

61 B. Patten, *Human Embryology*, 3rd edn (1968), 470.

62 Toxic substances appear invariably to have three effects, teratogenesis, mutagenesis and carcinogenesis, which accounts for the sexually indiscriminate nature of most toxins. Although scientists are unclear why toxins act in this way, it is thought that the substances act at a cellular level to alter the DNA; see J.F. Haas and D. Schottenfeld, 'Risks to the Offspring from Parental Occupational Exposures', *Journal of Occupational Medicine* (1979), 607.

63 General awareness of reproductive toxicity is to start with very limited: 'What is known about reproductive hazards is far outweighed by what is unknown … Much of the information on suspected reproductive hazards … is derived from animal studies,

which present problems of interpretation in extrapolating to effects in humans. There are consequently no reliable estimates as yet of the basic measures of reproductive risk in the workplace' (Office of Technological Assessment, *Health Hazards in the Workplace* (1985), 3).

64   Becker, *supra*, at 1236; Philips, *supra*, at 985–6.

65   Becker, *supra*, at 1236.

66   Hricko, *supra*, at c-8, c-9.

67   *SOEH Proceedings, supra*, at 91.

68   J. Mason and R. Simon, 'Effects of Lead on Mammalian Reproduction', in V. Hunt (ed.), *Work and Health of Women* (1979), 171, at 172–4.

69   According to Harrington and Gill, 'at least 15–20% of normal conceptions fail to reach full growth and normal delivery. These could be termed 'normal' spontaneous abortions ... . Congenital malformations have been reported in about 3% of all newborn children with a further 3% reported during postnatal or later development ... . Most abnormal pregnancy outcomes, however, have no known cause' (Harrington and Gill, *supra*, at 110). Genetic and environmental influences are known to account for only one in 20 abnormal pregnancy outcomes; see M. Harrington, 'Reproductive Outcome', *Occupational Health* (October 1987), 309, at 310.

70   Nothstein and Ayres, *supra*, at 244.

71   Letter from Eula Bingham to corporate medical directors, cited in Williams, *supra*, at 663.

72   'OSHA News', *Job Safety and Health*, **6**, (December 1978), 2.

73   *Encyclopedia of Health and Safety at Work, Law and Practice II* (London: Sweet and Maxwell, 1993), 4–1101, 4998/283.

74   'OSHA News', *supra*, n.62.

75   C. Assennato, R. Molinini, C. Paci *et al.*, 'Sperm Count Suppression Without Endocrine Dysfunction in Lead-Exposed Men', *Archive of Environmental Health*, **42**, (1987), 124.

76   I. Lancranjan, H.I. Popescu, O. Gavanescu, I. Klepsch and M. Serbanescu, 'Reproductive Ability in Workmen Occupationally Exposed to Lead', *Archive of Environmental Health*, **30** (1975), 396. Increases in sperm abnormalities may also be transmitted to subsequent generations; see Mason and Simon, *supra*, at 172–4.

77   M.L. Lindbohn, M. Sallmen, A. Antilla, H. Taskinen and K. Hemminski, 'Paternal Occupational Lead Exposure and Spontaneous Abortion', *Scandinavian Journal of Work Environment Health*, **17**, (1991), 95.

78   Preamble to OSHA Lead Standard, 43 Fed. Reg. (1975), 54,388.

79   886 F.2d 871 (7th Cir. 1989) at 889.

80   Draper, *supra*, at 93.

81   *Wright* v. *Olin*, *supra*. Benzene is a highly flammable colourless liquid. It is a known carcinogen and one of the top 12 chemicals by volume used in the United States (Note, 'Title VII – Employment Discrimination and Foetal Safety in Hazardous Work Environments – *Wright et al.* v. *Olin*', *Arizona State Law Journal* (1984), 211, at 212 n.8). Benzene is thought to be a mutagen affecting sperm morphology; see Haas and Schottenfeld, *supra*.

82   *Doerr* v. *B.F. Goodrich Co.*, 484 F.Supp. 320, 321 (N.D. Ohio 1980). Vinyl chloride is essential to the production of plastics. It has been shown to cause cancer of the brain, liver, lungs and lymphatic system, J. Wagoner, P. Infante and D. Brown, 'Genetic Effects Associated With Industrial Chemicals', *SOEH Proceedings*, *supra*, at 100. Male exposure to vinyl chloride has been associated with spontaneous abortion in unexposed partners; see Haas and Schottenfeld, *supra*.

83 Avtex Fibres Inc., a rayon manufacturer (Williams, *supra*, at 648). There is evidence suggesting carbon disulphide may cause birth defects in the offspring of exposed males (S. Blakeslee, 'Research on Birth Defects Turns to Flaws in Sperm', *New York Times* (1 January 1989), A1, 36).

84 DuPont, for example, excluded women of child-bearing capacity from workplaces that involved exposure to hexafluoroacetone which, according to DuPont's own study, damages sperm (Draper, *supra*, at 93).

85 A survey of 198 large chemical and electronics companies in Massachusetts found that 54 used glycol ethers, which have proved very toxic to sperm at low levels of exposure. None of the companies has restricted male access, while 37 have excluded or restricted the employment of women on the basis of potential reproductive harm; (see C. Daniels, M. Pauls and R. Rosofsky, *Family Work and Health* (Boston: Commonwealth of Massachusetts, 1988).

86 International Programme on Chemical Safety, *Environmental Health Criteria 114: Dimethylformamide* (Geneva: World Health Organization, 1991), 14.

87 A.M. Ducatman *et al.*, 'Germ Cell Tumours of the Testicle Among Aircraft Repairmen', *Journal of Urology*, **136**, 834–6; S.M. Levin *et al.*, 'Testicular Cancer in Leather Tanners Exposed to Dimethylformamide', *The Lancet* (1985), 1153.

88 D.L. Hoadley, 'Fetal Protection Policies: Effective Tools for Gender Discrimination', *Journal of Legal Medicine*, **12**, (1991), 85, at 101.

89 C. Atwell, 'Hazards to Female Reproduction', *Occupational Health* (October 1987), 312. See also R.P. Knill-Jones *et al.*, 'Anaesthetic Practice and Pregnancy – Controlled Survey of Women Anaesthetists in the UK', *The Lancet* (1972), 1326.

90 Equal Opportunities Commission, *Some Facts About Women 1993*, Employment By Industry (Manchester, 1993).

91 Draper, *supra*, at 95.

92 Ibid., at 94; also Becker, *supra*, at 1238.

93 The codes of practice provide for the removal of women from workplaces that expose them to blood lead levels of 40 µg/100 ml (para. 118(a)).

94 See ss. 74(*a*)–74(*f*).

95 *Oil, Gas and Atomic Workers* v. *American Cyanamid Co.*, 741 F.2d 444 (D.C. Cir. 1984).

96 697 F.2d 1127.

97 For example, *Johnson Controls* (7th Cir.) 886 F.2d 871.

98 *EEOC* v. *General Motors Corp.*, 76–538–E (S.D.Ind., filed 22 September 1976).

99 697 F.2d, at 1191.

100 726 F.2d 1543 (11th Cir. 1984).

101 886 F.2d 871 (7th Cir. 1989) at 889.

102 J.M. Stellman and M.S. Henifin, 'No Fertile Women Need Apply', in R. Hubbard (ed.), *Biological Woman – The Convenient Myth* (1982), 117, at 138.

103 A. Macfarlaine and M. Mugford, *Birth Counts: Statistics of Pregnancy and Childbirth* (London: HMSO, 1984), 9, Table A3.3: 'Age-specific fertility, England and Wales, 1939–1980'.

104 V. Stolte-Heisankanen, 'Fertility and Women's Employment Outside the Home in Western Europe', Table 7.4: 'Fertility Rates Specific for Age of Mother, Selected European Countries', in S. Kupinski (ed.), *The Fertility of Working Women: A Synthesis of International Research* (New York: Praeger, 1977), 250, at 259.

105 Ibid. In fact, only one in 5000 women between the ages of 45 and 49 has a child in any given year in the United States (US Department of Commerce Bureau of the Census, Statistical Abstract of the United States 1986, at 57).

106   See D. Rush, 'Socioeconomic Status and Perinatal Outcome', in S. Aladjem and A.K. Brown (eds), *Perinatal Intensive Care* (Saint Louis: CV Mosby, 1977), 14–17. Rush also illustrates the link between socioeconomic factors and infant mortality. More specifically, poor nutrition has been associated with fertility problems (A. Fletcher, *Reproductive Hazards at Work* (Manchester: Equal Opportunities Commission, 1985), at 24); neural tube defects such as spina bifida and anencephaly, (ibid.); low birth rate, (ibid., at 22); and may cause an increased sensitivity to teratogens (M. Wynn and A. Wynn, *The Prevention of Handicap of Early Pregnancy Origin* (London: Foundation for Education and Research in Childbearing, 1981)).

107   J. Bertin, 'Should "Fetal Protection" Policies Be Upheld? No: Fix the Job Not the Worker', *American Bar Association Journal*, **76** (1990), 39.

108   See Lytle, 'American Cyanamid Co.: Good Neighbor or Hazard?' *New Haven Reg.*, 16 December 1984, at 1, col. 1. See also Draper, who notes that the Bunker Hill Company, which operates a foetal protection policy that excludes women on the basis of exposure to lead, has been sued for exposing children to lead in the areas surrounding the companies facilities (Draper, *supra*, at 96).

109   Hoadley, *supra*, at 101.

110   'Facts of Knowledge' *supra*, at 175–6.

111   R. Siegel, 'Reasoning from the Body: A Historical Perspective on Abortion Regulation and Questions of Equal Protection', *Stanford Law Review*, **44**, (1992), 261, at 338.

112   This disappearance may, however, be placed within a broader social trend towards the disappearance of the body, as J.G. Ballard has written: 'Does the body exist at all, in any but the most mundane sense? Its role has been steadily diminished, so that it seems little more than a ghostly shadow seen on the X-ray plate of our moral disapproval' (J.G. Ballard, 'Project for a glossary for the Twentieth Century', in 'Incorporations', *Zones*, **6**, (1992), 269.

113   See C.A. Stabile, 'Shooting the Mother: Fetal Photography and the Politics of Disappearance', *Camera Obscura*, **28**, (1992), 179, at 194; A. Young, 'Decapitation or Feticide: The Fetal Laws of the Universal Subject', *Women: A Cultural Review*, **4**, (1993), 288; R. Petchesky, 'Foetal Images: The Power of Visual Culture in the Politics of Reproduction', in M. Stanworth (ed.), *Reproductive Technologies: Gender, Motherhood and Medicine* (Cambridge: Polity Press, 1987); V. Hartouni, 'Containing Women: Reproductive Discourse in the 1980s', in C. Penley and A. Ross (eds), *Technoculture* (Minneapolis: University of Minnesota Press, 1991).

114   See, Stabile, *supra*; Petchesky, *supra*; also E. Ann Kaplan, *Motherhood and Representation: The Mother in Popular Culture* (London: Routledge & Kegan Paul, 1992), 180–219.

115   Petchesky, *supra*.

116   See S. Sheldon, 'The Law of Abortion and the Politics of Medicalization', in J. Bridgeman and S. Millns (eds), *Law and Body Politics: The Legal Regulation of the Female Body* (Aldershot: Dartmouth, 1995).

117   Dr Bernard Nathanson, producer of *The Silent Scream*, interviewed in *Newsweek*, cited in Petchesky, *supra*, at 58.

118   Dr Michael Harrison, writing about 'foetal management', cited in Petchesky, *supra*.

119   M. Jacobus, E. Fox Keller and S. Shuttleworth, *Body/Politics: Women and the Discourses of Science* (London: Routledge, 1990), 6.

120   See E. Fox Keller and C.R. Grontkowski, 'The Mind's Eye', in S. Harding and M. Hintikka (eds), *Discovering Reality: Feminist Perspectives on Epistemology, Metaphysics, Methodology and Philosophy* (Dordrecht: Reidel, 1983).

121   Jacobus *et al., supra*, at 9.
122   E. Martin, 'Science and Women's Bodies: Forms of Anthropological Knowledge', in Jacobus *et al., supra*, at 69.
123   *UAW* v. *Johnson Controls* (7th Cir.), *supra* at 886.
124   The solicitor for the Freight Hire Company in the *Page* case claimed that Ms. Page had 'formed the view, as women's libbers and pro-abortionists do, that she had the right to decide the future of her own body and her own unborn' (*The Northern Echo*, 27 March 1980, 13).
125   M. Foucault, *Power/Knowledge: Selected Interviews and Other Writings, 1972–1977*, ed. C. Gordon (Brighton: Harvester Press, 1980), 58.
126   Jacobus *et al., supra*, at 4.
127   Young, *supra*, at 293.
128   J. Grbich, 'The Body in Legal Theory', in M.A. Fineman and N.S. Thomadsen (eds), *At the Boundaries of Law: Feminism and Legal Theory* (London: Routledge, 1991), 61, at 67.

6   New Reproductive Technologies: the (Post)modern Prometheus

I did not sleep, nor could I be said to think. My imagination, unbidden, possessed and guided me, gifting the successive images that arose in my mind with a vividness far beyond the usual bounds of reverie. I saw – with shut eyes, but acute mental vision – I saw the pale student of unhallowed arts kneeling beside the thing he had put together. I saw the hideous phantom of a man stretched out and then, on the working of some powerful engine, show signs of life, and stir with an uneasy and half vital motion. (M. Shelley, *Frankenstein* (London: Penguin Classics, 1992), author's Introduction, 9)

The child of fire is the child of disobedience. In revolt. The Promethean child steals the matches to strike a dangerous light in the dark. As he sets fire he has wicked thoughts. He will not get caught. The fire dies down. In the red embers he becomes aware. (D. Jarman, *Chroma* (London: Vintage, 1995), 37)

Storytelling becomes a vicarious pregnancy. (M.A. Rubenstein, '"My Accursed Origin": The Search for the Mother in *Frankenstein*', *Studies in Romanticism*, **15**, (1976), 165, at 173)

Introduction

In their introduction to *Body/Politics: Women and the Discourses of Science*, Jacobus, Fox Keller and Shuttleworth remark:

The more distant the historical period, the easier it becomes to identify [the] pressures that have framed scientific discourse; the Victorian medical and social discussions of the female body ... for example, offer themselves readily to ideological dissection, revealing the economic and gender assumptions at stake. As we move closer to our own time, when science wields an unprecedented cultural authority, and massive material investments guarantee its truths, demystification grows more difficult.[1]

Problems of proximity in dissecting present-day medical or scientific discourses are explicable, as Jacobus *et al.* assert, in part, in the privileging of science. Science does wield an unprecedented cultural weight. Yet obstacles to ideological dissection exist beyond this. If we understand the embodied subject as a product/materialism of discourse and practice, then analysis of contemporary discourse becomes problematic. We exist, and indeed are constituted within rather than without the discourses, practices and ideology we seek to understand. Yet particular processes, structures and networks of power and knowledge may be located within different discourses – both within the same period and within different historical periods. The networks mapped within consideration of historic discourses and practices provide us with interpretative tools, hinting at what may lie within that with which we may be too familiar.

Utilizing the networks mapped so far within reproductive discourses, the aim in this and the following chapter is to examine the new reproductive technologies.[2] These technologies have extended our vocabulary. We have what Derek Morgan and Robert Lee have called a 'new lexicon of life',[3] new possibilities both real and imagined, new language with which to know. Yet within this new lexicon and its discourses there exist familiar narratives. This chapter and Chapter 7 will illustrate how, as with the other reproductive discourses considered so far, the discourses and practices (the narratives) of the new reproductive technologies may be understood as technologies of gender.

In many ways repeating the approach adopted in Chapters 3 and 4, this chapter and the next consider the new reproductive discourses in the light of a reading of Mary Shelley's Gothic classic, *Frankenstein*. Subtitled *The Modern Prometheus*, the novel may easily be coopted as a fabled warning of the errors of (masculine[4]) interference in the creation of life, the 'supremely frightful ... effects of any human endeavour to mock the stupendous mechanism of the Creator of the world'.[5] Indeed, as Maurice Hindle argues: 'As a cautionary tale warning of the dangers that can be cast into society by a presuming experimental science, *Frankenstein* is without equal.'[6] Yet Shelley's work may be illustrative in further ways.

Shelley's text may animate consideration of the continued manner in which reproductive discourses define and are defined by gender. At this point, however, I introduce a temporary shift of emphasis. This chapter looks at the relationship between male gender and the evolution and management of the new reproductive technologies. While the nature of the relationship between masculinity and the management of reproductive choices has, to an extent, been implicit in the discussion so far, it is now necessary to provide a more explicit consideration. Utilizing *Frankenstein* places the emergence or evolution of the new reproductive technologies within a continuity of masculine creation mythology and desire. Understood in this light, the new reproductive technologies may be located within the understanding and critique of masculine creation that Shelley's text affords. This critique not only aids an understanding of masculinity, but also demands that we consider the status of the maternal within masculine creation projects. Assessing the status of the maternal within the new reproductive technologies, we find Shelley's suggestion that the maternal is circumvented and denigrated is supported. This is evidenced, as will be argued, not only at the experimental fringes of reproductive science but also in the general lack of consideration that is given to the very real health risks involved in many of these procedures.

Turning to the relationship between the female gender and the new reproductive technologies in Chapter 7, Shelley's text also allows a development of the arguments already pursued that understand 'bodies [as] made, not given'.[7] Importantly in this respect, *Frankenstein* proves illustrative of the historical association of the female body with not just the pathological but also the monstrous. In examining this association, the next chapter considers the primary statutory response to the new reproductive technologies in England and Wales, and looking at the provisions of the Human Fertilisation and Embryology Act 1990 (HFEA), considers the provisions which embody, in one form, this association between the female body and the monstrous.

Frankenstein

> [The novel] inculcates no lesson of conduct, manners, or morality ... it fatigues the feelings without interesting the understanding; it gratuitously harasses the heart, and only adds to the store, already too great, of painful sensation ... the reader [is left] after a struggle between laughter and loathing, in doubt whether the head or the heart of the author be the most diseased. (*Quarterly Review*, March 1818)

The anonymous publication of Mary Shelley's *Frankenstein* in 1818 was met by predominantly unfavourable reviews,[8] yet, while the *Quarterly Review* and others, evoked the author's depravity, Sir Walter Scott was to note the novel's 'uncommon powers of poetic imagination' and celebrate the 'author's original genius and happy power of expression'.[9] It is this latter verdict which appears to have endured, the novel recently being described as 'amongst the most celebrated events in literary and popular history',[10] the text, more precisely, being understood as one 'which is too complex, peculiar and interesting to be neglected'.[11]

Yet, although *Frankenstein* is familiar to us, the demands of popular culture have distorted the novel's cultural presence. Shelley's text has been subsumed by the privileged cultural space the Monster has attained: 'The afterlife of the novel in the popular imagination has been intensely focused on that monstrous body.'[12] The image of the reanimated Monster has proved so arresting and so enduring as to obscure the sources of its fascination.[13] While this is important, and a point to which I will return, given the continued reworking of the fable it is probably of value to return briefly to the novel's structure and content.

Part of the novel's complexity and interest derives from Shelley's choice of narrative structure. The novel, like Greenaway's *The Baby of Macon*, provides a story within a story, framing one narrative within another. Shelley develops this idea further, however, imbedding a tale within a tale within a tale. With what Brooks refers to as a 'nested narrative structure'[14] and what Rubenstein refers to as 'a series of concentric rings of narrative, each enclosing the next',[15] Shelley draws attention to the presence of the listener – the one who is to be warned.

The novel opens with, and exists within the parenthesis of, the explorer Robert Walton's letters to his sister, Mrs Saville. Walton's letters (to the silent and distant, and perhaps unreceiving sister – is she us, the reader?[16]) tell of his meeting with the near dead Victor Frankenstein on the Arctic ice flows. Walton's ship, on a perilous and heroic journey of exploration, has become fixed within the ice. Walton and his crew members provide a captive audience.[17] Frankenstein, recognizing that Walton may suffer his own fate, tells his tale. Within this narrative, however, the Monster tells his own story. The Monster's tale is told initially to Frankenstein, in turn to Walton and eventually to Mrs Saville/us. Within this complex structure, Shelley tells what has proved to be an enduring tale.

Guided through the narrative layers, we learn of the work of the gifted young student Frankenstein. Schooled in the teachings of the ancient alchemists – Cornelius Agrippa, Paracelsus, Albertus Magnus – Frankenstein pursues natural philosophy. Such ancient magic, however, does not retain its hold on the young Frankenstein for long. Observing the destructive power of lightning, he discovers the new magic of electricity and galvanism,[18] and 'set[s] down natural history and all its progeny as a deformed and abortive creation'.[19] With his new alchemy, Frankenstein challenges the boundaries of knowledge, aiming to 'banish disease from the human frame and render man invulnerable to any but violent death!'[20] Such noble and beneficent intentions play an important role in the fable, underpinning the dangers of even the best intentioned explorations. Soon the intention to cure disease is subsumed by more elemental and macabre desires:

> soon my mind was filled with one thought, one conception, one purpose. So much has been done, exclaimed the soul of Frankenstein, – more, far more, will I achieve: treading in the steps already marked, I will pioneer a new way, explore unknown powers, and unfold to the world the deepest mysteries of creation.[21]

In pursuit of these 'deepest mysteries', Frankenstein's path at this point is more faithfully reflected than most other aspects of the tale in its translation to film. Frankenstein produces a composite creature, monstrous in appearance and size.[22] Yet, after the Monster's genesis, the path taken by the novel and that pursued within popular retelling again diverges. Shelley in her introduction to the text tells how the image she started with at Lord Byron's Villa Diodati on the shores of Lake Leman in Switzerland in the May of 1816 was the absolute horror of the creator waking under the gaze of the created:

> His success would terrify the artist; he would rush away from his odious handiwork, horror-stricken. He would hope that, left to itself, the slight spark of life which he had communicated would fade; that this thing, which had received such imperfect animation, would subside into dead matter; and he might sleep in the belief that the silence of the grave would quench forever the transient existence of the hideous corpse which he had looked upon as the cradle of life. He sleeps; but is awakened; he opens his eyes; behold, the horrid thing stands at his bedside, opening his curtains and looking on him with yellow, watery, but speculative eyes.[23]

Incorporating this chilling vision into the tale, the Monster then disappears. His journey, actions and the observations of these 'speculative eyes' we learn of predominantly through the innermost of the narratives – the Monster's own tale. The Monster tells of his self-education, his discovery of language and his reading of Milton's *Paradise Lost*, Plutarch's *Lives*, and Goethe's *Sorrows of Werther*, a 'minimal Romantic *cyclopedia universalis*'.[24] Yet, driven by the reactions of others to his monstrous state, Frankenstein's creation seeks to exact revenge against his creator. The Monster's first murder is committed against Frankenstein's young brother, William. Having strangled him, the Monster removes a locket from the child and plants the evidence upon the family servant, Justine Moritz, who is in turn executed for the murder of the child. Having both temporarily sated the desire for revenge and demonstrated his malevolent power, the Monster seeks out his maker.

Frankenstein is found by his creation seeking solace, and perhaps forgiveness, in the Alps above Chamonix. Ascending to Montanvert and the Mer de Glace, Frankenstein expresses his desire to recapture the 'sublime ecstasy that gave wings to the soul and allowed it to soar from the obscure world to light and joy'.[25] In one of the many scenes of what Marc Rubenstein has called 'primal scene imagery', imagery which is 'pervasive and unmistakable ... penetrat[ing] into the very structure of the novel and becom[ing] part of a more deeply hidden search for the mother',[26] Frankenstein recognizes the power of (mother) nature, a power greater than his ill-advised and doomed act of creation:

> The immense mountains and precipices that overhung me on every side – the sound of the river raging among the rocks, and the dashing of the waterfalls around, spoke of a power mighty as Omnipotence – and I ceased to fear, or to bend before any being less almighty than that which had created and ruled the elements, here displayed in their most terrific guise.[27]

Within this primal scene, however, Frankenstein is, as he will be throughout the remainder of the novel, pursued and caught by his own primal act. The Monster denies Frankenstein his right of dismissal and asserts his own right to be heard by his creator. With great eloquence, the Monster tells of the acts of those for whom his physical state is repulsive. He recounts his loneliness, and his desire for Frankenstein to construct a female partner. Eloquence and an undertaking by the Monster that he would take his bride far from humankind is rewarded by Frankenstein's acquiescence. This acquiescence, however, is not sustained and, although Frankenstein embarks upon the creation of a second (female) Monster, his project is aborted; he dismembers and destroys his work. Appalled by the destruction of his mate, the Monster fulfils his promised revenge against his creator's family and ultimately against his creator's own bride/wife. This final act of revenge, of arguably Oedipal rage, seals as inevitable the ultimate pursuit of the Monster by Frankenstein and the death of both creator and created, again within a landscape of primal scene imagery.

Frankenstein: Text and Tradition

In exploring the 'fictions that address the body, that imbed it in narrative, and that therefore embody meanings: stories on the body, and the body in story',[28] Peter Brooks notes the complex questions of motherhood, fatherhood, gender and narrative that Shelley's text raises.[29] Within these questions, many of them written upon the monstrous body, are questions that may be aligned with current feminist challenges to the new reproductive technologies, yet before considering these questions, both in this and in the following chapter, it is necessary to place Shelley's text within its literary context, particularly within what may be seen to be a masculine culture. This process helps to locate the technologies under consideration within the critique Shelley offers. That is to say, the technologies may be positioned within the critique Shelley's text provides of androcentric reproductive myths and discourses.

Frankenstein deals with the construction of man-made realities, the creation of man by man. This androcentric desire has a distinguished literary genealogy. The novel's antecedents are the Promethean legends of Ancient Greece (*Prometheus pyrophoros*) and Rome (*Prometheus plasticator*), the *Book of Genesis* and, with a very self-conscious intertextual presence, Milton's *Paradise Lost*. Yet this masculine tradition is discernible not only in the complete male negation of the maternal, seen in these texts, but also in androcentric or sperm-centred representations of procreation. Aeschylus provides one such analysis. In *The Eumenides*, the last play of the *Oresteia*, the question is not whether Orestes actually cut Clytemnestra's throat – that is admitted – but whether the murder was wrong. Apollo, attempting to exonerate Orestes of his act of matricide, asserts that there exists no blood relation between mother and son.[30] Within this literary tradition the novel may be understood as part of a heritage of masculine creation. The novel creates a male God introducing life into his inert Adam. Frankenstein brings his Adam single-handed into a world where women are peripheral if not an afterthought.

Beyond literature, Promethean tales have a similarly illustrious heredity. Aristotle, for example, believed the woman an incubator for an embryonic ejaculate implanted by the man. The *catamenia* – a formless material from the menstrua – was animated by the *pneuma*, the life-giving power contained within the semen.[31] Coming closer to our own time and, perhaps more importantly, moving within the scientific model, the poet–doctor Erasmus Darwin offered a surprisingly similar model. Importantly, Darwin was one of the topics of conversation between Percy Shelley and Byron to which Mary Shelley had famously claimed to have been a silent witness.[32] In *Zoonomia*, published in 1794, Darwin highlighted the imaginative powers of the male in their generative effect, leaving the female almost as an inert receptacle.[33]

The tradition within which Shelley's text may be located, and which she ultimately critiques, involves not only the pre-Romantic desire of man making man, but also the Romantic Promethean desire of man *re*making man – the theory of perfectibility.[34] A theory largely championed by Shelley's father, William Godwin,[35] perfectibility espoused a belief in the possibility of the betterment of man. Godwin's theory was premised on a belief in man's inherent good, or at least his neutrality (man 'is not originally vicious'[36]), and in the overwhelming need to pursue truth.[37] Frankenstein's quest, conflating these ideals, provides a clear critique of Godwin's theory and optimism. Yet Shelley clearly locates perfectibility within its historical and masculine context, extending the critique to all androcentric models of reproduction. Recognizing perfectibility's genealogy, the text lays bare, as Paul Cantor observes, the 'nightmare of Romantic idealism, revealing the dark underside to all the visionary dreams of remaking man that fired the imagination of Romantic myth-makers'.[38]

Shelley's text subversively appropriates the myths of masculine creation in which perfectability is imbricated. The novel's intertextuality forms part of this subversion. Shelley draws together a history of male creation mythology suggesting a continuity of desire. The product of this desire is a monstrous and ultimately destructive body. The novel's intertextuality is deliberately brought to the reader's attention in many ways by the author – not least in the nested narrative structure employed by Shelley and noted above. The nature of the text is also embodied in the Monster's origins – in his composite nature – in the images of Frankenstein (Shelley) sorting through corpses (texts) in charnel houses and tombs for the beautiful and perfect. The body therefore becomes an intertextual product, male creation mythology embodied in a monstrous form. As such, within the novel's structure and the composite form of both Monster and text, Shelley draws our attention towards, and offers a strong critique of, male creative desires.

Shelley's warning against self-inseminating man is seen not only in the monstrous progeny and its monstrous acts, but also in the novel's clear symbolism. Perhaps the most clearly employed symbolism is in the (gendered) conflict that emerges between nature and the monstrous. While, as noted above, the novel is replete with primal scene imagery, this is in a way corrupt. As Brooks observes: 'virtually every time "nature" is involved in the novel, as moral presence presiding over human life, it appears to produce only the monstrous'.[39] With Frankenstein's assent of Montanvert and the Mer de Glace, again noted above, the Monster first seeks audience with his creator. The Monster's presence corrupts the 'sublime ecstasy'[40] of nature, telling of the errors of a presuming experimental and Promethean science. Throughout the novel the monstrous is placed between man and nature, tainting what Shelley sees as the moral presence of (mother) nature.

Within this challenge to a masculine tradition, Shelley offers a 'subversive and reflexive version of creation – the role of God is diminished and man celebrated as his own creator'.[41] In itself this is an important observation. It details the rise of the doctor. He is not only 'Father and Judge, Family and Law' but also (therapeutic) Priest.[42] Reproduction shifts within this period through the general rise in the medical profession and its colonization of all aspects of life. Yet integral to this critique is a recognition of the status of the maternal within this androcentric tradition. As Margaret Homans writes, 'Most succinctly put, the novel is about the collision between androcentric and gynocentric theories of creation, a collision that results in the denigration of maternal childbearing through its circumvention by male creation.'[43]

Within the novel and its textual ghosts we therefore see, not just the diminishment of the role of God, but also the desire for 'the obviation of the mother, the male quest for substitutes for the mothers'.[44] The text draws us to Clytemnestra's fate, Aristotle's catamenia and pneuma, Darwin's *Zoonomia*. It is this recognition of a circumvention or obviation of the maternal within male creative desires that I will focus upon. First, however, to better understand this, I consider the nature of masculine experiences of reproduction and note how the current episteme shapes this experience and simultaneously attempts to alter it.

Masculinity and Reproduction

Shelley's text may offer a graphic critique of Promethean desires. As has been suggested, this critique may be extended to the contemporary involvement of the masculine in the management of reproduction. Most helpfully in the positioning of these technologies within the historical tradition noted above, the text illuminates (and indeed is illuminated by) some of the analysis that has located the emergence of new reproductive technologies within a psychoanalytical understanding of gender and reproduction. Rosi Braidotti, offering arguably the most intelligent of these commentaries, has written:

> On the imaginary level ... the test-tube babies of today mark the long-term triumph of the alchemists' dream of dominating nature through their self inseminating, masturbatory practices. What is happening with the new reproductive technologies today is the final chapter in a long history of fantasy of self-generation by and for men themselves – men of science, but men of the male kind, capable of producing new monsters and fascinated by their power.[45]

While a continuity may be discerned, it needs to be asked why it exists. The masturbatory practices to which Braidotti refers may be understood as a product of what Mary O'Brien has described as the intellectual leap that men have to make within the process of reproduction. According to O'Brien, men's experience of paternity is uncertain. O'Brien claims they face a void, or nullity,[46] which has led to this Promethean quest to 'transcend natural realities with historical, man-made realities'.[47] However, it may be argued that there is not so much a void as a more prosaic need for proof of fatherhood, although this need for proof may stem from the same separation which O'Brien suggests. Ann Oakley, pursuing this argument, links the emergence of the new reproductive technologies with the historic need for 'assured paternity': 'These particular technologies enable men to achieve what they have always wanted – proof of fatherhood. It is not possible to understand why new reproductive technologies happen or what their implications are without asking and answering the question "What do men want?"'[48]

The social and political context of the new reproductive technologies is therefore both complex and simple. These technologies, it must be remembered, offer the possibility of child bearing to women and couples who experience their infertility or subfertility as a tremendous loss. They also contain many challenging possibilities, the responses to which will be considered in the following chapter. Yet, at the same time, these technologies allow something as simple as male security in the context of paternity.[49] Noting the complexity of effects that the new reproductive technologies have created, Carol Smart has argued: 'At the same time conception in the petri dish, as opposed to the uterus, not only allows subfertile couples to have their "own" children, it allows men for the first time in history, to be absolutely certain that they are genetic fathers of their future children.'[50]

The void experienced, the desire to transcend the natural realities of reproduction, and the need for assured paternity are clearly embodied in enduring narratives such as *Frankenstein*. More specifically, the text goes beyond this, suggesting the masturbatory and arguably narcissistic nature of the desire the novel critiques. As Jane Blumberg argues, Frankenstein's 'desire to have sole responsibility for his "son's" creation and his refusal to reproduce in the far simpler and natural way is a desire ... to see his creation as solely a projection of himself. He would like to see his being made flesh, objectified so it may be possessed.'[51] *Frankenstein*, therefore, is arguably illustrative of a masculinist culture which seeks to manage, regulate, tame and perfect. There is both a desire to know, to bridge the void men face during reproduction, and narcissistically to discipline the uncertainties and vagaries of *unassisted* reproduction. Margaret Homans, considering both *Frankenstein* and the creation of Eve in Milton's *Paradise Lost*, similarly notes this narcissistic element: 'These new creations in the image of the self are substitutes for the powerful creating mother and place creation under the control of the son.'[52] This desire to rewrite or renegotiate the relationship between men and reproduction may be understood at a more complex level. In terms of the contemporary manifestations of Promethean fantasy (in new reproductive technologies and the embryological experiments of self-generation or parthenogenesis, nucleus substitution or cloning), Rosi Braidotti locates this within the privileging of the visual in western epistemology. This privileging of the scopic problematizes the relationship between men and the experience/phenomenon of pregnancy:

> The woman's body can change shape in pregnancy and childbearing; it is therefore capable of defeating the notion of the fixed *bodily form*, of visible, recognisable, clear and distinct shapes as that which marks the contour of the body. She is morphologically dubious. The fact that the female body can change shape so drastically is troublesome in the eyes of the logocentric economy within which to *see* is the primary act of knowledge and *the gaze* the basis of all epistemic awareness.[53]

The epistemic primacy afforded to the visual may arguably explain the relational problem that men experience in terms of pregnancy. The reliance upon the visual problematizes not only the notion of the fixed bodily form but also questions of assured paternity. The failure to secure paternity (scientifically or visually) promotes the void to which O'Brien has referred. The desire to legitimate paternity within the dominant epistemic framework has been translated into a desire to extend the gaze to an area previously beyond the visual. This desire is clearly embodied in the increasingly complex management of the infertile female. Most noticeable within this management has been the increased visualization of the interior of the reproductive system. The visual becomes the main focus for contemporary Promethean desire. In the process of *in vitro* fertilization (IVF), for example, the woman may be subject to daily ultrasound, assessing the development of ova follicles. Once the follicles are mature, ova will be extracted and ultrasound scanning will visualize the ovaries guiding the laparoscope, facilitating aspiration of the ova. Importantly, this graphic visualization is very much part of an intense management of the body during IVF treatment.[54] The importance of the visual in this process is noted by Cathryn Vasseleu:

> Through [ultrasound and] the endoscope, the body's unknown volume unfolds as a framed and flattened topography. It is rendered as a surface over which purchase may be gained by the viewing subject. [With ultrasound and in] the endoscope's action of screening an image can be read a desire for purchase reminiscent of the camera obscura, whose images not only entertained but put things in perspective.[55]

The desire for purchase or control over the pregnant body places the new reproductive technologies themselves in perspective. Continuity is discernible in the nature of medical intervention in reproduction. Yet, whilst the new reproductive technologies may be contextualized in this way, it does not necessarily imply a tacit collusion between a (male) state and medicine. What it does suggest, however, is the male gendered position from which medicine may act, with at times medical and state interests converging. In the light of this it is worth noting that HFEA gives monopoly control over most infertility services to licensed clinicians, which both enforces and entrenches the medical management of reproduction and makes infertility services both visible and subject to regulation. In terms of the continuity in medical control of reproduction, Renate Duelli Klein has recognized little that is (ideologically) new in the 'new' reproductive technologies:

> Whether 'old' or 'new', these procedures have in common that they represent an artificial invasion of the human body – predominantly the female body. Increasingly more and more control is taken away from an individual's body and concentrated in the hands of 'experts' ... assessment of the 'old' as well as the 'new' reproductive technologies must recognise them as powerful socio-economic and political instruments of control.[56]

Again, clearly suggesting converging interests between medicine and state, one may be drawn to consider Foucault's concept of *biopower*, yet there is also present a contemporary manifestation of the Godwinian ideology of perfectibility, the privileging of the visual extending the notion of perfectibility retroactively. Unlike Romantic ideology, this remaking occurs not postpartum but prenatally and even preconceptually. Both the increasing possibilities for artificial procreation and increasingly complex interventions in the uterus (with foetal health monitoring and *in utero* surgery) may be understood in this context.

This complex motivation, the desire to assure paternity within an epistemology which privileges the visual, may, in part, make explicable the intense investment in assisted reproduction techniques when success rates may justifiably, for some procedures, be termed negligible.[57] As Frances Price writes: 'The vigour of research and the considerable publicity surrounding births following IVF, ET and GIFT belies the low success rate in establishing clinical pregnancies.'[58] The publicity itself forms an important part of the ideology of assisted conception, as Kathryn Pauly Morgan notes:

> The media are filled with pictures of beaming heterosexual couples bearing their tender one (or, often, ones) in their arms. Their bliss is taken as unconditional testimony to and endorsement of the deeply humane, life-orientated motivations of the theorists and empirical scientists who make the exciting breakthroughs and discoveries which enable the reproductive techniques to bring into existence new life on their behalf.[59]

This section has suggested that the new reproductive technologies may, in part, be understood as a (Promethean) response to the void men experience in terms of reproduction. It has also been argued that this void can be seen as a product of the privileged status of the visual within western epistemology. Following on from this, I now consider the degree to which these modern technologies may be seen to fall within the critique of masculine (pro)creative desires that Shelley provides by assessing how far the new reproductive technologies mirror *Frankenstein* – and the texts the novel critiques – in the circumvention of the maternal.

Circumventing the Maternal

It is easy to assert that at the fringes of reproductive research there has been movement towards a very explicit denial of the maternal. We have witnessed talk of male pregnancy.[60] We have also, illustrating the more macabre nature of some research, seen attempts to raise animals outside the maternal environment – the uterus, amniotic fluid and nutrients provided by scientists.[61] Importantly, the animals chosen for this, embryonic/foetal goats, are raised within an entirely transparent plastic uterus. The possibility of a wholly artificial pregnancy, plus the technology that will allow the maturation of ova taken from aborted foetuses,[62] may mean not only the removal of the maternal function from women but also the possible circumvention or removal of the procreative. The primacy of the visual has indeed impoverished the whole.[63]

While this impoverishment is evident at the experimental end of the new reproductive technologies, it is also evident in current normalized practices. As Michelle Stanworth argues, current assisted reproduction techniques 'deconstruct' the woman: 'in place of "mother", there will be ovarian mothers who supply eggs, uterine mothers who give birth to children and, presumably, social mothers who raise them'.[64] Sue Millns, similarly, notes: 'the new reproductive technologies have brought about fundamental change in the process of reproduction by the achievement of conception through deconstructed and dis-integrated female bodies, [a] radical break up of the processes of conception, gestation and rearing of children, and the distribution of these functions amongst different women'.[65] Women are deconstructed, pared down to the useful, 'women are being dismembered – split into separate reproductive parts which can be reassembled, perhaps in a different order, perhaps using parts from different women'.[66] Again, echoes of *Frankenstein*.

In *Frankenstein*, the maternal is removed, impoverished. As Mary Jacobus writes, noting the reworking of Milton's *Paradise Lost*, 'The most striking absence in *Frankenstein*, after all, is Eve's.'[67] That Frankenstein's mother is dead (importantly as a result of maternal sacrifice) is made evident at the beginning of *Frankenstein's* narrative.[68] The Monster itself is without a mother, and the possibility that Frankenstein's bride may conceive is denied by the Monster's vengeance for the denial of a monstrous bride. In terms of the murder of Frankenstein's bride, it is significant that the Monster kills her on her wedding night and in the marital bed before the marriage is consummated. This absence of the maternal is also emphasized in images of incest within the text, the relationships of Walton and Mrs Saville, Frankenstein and Elizabeth.[69] Similarly, this absence is highlighted in the primacy given to male relationships: father and son, Frankenstein and Walton, Frankenstein and Clerval, creator and created.[70] Considering the text and arguing that all scientific quests for the origins of life may be understood as essentially unconscious (homo?)erotic exercises, Jacobus offers some explanation: 'When the primary bond of paternity unites scientist and his creation so exclusively, women who get in the way must fall victim to the struggle.'[71] The status of the maternal in the novel clearly reflects the denigrated and endangered status of the maternal under the Promethean gaze. Frankenstein does not so much appropriate the maternal function as circumvent it, leaving the woman superfluous, if not, as has been argued in the case of possible future developments in reproductive technologies, dead:[72] 'Victor has gone to great lengths to produce a child without [female] assistance, and in dreams language, to circumvent her, to make her unnecessary, is to kill her, and to kill mothers altogether.'[73]

It has been noted that the maternal has been impoverished and circumvented at the research end of reproductive technologies, and in the general deconstruction of the woman within these technologies, but it is also apparent at what is perhaps a more pervasive and immediate level. What is suggested here is that the circumvention of the maternal that Shelley's text warns of is very much in evidence in the low priority given to the health risks that accompany many of the new reproductive technologies.[74]

No modern method of assisted reproduction appears free of risk, just as no pregnancy is free of risk. Yet the new reproductive technologies compound the risks of reproduction, introducing many new hazards to the act of procreation. In terms of risks to offspring, all manipulation of gametes and embryos involves risk of damage and abnormality.[75] Following recommendations within the Warnock Report,[76] the British Medical Research Council has created a central register to determine the comparable incidence of congenital malformation and other differences experienced by children conceived in this way.[77] While the Warnock Committee made such a recommendation, the risks posed to those receiving treatment services warranted no similar provision.

Although methods of assisted reproduction are diverse, and as such carry diverse risks to health, I concentrate here solely on the risks associated with IVF.[78] As the most developed and commonly practised of the technologies, IVF may be used to highlight the risks involved in the more advanced forms of assisted conception. As indicated above, I will concentrate on the health risks, and will go on to outline the emotional costs of treatment, but it should be emphasized that, of course, women's experience of IVF/assisted conception varies dramatically. Many women will be unaffected by the risks involved in these procedures which may, after all, be understood as only statistical possibilities. In emotional and psychological terms, many women may similarly experience assisted conception as a wholly positive or at least benign experience. It is important to understand the possible adverse consequences of any medical treatment or service, but it is not intended either to portray these technologies as wholly negative or oppressive, or to homogenize the women who receive them as victims.

Physical Risks to the Woman and the Foetus

With IVF male and female gametes are brought together to allow fertilization outside the uterus. Two to three days later, the pre-embryo is placed in the uterus via a catheter placed along the cervical canal. Originally, removal of the female gametes involved making an incision in the abdominal wall and removing mature ova using a laparoscope. As the 'harvesting' involved general anaesthetic, the procedure involved the risks typically associated with any general anaesthetic. With the insertion of the laparoscope, there were risks of damage to the ovaries, pelvis and intestines and of excessive internal bleeding. The current procedure involves the insertion of a needle through the vaginal wall, through which the mature ova are extracted. Whilst the risks presented by general anaesthetic have been removed, possible internal damage by the needle remains.[79]

In order to attempt to improve the low success rate of IVF, a number of pre-embryos are cultured *in vitro*. Multiple pre-embryos are then transferred to the woman's uterus. The increased rate of pregnancy with the greater number of pre-embryos introduced has encouraged IVF centres throughout the world to transfer three, four, five or six pre-embryos in clinical practice.[80] For one United Kingdom clinic, the number of transferred pre-embryos was reported to be as high as 12 and rumoured to be even higher.[81] There are a number of resulting harms associated with this aspect of IVF. In order to produce multiple pre-embryos drug therapy is utilized to stimulate the ovaries into releasing a number of eggs. The drugs used to stimulate the ovaries may cause ovarian hyperstimulation and may lead to ovarian cysts, resultant discomfort or severe pain, and the possibility that the cysts may rupture, causing internal bleeding. This may necessitate the removal of all or part of the affected ovary.[82] Hyperstimulation may also lead to temporary or permanent ovarian dysfunction.[83] Ovarian drug therapy may also cause intense headaches, fatigue, nausea, weight gain and lack of concentration.[84] Wagner and St Clair summarize:

> Complications linked with the induction of superovulation by fertility drugs include ovarian hyperstimulation syndrome, cysts, coagulation abnormalities leading to thromboembolism, stroke, myocardial infarction, mola pregnancy, and ovarian cancer. Ectopic pregnancy rates are high, but it is not clear whether this is due to IVF/Embryo Transfer or to pre-existing tubal disease.[85]

Fertility drug therapy may also increase health risks by increasing the incidence of multiple pregnancies. This was perhaps most dramatically seen in 1996, with the case of Mandy Allwood, whose octuplet pregnancy was reported to be the result of her having intercourse against her doctor's instructions while taking fertility drugs.[86] High order pregnancies may also result from the practice of embryo transfer (ET) itself. As noted above, multiple embryos are transferred in an attempt to increase the success rate of implantation. Yet should more than one embryo implant – whether as a result of fertility drugs, embryo transfer or unassisted reproduction – the woman is subject to the almost exponentially increasing perinatal stresses and risks associated with twins, triplets, quadruplets and higher order pregnancies. IVF/ET appears to greatly increase the possibility of a multiple pregnancy. Approximately one-quarter of IVF/ET live birth pregnancies in the United States are multiple.[87] In Australia and New Zealand, the transfer of three or more embryos during treatment involves a threefold increase in the incidence of multiple pregnancies.[88] Compounding general risks and stresses, IVF, as a direct result of this increased incidence of higher order pregnancies, also increases the necessity for Caesarean delivery.[89] In Australia and New Zealand, 62.7 per cent of multiple pregnancies are delivered by Caesarean section.[90]

With twins and other multiple pregnancies, the risks of maternal and foetal morbidity and mortality are greatly increased. In Australia, IVF/ET neonatal mortality is twice the national average, whilst perinatal mortality is four times the rate of the normal population. Multiple births may also lead to prematurity and placental insufficiency. This increases the vulnerability of neonates, particularly when they are pre-term and with low birth weight.[91] The risk of low birth weight appears dramatically increased by IVF/ET. Whilst the incidence of low birth weight in Australia is predicted at 5.8 per cent of all live births, for IVF newborns the rates are 17 per cent of single births and 65.4 per cent of multiple births.[92] Neurological and sensory impairments occur more frequently with low birth weight.[93] Children surviving higher order births also have a greater risk of suffering the disabilities associated with congenital problems such as cerebral palsy.[94] Whilst general maternal and infant mortality rates have declined dramatically, the same rates of reduction are not seen with multiple pregnancies. Beyond questions of mortality and morbidity, the strains on both parents and the health service created by multiple births are many:

> If they do survive the neonatal period their care-takers face extraordinary demands in relation to the provision of food, nurturance and physical care. Little is known ... about how parents cope or the extent to which they can obtain help and support. [In terms of] community provision higher order multiple births [have] become of increasing concern. The unusual demands made on behalf of these children are not only on the health services but also on social services, which are already stretched as a consequence of the implementation of welfare policies transferring care to the community.[95]

Another consequence of introducing multiple pre-embryos and the resultant increased incidence of higher order pregnancies has been the use of selective reduction.[96] Selective reduction is facilitated by the injection of potassium chloride into the amniotic sac or into the heart of the foetus; alternatively, the foetus may be exsanguinated or aspirated.[97] Whilst such terminations had previously been used where only one of two or more carried foetuses suffered from an abnormality,[98] it has become increasingly common to reduce pregnancy size in this manner. The first such reported case was carried out in 1986 in Holland, where a quintuplet pregnancy was reduced to a twin pregnancy.[99] In the same year, a similar selective abortion was reported in the United Kingdom.[100]

As with all invasive procedures, there are physical risks involved, even though these may be considerably less than the risks involved in carrying a multiple pregnancy to term. However, with selective reduction there arise some of the concerns that are evident within consideration of reproductive technologies generally. In terms of the mechanics of selective reduction, the role of the visual is again apparent. The possibility for selected reduction has been created by advances in ultrasound imaging technology which is needed to visualize the foetal heart beat.[101] More generally, there again emerge questions regarding the medical control of reproduction. Frances Price refers to selective reduction as the 'tailoring of multiparity'.[102] The French reproductive clinician, Salat-Baroux, talks of the 'management of multiple pregnancies after IVF'.[103] In this, and as with other practices within reproductive medicine, selective reduction may be understood as a challenge to the meaning of motherhood.[104] The foetuses that the woman carries become a clinical decision, a managed medical exercise. The public response to Mandy Allwood was, to a large extent, shaped by her refusal to follow medical advice and allow her pregnancy to be selectively reduced. This failure to follow medical advice, both in terms of her behaviour while taking the fertility drug and her subsequent desire to carry all eight foetuses to term, marked her for public censure. In the public imagination, her pregnancy was a clinical issue with which she should not interfere.[105]

Emotional and Psychological Risks

While a limited literature highlights some of the physical harms and re-source allocation questions created by technologically advanced assisted reproduction, the many emotional and psychological risks are left largely unconsidered. The emotional costs of assisted reproduction are clearly illus-trated in considering the responses of women to IVF treatment. The degree of emotional trauma reflects the degree of intensity of the programme and its arguably regulatory and disciplinary nature.[106] To illustrate the emotional costs involved, the following draws heavily on the research of Linda Williams, who shadowed and interviewed 20 Canadian women through their infertility treatment. The nature of the emotional costs borne may best be represented chronologically, illustrating the changing experiences associated with each stage of the treatment. Although many of these burdens could, individually, perhaps be dismissed by some as *de minimus*, the overall 'process' appears to have an amplifying effect. In the process of IVF treatment the emotional (and physical) burdens appear immediate:

> ANNE – You get up so early and you have to be downtown at 7:30 and then you're rushing from the lab to the hospital to have your ultrasound done, and you seem to be waiting there forever and all you can think of is getting back to your job, onto the desk 'cause no one's covering you while you're gone for most of the morning. Most times I didn't get back until 11:30. The morning is shot and then you had to leave work at 3:30 or so to get downtown just to wait for the doctor to let you know if you needed Perganol or whether you were kicked off the program (cancelled). Then come home and have supper and kind of hop into bed. You're like a zombie those days. You're tired and you know you have to get up so early again the next morning. And depending on what time of year you're going you're not only fighting the traffic but you could be into winter weather on top of it.[107]

The nature of the experience at this stage is also shaped by the fact that ultrasound requires a full bladder, leading, at times, to great discomfort.[108] The repeated blood tests may also heighten the negative experiences of this stage.[109] Uncertainty appears a major cause of anxiety and stress. This results both from the fluidity of the group of women who may share the experience, and the ever present possibility that any stage of the process may fail and the woman be 'cancelled':

> JANICE – It was a waiting game. There were four of us who would meet and have breakfast together and things like that. When Amy got cancelled that's when I first realised the hurt of being cancelled. All of us lived in the fear all week of being the ones that would be cancelled at any time. And I would ask about my levels of oestrogen and you compare. And you compare sizes of follicles.[110]

While the waiting was obviously traumatic, to actually be cancelled proved emotionally disturbing for many women:

> MARILYN – I was really disappointed. I was really upset. Andrew took me out for dinner, and I don't drink, but I had a drink because I was really upset. And he didn't know what to do for me. So it was very trying at that point. And again, I had felt I had let him down, I'd let myself down. I think it was more of a rude awakening, because I had done so well in July and I went through the whole program, how the hell did I get cancelled? So you go through a lot of what did I do wrong? I didn't do anything. Every period is different and your body reacts differently each time.

> LOIS – I remember getting into the car and crying all the way home. I'm never going back there! They've had enough! [She laughs nervously] And I thought – this is it. I'm not doing this again. But about two days afterwards it was, okay, let's go back in [she laughs].[111]

In some ways the experience of IVF illustrates not only the often ignored emotional costs of assisted reproduction but also the degree to which the intense concentration on the body affects the woman's relationship with her corporal self. As Williams remarks, after the eventual embryo transfer: 'Most of the women who made it to this stage of the procedure reported that they became intensely preoccupied by their bodies and severely limited their movements.'[112]

> MARILYN – The weird part of it is that you could have discharged the embryo hours after coming home or a day after coming home. And it's microscopic and you can't see it, but every woman you ever talk to, no doctor can understand it, will get up from peeing and look in the toilet to see something wave at you, because you are sure you have lost it. So every time you go to the bathroom you don't push and you walk like you are walking on eggs … You don't move. You get up slowly. You don't want to lift anything. You rub your stomach. You just do these things naturally. I think it is also a reaction to still having Perganol and Clomid still in your body, because your body thinks it's pregnant. Your mind's

going, what the hell are you doing? And that's where you're playing basketball with your emotions, you're up and down like a yo-yo. So it is incredibly hard on you, it's incredibly hard on your spouse, because he doesn't know what to make of you because one moment you're laughing, and the next you're crying. Two weeks becomes virtually two years. It's the longest time.[113]

The nature of the procedure appears to fissure the woman from her corporal self. The deconstruction and disintegration to which both Stanworth and Millns refer are physically and psychologically manifest. This is reminiscent of Emily Martin's observation that women often experience their 'self' as something divorced from their corporal self.[114] Arguably, this fissuring results from the insertion of the masculine (Promethean) gaze. The desire to replace the natural with the man-made distances the woman from her experience of maternity while drawing in the male. The extreme physical and mental stress of the entire procedure from drug therapy through to embryo transfer is graphically retold by the last of Williams' respondents:

JOANNE – [The most stressful aspect of IVF was] getting through it. Day by day. A friend had been through it and she said, 'It's going to be really hard on you.' And I, Miss Naïveté then too said, 'Oh no, after all I've been through, I don't think that will be too bad.' Wrongo, that was really stressful. It was so bad, so stressful. And I consider myself pretty good at coping with things usually. But at one point, and it was into the thing too, I think it was even past the laparoscopy, anyways, at one point honest to God I almost packed up and left. I thought, I cannot stand this another second. It was like a time capsule of all your expectations and all your stress just jam packed into five days or six days or whatever it was. And you never got any relief from it. You made it through one day and then you couldn't celebrate because you may not make it through the next day. And so you were just constantly so upset. And those around you were just dropping like flies perhaps. There were girls on the program who would leave in tears who didn't get as far as you were. That was terrible. The day by day pain of trying to get through each hurdle with no relief until the end.[115]

Conclusions

While *Frankenstein* may be understood as a grotesque parody and critique of a masculinist tradition of self-inseminating desire, such a parody endures to aid our understanding of contemporary manifestations of the same desire. Shelley's self-consciously intertextual novel reveals a continuity of intent, an intent to renegotiate or redefine reproduction. Morgan and Lee's 'new lexicon of life' – *in vitro* fertilization, embryo transfer, gamete intra-fallopian transfer (GIFT), zygote intra-fallopian transfer (ZIFT), peritoneal oocyte and sperm transfer (POST), vaginal intra-peritoneal sperm transfer (VISPER) and so on – refigure this (enduring) Promethean legend. The costs of this refiguring are considerable. The disappearance of the woman, her circumvention and negation, in this and other reproductive discourses, negates consideration of the very real physical and psychological risks to which the woman is exposed. This disappearance may, in part, explain why a procedure which many understand as experimental has been normalized and as such unregulated by the normal strictures imposed upon experimental treatments. As Wagner and St Clair write, 'No new treatment should become standard until after rigorous evaluation. Until then, it must remain experimental, guided by the principles covering research on human subjects.'[116] The new reproductive technologies have not been scrutinized in this way. As Wagner and St Clair continue, 'The public health position ... requires that efficacy and risks be known before the procedure becomes standard. We should heed the lessons of the "Dalkon Shield", diethylstilboestrol and thalidomide.'[117]

The Promethean desire to regulate pregnancy, or perhaps to assure paternity, has, as has just been shown, very real implications for women's health. The Human Fertilisation and Embryology Act makes no requirement that the Human Fertilisation and Embryology Authority monitor the physical and psychological effects of the new reproductive technologies upon women. The 1990 legislation in this way affirms the process of removal/disappearance and the effect this has on women's health. As Gillian Douglas writes: 'the long-term health risks for women of fertility drugs and invasive procedures are not yet clearly known. By omitting a specific requirement to consider these, the invisibility of the woman who takes the risks is once again reinforced. Inclusion would have been *symbolically* valuable, at least.'[118]

The heuristic aid that *Frankenstein* has provided within this chapter is only part of what can be taken from Shelley's text. What I also want to look at is the manner in which Shelley's novel reveals other desires. Chapter 7 looks more closely at the figure of the Monster, and the idea of the monstrous more generally. The monstrous is located as an object of fascination and horror. Examining the female subject of the Human Fertilisation and Embryology Act 1990, it will be argued that this figure is similarly an object of fascination and horror. It therefore assists our understanding of the new reproductive technologies and their regulation if we inquire into what place the monstrous has achieved within our discursive order. Importantly, the examination of the association between the female body and the monstrous has repurcussions beyond our understanding of the new reproductive technologies. It informs our understanding of bioscientific/medical involvement in the reproductive and non-reproductive female body generally.

Notes

1   M. Jacobus, E. Fox Keller and S. Shuttleworth (eds), *Body/Politics: Women and the Discourses of Science* (London: Routledge & Kegan Paul, 1990), 4.

2   In referring to modern techniques of assisted reproduction as 'the new reproductive technologies' I do not want to suggest that assisted reproduction is a new phenomenon. Rather, the nomenclature suggests merely recent developments and the level of technological involvement. See C. Carver, 'The New – and Debatable – Reproductive Technologies', in C. Overall (ed.), *The Future of Human Reproduction* (Toronto: The Women's Press, 1989), 46.

3   D. Morgan and R.G. Lee, *The Blackstone's Guide to the Human Fertilisation and Embryology Act 1990* (London: Blackstone Press, 1991), 118.

4   Brian Easlea, for example, has understood *Frankenstein* as an 'indictment of masculine ambition' and 'the compulsive character of masculine science' (B. Easlea, *Fathering the Unthinkable: Masculinity, Scientists and the Nuclear Arms Race* (London: Pluto Press, 1983), 28, 35).

5   M. Shelley, *Frankenstein* (London: Penguin Classics, 1992), Author's Introduction to the Standard Novels Edition (1831), 9. (Unless stated, all other references are to this edition.)

6   M. Hindle, Introduction, in M. Shelley, *Frankenstein* (London: Penguin Classics, 1992), *vii*. This element of the novel is clearly reflected in Richard Brinsley Peake's aptly titled *Presumption: or the Fate of Frankenstein*, the first dramatic adaptation of *Frankenstein* which played at the English National Opera House in 1853. See M. Butler, *Introduction to Frankenstein* (Oxford: Oxford University Press, 1994), *xlix*.

7   R. Diprose, *The Bodies of Women: Ethics, Embodiment and Sexual Difference* (London: Routledge & Kegan Paul, 1994), 21.

8   Shelley broke her anonymity with the 1823 edition of *Frankenstein*.

9   Cited in Hindle, *supra*, at vii–viii.

10   J. Blumberg, *Mary Shelley's Early Novels* (London: Macmillan, 1993), 30.

11   P. Brooks, *Body Work: Objects of Desire in Modern Narrative* (London: Harvard University Press, 1993), 199.

12   Ibid.

13   M.A. Rubenstein, '"My Accursed Origin": The Search for the Mother in *Frankenstein*', *Studies in Romanticism*, **15**, (1976), 165, at 175.

14   Brooks, *supra*, at 200.

15   Rubenstein, *supra*, at 172.

16   Rubenstein suggests that Mrs Saville – the passive listener – may be Mary Shelley. Rubenstein argues that Shelley had been a devout but nearly silent listener at the Villa Diodati. Transferring this to the novel, her 'presence is implied … the passive but enveloping transmuting persona of the author herself creating the novel's outermost narrative circle' (ibid., at 173).

17   Walton is attempting to visit the North Pole, believing there 'the sun is ever visible' (Shelley, *supra*, at 13). This quest is not without its narrative significance. Light to the Romantics and the gnostics of antiquity existed as a motif denoting Divinity. See Hindle, *supra*, at *xxxii–xxxiii*.

18   Given the introduction of techniques of galvanism to gynaecology in the nineteenth century, it is perhaps intentional that this should form the basis for an *unnatural* birth. See R. Ellis, 'The Galvanic Cautery in the Treatment of Uterine Disease', *BMJ* (14 May 1853), 443; R. Ellis, 'On Cauterisation by Electric Heat in the Treatment of Certain Diseases of Women', *BMJ* (4 January 1862), 20; E.C. Mann, 'Displacement

of the Uterus Treated by Electricity', *BMJ* (6 December 1873), 666; W.S. Playfair, 'Electricity in the Treatment of Uterine Disease', *BMJ* (11 June 1887), 1303; M. Tripier, 'Electricity in Cases of Antiflexion and Retroflexion', *BMJ* (27 March 1875), 415.

19 Shelley, *supra*, at 41.

20 Ibid., at 40.

21 Ibid., at 47.

22 The obvious exception to the faithful representation of this element of the text is *Frankenstein: The True Story* (1974) written by Christopher Isherwood and Don Bachardy. The screenplay introduces us to a beautiful Monster and perhaps plays on the homoerotic potential of femaleless reproduction. *Andy Warhol's Frankenstein* (1973) also proves an exception, where the Monster is both beautiful and female.

23 Shelley, Author's Introduction, *supra*, at 9.

24 Brooks, *supra*, at 205.

25 Shelley, *supra*, at 94.

26 Rubenstein, *supra*, 165.

27 Shelley, *supra*, at 91.

28 Brooks, *supra*, at xi.

29 Ibid., at 199.

30 The mother is no parent of that which is called
Her child, but only nurse of the new planted seed
That grows. The parent is he who mounts. A stranger she
Preserves a stranger's seed ...
(Aeschylus, *The Eumenides, Oresteia*, vol. II, trans. R. Lattimore (Chicago: University of Chicago Press, 1953), 558–661.

31 Aristotle, *De Generatione Animalium*, in *The Works of Aristotle*, Vol.V, trans. A. Platt (Oxford: Clarendon Press, 1912).

32 Shelley, Author's Introduction, *supra*, at 8.

33 See E. Darwin, *Zoonomia*, Vol. I, (Dublin: 1794), 565–570.

34 Percy Shelley had been an energetic proponent of perfectibility. As Mary Shelley notes, ironically in her editorial notes to *Prometheus Unbound*: 'The prominent feature of Shelley's theory of the destiny of the human species was, that evil is not inherent in the system of creation, but an accident that might be expelled ... Shelley believed that mankind had only to will that there should be no evil, and there would be none ... That man could be perfectionized as to be able to expel evil from his own nature, and from the greater part of creation, was the cardinal point of his system' (M. Shelley (ed.), *The Works of Percy Bysshe Shelley* (London: Edward Moxon, 1854)). Rather incestuously, Percy Shelley gave his own version of his understanding of perfectibility in an anonymous review of *Frankenstein*: 'Treat a person ill, and he will become wicked. Requite affection with scorn; – let one being be selected, for whatever cause, as the refuse of his kind – divide him, a social being, from society, and you impose upon him the irresistible obligations – malevolence and selfishness' (P.B. Shelley, 'On Frankenstein; or the Modern Prometheus', in R. Ingpen and W.E. Peck (eds), *The Works of Percy Bysshe Shelley*, Vol. VI (London: Ernest Benn Ltd., 1929), at 264. For a discussion of the development of Shelley's critique of Radical/Romantic ideology within the text, see Blumberg, *supra*.

35 Particularly in *Enquiry Concerning Political Justice* (London: 1793). These ideas and principles were dramatized in perhaps his most famous novel, *Caleb Williams*.

36 Godwin, *Political Justice*, *supra*, Vol. II, at 210.

37 In this latter respect, *Frankenstein* appears to take from, or parody, Godwin's drama-

tization of this pursuit in his novel *Caleb Williams*. Victor Frankenstein embraces unquestioningly the Godwinian ideal of the pursuit of knowledge. This similarity was noted contemporaneously by the *Edinburgh Magazine*, which remarked that the novel had clearly been 'formed in the Godwinian manner' (*Edinburgh Magazine*, 2nd Series, **2**, (March 1818), 249–53).

38   P. Cantor, *Creature and Creator: Myth-Making and English Romanticism* (Cambridge: Cambridge University Press, 1984), 109.

39   P. Brooks, '"Godlike Science/Unhallowed Arts": Language, Nature and Monstrosity', in G. Levine and U.C. Knoepflmacher (eds), *The Endurance of Frankenstein: Essay's on Mary Shelley's Novel* (Berkeley: University of California Press, 1979), 205, at 206.

40   Shelley, *supra*, at 94.

41   Blumberg, *supra,* at 45.

42   M. Foucault, *Madness and Civilisation: A History of Insanity in the Age of Reason* (London: Tavistock, 1989), 272.

43   M. Homans, *Bearing the Word* (London: University of Chicago Press, 1986), 113.

44   Homans, *supra*, at 104.

45   R. Braidotti, *Nomadic Subjects: Embodiment and Sexual Difference in Contemporary Feminist Theory* (New York: Columbia University Press, 1994), 88. Nietzsche makes a more general link between science and sorcery or alchemy: 'Do you really believe that the sciences would ever have originated and grown if the way had not been prepared by magicians, alchemists, astrologers, and witches whose promises and pretensions first had to create a thirst, a hunger, a taste for *hidden* or *forbidden* powers? Indeed, infinitely more had to be promised than could ever be fulfilled in the realm of knowledge' (F. Nietzsche, *The Gay Science* , trans W. Kaufman (New York: Vintage Books, 1974), 240.

46   M. O'Brien, *The Politics of Reproduction* (London: Routledge & Kegan Paul, 1981), 43.

47   Ibid., at 54.

48   A. Oakley, 'From Walking Wombs to Test-Tube Babies', in M. Stanworth (ed.), *Reproductive Technologies: Gender, Motherhood and Medicine* (London: Polity, 1987), 39, at 53.

49   This of course relies on the honesty and good practice of the doctor. A case from the United States, where a doctor substituted his own semen for the semen his clients were expecting to receive, gives ready warning of the fragility of this assured paternity.

50   C. Smart, '"There is of course the distinction dictated by nature": Law and the Problem of Paternity', in Stanworth (ed.), *supra*, 98, at 100.

51   Blumberg, *supra*, at 45 (reference omitted). Narcissism is also suggested in the act of creation, and not the object of creation, existing as the focus of desire. As Frankenstein records in his journal: 'I had desired it with an ardour that far exceeded moderation; but now that I had finished, the beauty of the dream vanished and disgust filled my heart' (Shelley, *supra*, at 56).

52   Homans, *supra*, at 105.

53   Braidotti, *supra*, at 80.

54   For an account of IVF treatment which recognizes the intense management/discipline of the body, see L.S. Williams, 'No Relief Until the End: The Physical and Emotional Costs of In Vitro Fertilization', in Overall (ed.), *supra*, 120, at 121–3.

55   C. Vasseleu, 'Life Itself', in R. Diprose and R. Ferrell (eds), *Cartographies:*

Poststructuralism and the Mapping of Bodies and Spaces (Australia: Allen & Unwin, 1991), 55, at 56.

56   R.D. Klein, 'What's "New" about the "New" Reproductive Technologies?', in G. Corea *et al.,* (eds), *Man-Made Women: How New Reproductive Technologies Affect Women* (Bloomington, Indiana: Indiana University Press, 1985), 64, at 65. See also K.P. Morgan, 'Of Woman Born? How Old Fashioned! – New Reproductive Technologies and Women's Oppression', in Overall, *supra,* at 60.

57   Marsden Wagner and Patricia St Clair, for example, conclude that, while there exists no reliable data on the number of live births per stimulation cycle, it may be estimated that the success rate is only 4 to 5 per cent. See M. Wagner and P. St Clair, 'Are *In Vitro* Fertilisation and Embryo Transfer of Benefit to All?', *The Lancet* (28 October 1989), 1025. Similarly, in the United States in 1986, only 4 to 5 per cent of all IVF attempts resulted in a live birth. See C.A. Raymond, 'In Vitro Fertilization Enters Stormy Adolescence As Experts Debate the Odds', *Journal of the American Medical Association,* **259**, (22 January 1988), 464, at 469. Perhaps one of the clearest indicators of the poor efficacy of IVF and embryo transfer (ET) is the incidence of women accepted onto treatment programmes who nonetheless conceive naturally either before treatment has begun or subsequent to discontinuation of treatment. Reviewing studies of women who have begun or concluded treatment programmes and yet have experienced a treatment-independent pregnancy, Wagner and St Clair note that between 7 per cent and 28 per cent of women accepted for IVF/ET conceive unassisted either before treatment or within two years of discontinuation of treatment (Wagner and St Clair, *supra,* at 1028). One clinic in Australia reported 450 treatment-independent pregnancies in women on treatment waiting lists between 1980 and 1985 (D.M. Saunders, M. Matthews and P.A.L. Lancaster, 'The Australian Register: Current Research and Future Role', *Annals of the New York Academy of Science* **541**, (1988), 7–21).

58   F. Price, 'Establishing Guidelines: Regulation and the Clinical Management of Infertility', in R. Lee and D. Morgan (eds), *Birthrights: Law and Ethics at the Beginning of Life* (London: Routledge & Kegan Paul, 1989), 37, at 42. Williams makes a similar observation, noting how 'the harsh reality of the IVF experience is never completely portrayed, and the limited accounts which are available are overshadowed by the happy endings being reported' (Williams, *supra,* at 120).

59   K.P. Morgan, *supra,* at 61.

60   Connie Clement, for example, has noted how the renowned geneticist Jerome Lejeune testified before a court in 1983 that 'human embryos rely on their mother only for shelter and sustenance. He said a fetus is so independent it could be implanted in a man's abdominal cavity and grow to maturity' (C. Clement, 'Science Fiction/Science Fact', *Healthsharing,* **6**, (1985), 18). Lejeune's statement, in its similarity to historic sperm-centred accounts of reproduction, illustrates a connectedness between historical and modern Promethean discourses. The discourse of male pregnancy has become of increasing media interest. Its high point so far may well be the Arnold Schwarzenegger film, *Junior!*

61   'Two Lives', *Horizon* (3 February 1995).

62   However, it should be noted that the use of embryonic tissue in infertility treatment has now been prohibited under section 1(5)(6) of the Criminal Justice and Public Order Act 1994, which inserts a new section 3(*a*) into HFEA.

63   E. Martin, 'Science and Women's Bodies: Forms of Anthropological Knowledge', in Jacobus *et al.* (eds), *supra,* at 69.

64   M. Stanworth, 'Reproductive Technologies and the Deconstruction of Motherhood', in Stanworth (ed.), *supra,* 10, at 16.

65   S. Millns, 'Making "Social judgements that go beyond the purely medical": The Reproductive Revolution and Access to Fertility Treatment Services', in J. Bridgeman and S. Millns (eds), *Law and Body Politics: The Medical Regulation of the Female Body* (Aldershot: Dartmouth, 1995), 79, at 82.

66   Klein, *supra*, at 66.

67   M. Jacobus, *Reading Woman: Essays in Feminist Criticism* (New York: Columbia University Press, 1986), 99.

68   Shelley, *supra*, 42.

69   The strongest image of incest appeared in the 1818 text where Frankenstein and Elizabeth were cousins. At one point Frankenstein informs his father: 'I love my cousin tenderly and sincerely. I never saw any woman who excited, as Elizabeth does, my warmest admiration and affection. My future hopes and prospects are entirely bound up in the expectation of our union' (Shelley, *supra*, at 146). By the 1831 text, Elizabeth had become an abandoned orphan. This element of the text is graphically played out in *Andy Warhol's Frankenstein* (1974) where Frankenstein (Udo Kier) is both brother and husband to the Baroness (Monique van Voonen).

70   In discussing the friendship between Frankenstein and Walton, Brooks talks of 'the longing of two incomplete creatures for fullness in androgynous fusion' (Brooks, 'Godlike Science/Unhallowed Arts', *supra*, at 219). Importantly, it should be noted that Walton, like Frankenstein, yearns for a male companion, not a female. He writes in his second letter to Mrs Saville of a need for 'the company of a man who could sympathize with me, whose eyes would reply to mine' (Shelley, *supra*, at 17).

71   Ibid. This is similarly suggested by Brooks, who talks of the 'Monster put[ting] his body in the way of Frankenstein's desire' (Brooks, 'Godlike Science/Unhallowed Arts', *supra*, at 212). Also Homans suggests, 'The demon appears where Frankenstein's wife should be, and his murder of her suggests not so much revenge as jealousy' (Homans, *supra*, at 104).

72   See R. Rowland, 'Motherhood, Patriarchal Power, Alienation and the Issue of "Choice" in Sex Pre-Selection', in Corea *et al.*, *supra*, at 75.

73   Homans, *supra*, at 103.

74   This may be contextualized within a broader subordination of general health considerations to the medical regulation of the female body. This includes risks associated with the regulation of both the reproductive and non-reproductive body. Within the context of the reproductive body, there has been a disregard for risks to health in connection with, for example, the contraceptive pill, which has recently been associated with thrombosis (see *The Sunday Times*, 7 May 1995); the synthetic oestrogen DES, prescribed to prevent spontaneous abortion (see H. Simand, '1938–1988: Fifty Years of DES – Fifty Years Too Many', in Overall (ed.), *supra*, 95–104; and the Dalkon Shield (see R. Graycar and J. Morgan, *The Hidden Gender of Law* (Annandale: Federation Press, 1990), 314 – 18). Within the context of the more general regulation of the female body, there has been a disregard for health risks associated with many aspects of cosmetic surgery (see N. Wolf, *The Beauty Myth* (London: Vintage, 1990), 214–49).

75   See, J.D. Biggers, 'In vitro fertilisation and embryo transfer in human beings', *New England Journal of Medicine*, **34**, (1981), 336–42. Yet the literature appears to conflict as to the causal incidence of abnormality. See, for example, Carver, *supra*, at 53; Price, *supra*, at 40; Wagner and St Clair, *supra*, at 1028.

76   Paragraph 13.9. See also para. 10.2, which recommends that frozen ova not be used until research has shown that there exists no unacceptable risk.

77   The effects of IVF and other methods of assisted reproduction may be not only

physical but also psychological. See D.N. Mushin, M.C. Barreda-Hansen and J.C. Spensley, 'In vitro fertilization and children: early psychosocial development', *Journal of In Vitro Fertilization and Embryo Transfer* (1986), 247; and F. Wirth, N. Morin, D. Johnson, M. Frank, H. Presberg, V. Vanderwater and J. Mills, 'Follow-up study of children born as a result of IVF', paper given at the Fifth World Congress on In Vitro Fertilization and Embryo Transfer (Norfolk, Virginia: 1987).

78   See Williams, *supra*, generally for risks associated with other methods of assisted conception.

79   Ibid., at 51–2.

80   Price, *supra*, at 42. However, it may be that with a large number of embryos transferred it becomes increasingly unlikely that any of them will complete gestation. Their cumulative presence also endangers the woman's permanent health, perhaps fatally. See B. Dickens, 'Reproductive Technologies and the "New" Family', in E. Sutherland and A. McCall Smith (eds), *Family Rights: Family Law and Medical Advance* (Edinburgh: Edinburgh University Press, 1990), 21, at 32. The Human Fertilisation and Embryology Authority has acted against this practice, limiting the number of embryos or eggs that may be transferred to three. See Human Fertilisation and Embryology Authority, *Codes of Practice*, 2nd revision (December 1995) at para. 7.9.

81   Price, *supra*, at 44. The American Fertility Society has found that, in the United States, up to nine embryos are transferred (Medical Research International, American Fertility Society Special Interest Group, 'In Vitro Fertilization/Embryo Transfer in the United States: 1987 Results from the National IVF/ET Registry', *Fertility and Sterility*, **51**, (1989), 13–18.

82   Raymond, *supra*, at 464–5.

83   Ibid.

84   Williams *supra*, at 127–9.

85   Wagner and St Clair, *supra*, at 1028.

86   See *Abortion Review* (Summer 1996), no. 61, 5–6. Also S. Sheldon, 'Multiple Pregnancy and Re(pro)ductive Choice', *Feminist Legal Studies*, **5**, (1997), 99.

87   Wagner and St Clair, *supra*, at 1028.

88   National Perinatal Statistics Unit and Fertility Society of Australia, *IVF and Gift Pregnancies: Australia and New Zealand, 1987* (Sydney: National Perinatal Statistics Unit, 1988).

89   The question of *necessity*, however, may well be questioned here, as elsewhere in the practice of Caesarean delivery. See M. Thomson, 'After *Re S*', *Medical Law Review*, **2**, (1994), 127, at 135.

90   National Perinatal Statistics Unit, *supra*.

91   Price, *supra*, at 42.

92   Wagner and St Clair, *supra*, at 1028.

93   Ibid.

94   P.W. Howie, 'Selective Reduction – Medical Aspects', in A.A. Templeton and D.J. Cusine (eds), *Reproductive Medicine and the Law* (Edinburgh: Churchill Livingstone, 1990), 25, at 26–7.

95   Price, *supra,* at 43.

96   For a discussion of the legality of selective reduction, see Morgan and Lee, *supra*, at 55–60; Howie, *supra*; Z. Pickup, 'Selective Reduction, Abortion and the Law', in Templeman and Cusine, *supra*; I. Kennedy and A. Grubb, *Medical Law: Text with Materials*, 2nd edn (London: Butterworths, 1994), 920–22; D. Price, 'Selective Reduction and Foeticide: the Parameters of Abortion', *Criminal Law Review* (1988),

199; J. Keown, 'Selective reduction of multiple pregnancy', *New Law Journal*, **137**, (1987), 1165–6; D. Brahams, 'Assisted reproduction and selective reduction of pregnancy', *The Lancet*, **II**, (1987), 1409–10.

97   Morgan and Lee, *supra*, at 56.

98   C.H. Rodeck, R.S. Mibastion, J. Abramowicz and S. Campbell, 'Selective feticide of the affected twin by fetoscopic air embolism', *Prenatal Diagnosis* (1982), 189. This practice was recorded in the United States in 1978: A. Aberg, F. Mitelman, M. Cantz and J. Gehler, 'Cardiac puncture of fetus with Hurler's disease avoiding abortion of unaffected co-twin', *The Lancet*, **II**, (1978), 990.

99   H.H.H. Kanhai, E.J.C. Van Rijssel, R.J. Meerman and J. Bennebroek Gravenhorst, 'Selective terminations in quintuplet pregnancy during first trimester', *The Lancet*, **II**, (1986), 1447.

100   C.H. Rodeck, 'The twin fetus', paper given at a Symposium on Multiple Births at the Institute of Obstetrics and Gynaecology (University of London, 1986). See also J. Salat-Baroux, J. Aknin and J.M. Antoine, 'The management of multiple pregnancies after IVF', paper presented at the Third Meeting of the European Society of Human Reproduction and Embryology (Cambridge, 1987).

101   Morgan and Lee, *supra*, at 57.

102   Price, *supra*, at 44.

103   Salat-Baroux *et al.*, *supra*.

104   B.K. Rothman, 'The Products of Conception: the Social Context of Reproductive Choices', *Journal of Medical Ethics*, **11**, (1985), 188–92.

105   See Sheldon, *supra*.

106   M. Foucault, *Discipline and Punish* (London: Penguin, 1977).

107   Williams, *supra*, at 125.

108   Ibid, at 126.

109   Ibid., at 126–7.

110   Ibid., at 129.

111   Ibid., at 130.

112   Ibid., at 133.

113   Ibid., at 133–4.

114   E. Martin, *The Woman in the Body: A Cultural Analysis of Reproduction* (Milton Keynes: Open University Press, 1987).

115   Williams, *supra*, at 136–7.

116   Wagner and St Clair *supra*, at 1027.

117   Ibid., at 1029.

118   G. Douglas, *Law, Fertility and Reproduction* (London: Sweet & Maxwell, 1991), 117.

7 Legislating for the Monstrous: the Monstrous Feminine and Access to Reproductive Services

I thought I saw Elizabeth, in the bloom of health, walking in the streets of Ingolstadt. Delighted and surprised, I embraced her; but as I imprinted the first kiss on her lips, they became livid with the hue of death; her features appeared to change, and I thought that I held the corpse of my dead mother in my arms; a shroud enveloped her form, and I saw the grave-worms crawling in the folds of the flannel. I started from my sleep with horror; a cold dew covered my forehead, my teeth chattered, and every limb became convulsed; when, by the dim and yellow light of the moon, as it forced its way through the window shutters, I beheld the wretch – the miserable monster whom I had created. (M. Shelley, *Frankenstein* (London: Penguin Classics, 1992), 57)

Introduction

In the preceding chapter, the new reproductive technologies were located within a historical continuity of masculine (pro)creative desires. Within this was detailed the circumvention of the maternal inherent in these androcentric projects. The present chapter builds upon this by providing a quite different and yet related analysis, a consideration of the female subject constructed within the Human Fertilisation and Embryology Act 1990 (HFEA). More specifically, this figure is considered within the conceptual framework of the monstrous feminine. The chapter starts by briefly examining the association within the male imaginary of the female (particularly the maternal) and the monstrous. This association is illustrated through a consideration of both fictional and medical narratives. Reading these narratives it is asserted that the monstrous and the feminine share a cultural space that is character-

171

ized by both horror and fascination. Within contemporary discourse it is seen that this association has become imbricated with more general anxieties regarding technology.

Examining the provisions of HFEA, it is argued that the woman constructed through the provisions governing embryo experimentation and access to reproductive services is indeed an object of horror and fascination. Most notably, it is in the exclusion of certain women from access to these technologies that the association between the monstrous and the feminine/maternal is most clearly evident. Although this chapter considers the monstrous within the regulation of the new reproductive technologies, it is not meant to be suggested that these technologies are purely disabling. Whilst the focus is on the issue of regulation, there is an implicit recognition of the possibilities that these technologies create.

The Monstrous Feminine

Relying on the work of Julia Kristeva, Rosi Braidotti has argued that, within the male imaginary,

> the maternal body [is] the site of the origin of life and consequently also of the insertion into mortality and death. We are all of women born, and the mother's body as the threshold of existence is both sacred and soiled, holy and hellish; it is attractive and repulsive, all-powerful and therefore impossible to live with.[1]

This duality is important in a number of ways, and may also be reached in a number of ways. Braidotti, in considering the conceptual interrelationship of women, the biological sciences and technology, the 'configuration of ideas ... mothers, monsters, machines'.[2] relies, in part, on the construction of the monster as a reflection of the 'monster's' status as *other*. She reflects that 'monsters, deviants or anomalous entities [are] paradigmatic of how differences are dealt with within scientific rationality'.[3] In terms of physiology and the biological sciences, this scientific rationality has seen the male body – from Aristotelian times – provide the norm. The female is, therefore, anomalous, 'a variation on the main theme of mankind'.[4] This body, as a result, becomes imbricated in tales of the monstrous/anomalous, as Braidotti continues:

> the association of femininity with monstrosity points to a system of pejoration that is implicit in the binary logic of oppositions that characterises the phallogocentric discursive order. The monstrous as the negative pole, the pole of pejoration, is structurally analogous to the feminine as that which is other than the established norm, whatever that may be.[5]

Telling Tales

The Novel

The association between the monstrous and the feminine, the configuration of ideas (mothers, monsters, machines) to which Braidotti refers, may best be explored through literature, perhaps most graphically by returning to Mary Shelley's *Frankenstein*. As was noted in the preceding chapter, *Frankenstein* may be read as an intertextual analysis and critique of masculine (Promethean) creation mythology and desire. More pertinently, it may be read as a commentary on the denigrated status of the maternal within such mythology. Within the text, however, there is a greater complexity which builds upon this denigrated status. Frankenstein's nightmare, noted at the beginning of the chapter, which he experiences after his act of creation, clearly suggests a sexual ambiguity in the figure of the Monster. Recognizing a general sexual ambiguity, it has been suggested that the Monster is female or, possibly, at a more abstract level, Woman. Marc Rubenstein, for example, writes: 'There is a hidden spirit of androgyny in [Shelley's] story. The creation of the monster might even be considered a hermaphroditic act. The monster himself seems transiently a woman in the throes of orgasm as Frankenstein applies "instruments of life".'[6] Margaret Homans recognizes a less transient sexual/gender ambiguity:

> That the demon is a revision of Eve, of emanations, and of the object of desire, is confirmed by its female attributes. Its very bodiliness, its identification with matter, associates it with traditional concepts of femaleness. Further, the impossibility of Frankenstein giving it a female demon, an object of its own desire, aligns the demon with women, who are forbidden to have their own desires.[7]

Whilst the Monster is clearly aligned with what Homans refers to as 'femaleness', it is nonetheless referred to as 'he'.[8] Yet Shelley's (subtextual) positing of the monstrous and the female clearly animates Kristeva and Braidotti's assertion of the maternal body as both *holy and hellish*. In reading Milton's *Paradise Lost*, one of the Romantic texts with which the Monster learns to read, the Monster understands his literary origins, berating his creator: 'I ought to be thy Adam, but I am rather the fallen angel.'[9] The conflict in *Frankenstein* of the monstrous and the image of God mirrors not only, as Paul Cantor has argued, the Shelleyan fear of the disjuncture between inspiration and composition,[10] but also, subtextually, the perceived duplicity of the female body. Again, this is clearly seen in Frankenstein's nightmare where Shelley poignantly conflates the female body with the dead and diseased, and ultimately with the monstrous.[11]

Frankenstein lends substance to Braidotti's argument that the monstrous is a figure of devalued difference within the binary logic of our discursive order. '"She" is forever associated to unholy, disorderly, subhuman, and unsightly phenomena.'[12] The female is an object both of desire and of fear, sexual fascination and horror. These associations, of desire and fear, of the monstrous and the necrophilial, have, importantly, been clearly retained and developed within the *Frankenstein* of film.[13]

Medical Stories

Fiction is not the only narrative form where we may locate images of the monstrous feminine. The association to which Braidotti refers is clearly discernible within medical discourse. A graphic example may be found in Frederick Leboyer's influential book, *Birth Without Violence*:

> One day, the baby finds itself a prisoner ... the prison comes to life ... begins, like some octopus, to hug and crush ... stifle ... assault ... the prison has gone berserk ... with its heart bursting, the infant sinks into this hell ... the mother ... she is driving the baby out. At the same time she is holding it in, preventing its passage. It is she who is the enemy. She who stands between the child and life. Only one of them can prevail. It is mortal combat ... not satisfied with crushing, the monster ... twists it in a refinement of cruelty.[14]

While we have seen political shifts in language and obstetrics, such sentiments may still be read, albeit recoded within the language and rationality of the 1990s. One clear example has been the emergence of a neo-Darwinian foetal–maternal model premised on conflict. This model has a number of similarities to the traditionally dominant model of foetal/maternal independence, but it also characterizes present-day representations of the monstrous feminine. As with Leboyer's description, the woman is constructed as the *enemy*. This is made explicit with the discourse of war. Discussing the evolutionary biologist David Haig's work, Lucy Hodges talks of 'the womb [as] a battleground, the site of a Darwinian struggle between mother and offspring'.[15] Importantly, the woman's body is constructed as the aggressor, the foetus waging biological warfare for its very survival. Haig talks of genetic conflict between the foetus and the woman:

> [In certain circumstances] it is advantageous for a woman to miscarry.... . The foetus, however, is trying to survive, so it is doing everything it can to stop rejection by its mother's body. To this end it has developed a method for reducing the chances of miscarriage ... . The foetus is now in control, ensuring that it will survive by interfering with the mother's hormonal communication.[16]

The inference is clear, with the (monstrous) maternal as aggressor, the foetus vulnerable and endangered. Importantly, David Haig's theories are described as unsubstantiated, defended merely as 'a new way of looking at the physiology of pregnancy'.[17]

Focusing on the association between the monstrous and the maternal I want now to consider the provisions of HFEA: more specifically, I want to consider how this association is reflected within the provisions and embodied subjects of the Act. It will be suggestted that the association has influenced the provisions of the Act in terms both of regulating embryo research and of delimiting access to reproductive services. In this latter respect, the role of the monstrous in affirming gender roles is also explored. While the association with the monstrous is considered, it is not intended to suggest that this was the sole motivating element in the determination of the Act or of the figures constructed within it. During the debates it was clear that many concerns were being played out. There were, for example, obvious concerns regarding the nature and speed of scientific advance and also fiscal concern regarding state support for single-parent families. Nor does this analysis seek to suggest a reduction of the law to a reflection of a homogenous male interest. As with other legal provisions, HFEA exists as the product of an exercise in conflict, contradiction and compromise.

HFEA: Prometheus Legislated

> Woman as a sign of difference is monstrous. If we define the monster as a bodily entity that is anomalous and deviant vis-à-vis the norm, then we can argue that the female body shares with the monster the privilege of bringing out a unique blend of *fascination and horror*.[18]

Braidotti asserts as a privilege the ability the female body and the monstrous share to evoke fascination and horror. While the concept of privilege may well be questioned, the presence of these features is perhaps without dispute. This is very clearly seen within the discourses and practices of the new reproductive technologies. E. Ann Kaplan importantly and illustratively connects the emergence of the new technologies of assisted conception with new representations of the monstrous: 'Science's new interest in the foetus coincides with renewed images of distaste for women's bodies and biological processes. Patriarchy's age-long distaste has been well-documented, but the renewed representations in such films as *Aliens*, for example, are significant as they dovetail with medical reproductive technologies.'[19] This reference to James Cameron's 1986 film, *Aliens*, is worth expanding upon as a preface to the subsequent analysis. The film with great clarity characterizes the association Braidotti details, particularly the shared features of horror and fascination.

Cameron's film is replete with images of the horrific maternal. The alien-mother of the film is an 'endlessly proliferating, ghastly body, consisting of sticky, sucking tubes which smother all in its path, emblem[izing] a whole host of male fears'.[20] H.R. Giger's design and artwork for the film relies on monstrous and brutal parodies of female genitalia. The alien itself is de-signed as *vagina dentata*, a vagina with teeth. The film very explicitly plays with the idea of castration.[21] This extends beyond the physical nature of the monster to what appears to be female asexual reproduction – the fear of the impotent, superfluous male. In the alien's design, its prolific asexual pro-creation, and in its insemination and murder of the male crew members the alien embodies many present-day horrors surrounding female sexuality. Yet there is also fascination.

The alien is described as *perfection*, the *perfect organism*. The alien, or rather the alien's progeny, are subject to medical scrutiny, dissection, the *medical gaze*. The ship's medical and scientific officer values the alien-mother's ability to destroy, her military potential. Corporate interests under-stand commercial potential, the fortune to be made from understanding and controlling this alien-mother. Horror, fascination and commerce rather poign-antly converge. In this, Kaplan's assertion that the new representations dovetail with the new reproductive technologies is clearly correct.

The discourses and practices of the Human Fertilisation and Embry-ology Act may be located within this textual field. This analysis, however, may be extended and placed more explicitly in line with earlier chapters. In providing reproductive medicine and science with a comparatively per-missive regulatory framework, a framework which more or less accepted existing medical standards and practice, the Act may be understood as codifying and legitimizing the productive and constitutive nature of scien-tific discourse: 'Scientific practice *is* writing. It makes things up. Its figurative strategies are constitutive of the objects whose essence they describe and its knowledges are textual and intertextual.'[22] Consequently, the medico-legal discourses of the new reproductive technologies become located within the continuity of discourses that have been mapped so far. That is to say, they may be read as powerful and privileged technologies which are productive of the gendered body. The gendered body con-structed at this axis is a figure of fascination and horror, she is the mon-strous feminine. While it is argued that this figure is constructed within the medico-legal discourses of the new reproductive technologies, it is evident that she inhabits other reproductive discourses. This is perhaps clearest in the continued pathologizing of the female body seen through-out the earlier chapters.

The following analysis, as has been noted, argues that the association between the monstrous and the maternal is evident within HFEA. More specifically, it is evident in the figure of fascination and horror that is constructed within the legal provisions. HFEA legitimizes the Promethean fascination and desire to know, as detailed in the preceding chapter, as well as recognizing the feared potential for reproductive technologies to operate outside current heterosexual, family-centred and masculinist notions of procreation. That is to say, the Act largely safeguards the medical *gaze* and its desire to control while securing against the fear of the 'proliferating, ghastly' feminine body with its new ability to marginalize, lay impotent or castrate the masculine in reproduction.[23] Braidotti's and Kaplan's observations prove insightful.

Fascination

As has just been noted, the Human Fertilisation and Embryology Act may be seen as comparatively permissive legislation. This is perhaps most evident in the regulation of research. It is arguable that in this context HFEA gives licence to exploration motivated by fascination. In terms of embryo research, the Act allows research up to the appearance of the *primitive streak*,[24] subject to supervision and licensing by the Human Fertilisation and Embryology Authority (HUFEA).[25] The licensing system is clearly structured with authorization for specific research granted for a maximum duration of three years.[26] To award a licence, the Authority must be assured that the research falls broadly within the expressed research aims outlined within the Act.[27]

While providing these general guidelines, the Act also provides a limited number of prohibitions within research practice. Not only does s.3(3) preclude research after the development of the primitive streak, but it also prohibits the placing of a human embryo in any animal, keeping or using an embryo in contravention of regulations, or the performing of nucleus substitution (otherwise known as cloning).[28] Beyond these limited prohibitions, the system of licensing merely provides that a licence will only be granted for research under the supervision of a named individual and upon specified premises.[29] A licence granted by HUFEA will only be valid for one research project, each project requiring a separate licence.[30] Although both research and treatment licences may authorize storage of embryos, treatment and research will require separate licence applications.[31] Any licence may impose conditions of practice.[32]

Whilst these provisions may appear restrictive, the research aims appear broad enough to legitimate most research not explicitly prohibited by the

Act. Perhaps more importantly, the scope of research permitted by the Act fares favourably, in clinical terms, in comparison with provisions in other jurisdictions. The Australian states of South Australia and Victoria, and the legislatures of Eire, Denmark, Germany, Norway and Portugal have all prohibited research using human embryos.[33] In this context, the 1990 legislation may appear comparatively liberal. It may, arguably, be read as legislating for *fascination*, giving licence to the desire to manage reproduction and challenge the vagaries of gynocentric reproduction. This is perhaps most clear from the provision of paragraph 3 of schedule 2, which legitimates research which is 'generally for the purpose of increasing knowledge about the creation and development of embryos and enabling such knowledge to be applied'. It is not stated to what ends such knowledge is to be applied.

As noted above, the Act embodies both *fascination* and *horror*. Horror emerges most clearly in the regulation of treatment services. It is at this point that the Act may be most clearly located within the framework of the monstrous feminine. It is also at this point that Kaplan's reference to new representations, as well as a knowledge of more enduring images, become valuable.

Horror

The licensing of treatment services is subject to the general provisions which are incorporated into every treatment, research or storage licence.[34] Schedule 2, paragraph 1 defines more specifically the parameters of a treatment licence.[35] Again, these provisions appear to fare well in an international context. Before considering the statutory limitations on the provision of treatment services, it is worth briefly outlining the German legislation, which provides a good comparison for the regulation of both embryo research and treatment services. Contrary to the provisions of HFEA, the Act, passed by the Bundestag on 24 October 1990, provides that eggs harvested for IVF may only be used for the purposes of the impregnation of the donor woman. Any embryo created may only be done so with the intention that it be returned to the donor's uterus. Any embryo treated outside the uterus may only be done so for therapeutic reasons. As in HFEA, both genetic manipulation and cross-species fertilization – the development of chimeras – are prohibited.[36] The fascination/horror duality of the 1990 HFEA legislation is highlighted by comparing it with the more consistent restrictive approach of the German legislation. Whilst both embryo research and treatment services appear to be more permissively legislated for under HFEA, the restriction of access to treatment services is, to a degree, a shared feature. Although the German legislation achieves this by clearly limiting access to IVF and other services, HFEA creates limits in a less direct manner, which will be considered in detail below.

While licensing fascination and appearing comparatively permissive in an international context, the Act nonetheless restricts the possibilities for access to infertility services for women not within 'standard' relationships. The Act, if not the practice,[37] restricts the possibilities of assisted reproduction, maintaining a heterosexual model, or at least a visible, physical male presence. Indeed, Millns observes: 'It [can] be argued that the ideology which underpins access to reproductive technologies is one which seeks the reconstruction of the heterosexual family despite the widely-acknowledged breakdown of this institution, and despite the deconstruction of the female body in the new process of reproduction.'[38] In this privileging of the heterosexual family, the Act denies many (though not all) of the possibilities that the technologies create. These possibilities include greater access to reproduction and child rearing for lesbian couples, single women and non-standard non-*nuclear* forms of 'family'. The technologies which the Act regulates also create the possibility of a more general reconsideration of reproduction and reproductive relations. As Barbara Katz Rothman writes,

> I think that the new technologies of reproduction offer us an opportunity to work on our definitions of parenthood, of motherhood, fatherhood and childhood, to rethink and improve our relations with each other in families. Freed from some of the biological constraints, we could evolve better, more egalitarian ways of relating to ourselves and each other in reproduction. The technology is a promise, beckoning us with new possibilities ... giving us new control.[39]

Although recognizing that such possibilities exist within the technologies (and therefore within the technologies that lie outside the regulation, or where the regulations are liberally interpreted), the Act nonetheless manifests a fear (horror) of such a rethinking. The Act manifests anxieties that are discernible in contemporary representations, in films like *Aliens*. It is also possible to return to *Frankenstein* and Frankenstein's refusal to create a female monster. Frankenstein understands the monstrous female as possibly more threatening than the (ambiguously) male Monster that already haunts him: 'I looked towards its completion with a tremulous and eager hope which I dared not trust myself to question, but which was intermixed with obscure forebodings of evil, that made my heart sicken in my bosom ... she might become ten thousand times more malignant than her mate.'[40] Not only does he fear that she may be 'ten thousand times more malignant' – building on Braidotti's assertion of the nexus between the monstrous and the feminine – but also that she may populate the world with her monstrous progeny, 'a race of devils would be propagated upon the earth'.[41] The ambiguous nature of the Monster's sex and the desire for a female mate manifests an anxiety regarding the sanctity of heterosexual reproduction. As the monstrous may be understood as a response to difference, the monstrous progeny may here be understood as the product of new (different) reproductive relations. These anxieties, and the assertion of a heterosexual ideology, are clear within the discourses and practices of assisted reproduction, as Morgan and Lee note: 'Assisted conception is to be, for the most part, for the married, mortgaged middle-classes; a conclusion which is entirely consonant with infertility services being unavailable on any scale through the National Health Service.'[42] This very narrow ideology is most visible in section 13(5).

Section 13(5)

In their introduction to a consideration of treatment services and licences, Morgan and Lee unambiguously write: 'The Government's clear intent in its introduction to the legislation was to place a restraint on the provision of certain modes of assisted conception to certain groups or types of women or couples.'[43] This intent was expressed, to a degree, within the *Report of the Committee of Inquiry into Fertilisation and Embryology* (the Warnock Report) which formed the basis for the legislation:

> Many believe that the interests of the child dictate that it should be born into a home where there is a loving, stable, heterosexual relationship and that, therefore, the deliberate creation of a child for a woman who is not a partner in such a relationship is morally wrong ... . We believe that as a general rule it is better for children to be born into a two-parent family, with both father and mother, although we recognise that it is impossible to predict with any certainty how lasting such a relationship will be.[44]

This intention to define appropriate or acceptable recipients for assisted conception is achieved primarily, though not exclusively, through s.13. This section provides a series of conditions which form prerequisites for the granting of every treatment licence under paragraph 1 of schedule 2. Failure to adhere to these conditions may result in the revocation of a treatment licence.[45] Subsection 5 provides the following condition:

> A woman shall not be provided with treatment services unless account has been taken of the welfare of any child who may be born as a result of treatment (including the need of that child for a father), and of any other child who may be affected by the birth.[46]

This section, which provides the clearest statement of appropriate recipient status, proves interesting in a number of ways. At its most immediate it is clear that the provision privileges a particular model of female sexuality – the stable, secure heterosexual. Yet perhaps more interesting is the explicit moral role that has been sanctioned for clinicians. The doctor (normally figured as male) is again clearly constructed as a normalizing moral agent, he is 'Father and Judge, Family and Law.'[47] In many ways the role of the doctor here is very similar to the role constructed within the Abortion Act 1967 and considered above. Yet here the question of moral judgment and the role of the doctor as *parallel judge* is more explicit. This construction of the doctor is emphasized in the Lord Chancellor's assertion that this is a responsibility which clinicians must already be fulfilling: 'The amendment will place on clinicians in statutory form a responsibility which I believe most, if not all, of them already perform. I accept that that is an important responsibility and it may in particular cases be far from easy to discharge.'[48] Under HFEA, therefore, the doctor appears to act as a mediator between society and those seeking treatment services. As Gillian Douglas writes, 'section 13(5) [and therefore the licensed clinician] limits treatment to those people we, as a society, think are worthy of parenthood'.[49]

Yet, arguably, the doctor's role goes beyond limiting treatment to the *worthy*. The doctor's role constructed under s.13(5) acts to define gender. This may also be considered in terms of the monstrous, particularly if we understand the monstrous as a response to difference. Peter Brooks, responding to Shelley's text, draws gender and the monstrous together, providing the following catechism: 'What then is a monster? The monster would thus be woman … . "What is a monster?" A monster may also be that which eludes gender definition … a monster is that which calls into question all our cultural codes.'[50] As gender is a cultural code, 'to call it into question' is monstrous. Section 13(5) is premised on dominant modern gender definitions. The doctor defines which women exist within these definitions, therefore also defining those – the monstrous – who fall outwith. Those who fall outwith remain in need of normalizing medical intervention. Offending against 'Father and Judge, Family and Law' thus provides an inner (monstrous) narrative. This role further complicates the interrelationship of woman, the biological sciences, the monstrous and technology. Bioscience's ability to define the monstrous shifts beyond responses to physiology, defining, or at least affirming, social relations. As earlier chapters have detailed, this constitutive and productive role is in no way a unique product of HFEA.

Importantly, this mediating, normalizing presence is seen as more efficient in regulating reproductive behaviour than a more explicit prohibition. As with the Abortion Act, the persuasive moral role of the doctor is once more relied upon. Again, the possible distance between the intended effect of the Act and clinical practice must be recognized. Considering an amendment that would have excluded single and unmarried women from access to treatment services, the Lord Chancellor expressed his concern that such women would merely go elsewhere:

> On the other hand, if the law recognises that in a very small number of cases single women will come forward for treatment, it may be better to encourage them to seek advice. With the child and welfare amendments we have just discussed there is a likelihood that through counselling and discussion with those responsible for licensed treatment they may be discouraged from having children once they have fully considered the implications of the environment into which their children would be born or its future welfare.[51]

The provision of s.13(5) may therefore be seen as directly regulatory. The legislation aims to achieve the same heterosexual and discriminatory ends provided for in other jurisdictions, such as Germany, and yet seeks what is believed to be a more efficient method. This pragmatism is explicitly reiterated by the Lord Chancellor later within consideration of the same amendment:

> We wish to achieve a result. One has to seek to achieve it against the backdrop of the actual and real world and what people may do in that world. On the whole there is much to be said for seeking not to make a completely watertight rule that may bar all consideration of particular situations, but to allow people, whatever their situations, to come forward to have their situation and the consequences of what they wish to do considered. I believe that in the end that may better achieve the purpose of my noble friends Lord Ashbourne and Lord Lauderdale [the exclusion of the unmarried from treatment services], an aim shared, I am sure, by other noble Lords.[52]

As has been noted, there is an unmistakable parallel between the normalizing role constructed for the clinician within the Act and that constructed within the abortion legislation. In both instances the doctor performs a clearly ideological role. Asserting appropriate gender behaviour, he may offer 'guidance'.[53] In terms of the Abortion Act, the guidance appears primarily aimed towards maternity. Under HFEA, he offers guidance away from maternity for those perceived as unsuitable. As already noted, the unsuitable are the lesbian, single or unmarried.

Managing the Unsuitable (or Talking Welfare)

While the role constructed for the doctor is important, there is a need to locate it within an understanding of the concept of welfare utilized within the Act. During, and indeed before, the passage of the Bill, considerable concern and hostility was expressed towards the idea of single or unmarried women or lesbian couples gaining access to treatment services. Concern was perhaps strongest regarding the absence of a male partner.[54] Again there are echoes of *Aliens* and the endlessly proliferating, asexual monster. Indeed, the idea that treatment services should be restricted to married women received much support. The amendment introduced in the House of Lords by Lady Saltoun, which would have made it a criminal offence to provide treatment services to unmarried women, was defeated by only a single vote.[55] The fear that gender relations may be realigned by unrestricted access to the technologies of assisted reproduction resulted in emotional pleas. For many, such concern became vocalized as concern for the preservation of the family, the possibilities of artificial insemination becoming part of a much broader moral panic surrounding the breakdown of the family and of family values.[56] As in the abortion debates of 1966–7 and of the previous century, *the family* was given an almost mythical importance.[57] As in these periods, the family was constructed as central to the nation's well-being and as such its preservation was essential:

> It is certainly necessary for us to reflect very carefully before we do anything either in relation to legislation or in statements about government policy which detracts from the stability of the family, for the health of the family is largely at the heart of the continuing health of our society.[58]

While the *status* of the woman may be understood as the primary concern, this appears to have been translated, not only into a concern for the family (that *'natural unit'*[59]), but also within statute into the broad welfare provision seen in s.13(5).[60] As Douglas writes: 'It may be noted that *welfare* of the child replaced the *status* of the woman as the appropriate criterion. This is much vaguer and less objectionable than overtly discriminating against women on the basis of marital status or sexual orientation.'[61] The concept of *welfare* may therefore be understood as signifying a great deal beyond an objective assessment of the well-being of any child born as a result of treatment services. The concept of welfare expressed here appears to assert a subjective assessment of what forms of sexual and social relations and parenting are acceptable.[62] It is also worth noting that, in translating 'status' to 'welfare', there remains a suggestion of dangerousness in the woman as status remains implicit in the discussion of welfare. The fluidity of the use of the concept 'welfare' is illustrated by Lord MacKay. Introducing the welfare amendment, the Lord Chancellor observed:

> I think everyone would agree that it is important that children are born into a stable and loving environment and that the family is a concept whose health is fundamental to the health of society in general. A fundamental principle to our law about children ... is that the welfare of children is of paramount consideration. I think it is, for these general reasons, entirely right that the Bill should be amended to add that concept. It could be argued that the concept of the welfare of the child is very broad and indeed all-embracing. That I think is inevitable given the very wide range of factors which need to be taken into account when considering the future lives of children who may be born as a result of technologies to be licensed under the Bill.[63]

The requirement of s.13(5) may, therefore, be understood as very broad, 'indeed all-embracing'. The section allows the government's pro-family agenda to be implemented in an apparently non-discriminatory manner. This need to avoid direct discrimination is affirmed by the Codes of Practice, which provide that 'in deciding whether or not to offer treatment services ... [centres] should avoid adopting any policy or criteria which may *appear* arbitrary or discriminatory'.[64] It is the issue of *appearance* and not discrimination that is given primacy. This was also evident in the case of *R v. Ethical Committee of St Mary's Hospital (Manchester), Ex parte Harriott*, decided before the passage of HFEA.[65] The case reviewed a decision by the ethics committee and medical team to remove Mrs Harriott from the IVF waiting list on the basis of her convictions for soliciting and running a brothel. Although finding the committee's advice unobjectionable (the committee had advised the medical team to make up their own mind), the judge did not rule out future judicial review of committee decisions. Yet, indicative of the nature of what the court may 'object' to, Schiemann J observed: 'If the committee had advised, for instance, that the IVF unit should in principle refuse all such treatment to anyone who was a Jew or coloured, then I think the courts might well grant a declaration that such a policy was illegal.'[66] Schiemann J's opinion, and the provisions of the Codes of Practice, suggest an acceptability of all but the most blatant forms of discrimination in the provision of treatment services. Welfare, in its 'all-embracing' form, may be understood as a form of indirect discrimination which is permissible and utilized to ensure the provision of treatment services to the *acceptable*.

Read in this way, s.13(5) may be understood as reflecting more a fear of the monstrous feminine, a fear of male exclusion and the redefining of reproductive relations, than a concern for the psychosocial development and welfare of any child born as a result of treatment services. Such fears are recoded as family- and child-centred welfare policies. These welfare arguments may be understood as a new form of essentialism tying women to traditional concepts of gender. As Carol Smart notes, there should be concern

> not so much for the vision of a brave new world peopled only by men and 'mother-machines', but for the way in which these developments will bind women more securely to the confines of the patriarchal, nuclear family – not through marriage as in the past, but for the sake of the children.[67]

Statements of concern for child welfare may therefore obfuscate other concerns. Beyond this, reliance on a claim that for normal psychosocial development a child needs two parents, one of each sex, is problematic. Interestingly, in asserting the welfare needs of a child – that is for two parents of different sexes – little empirical evidence was provided in support of this contention. Typically, as the Earl of Lauderdale illustrates, the proposition was supported by 'common sense':

> To allow and encourage by state provision – it is at the tax payers' expense ultimately – begetting of children into what are designed to be one-parent families does not make sense as regard serious sociological responsibility. Whether one is a Christian, a Muslim, a Jew or whatever, it does not make sense. The spirit behind the amendment [s.13(5)] is sound. It is not a specifically Christian matter. It is not a specifically Islamic matter. It is merely common sense from the point of view of society.[68]

While research in this area is limited, what little does exist appears to offer a serious challenge to such perceived 'common sense'. Assessing the research, Morgan and Lee recognize that, while a correlation may exist between single-parent families and emotional and behavioural problems, such a correlation, if it is shown to exist, may well be caused by the poverty and isolation such families often experience.[69] Consequently, the welfare of the child in these circumstances appears to be determined by a failure of state welfare provisions, rather than the parenting skills of the single parent.[70] The hostility reserved for the question of lesbian parents also appears to have little foundation. Rather, it appears to exist within a social policy continuity which creates a presumption in favour of heterosexual parenting.

Beyond s.13(5)

Conscientious objection   Section 13(5), however, is not the only means whereby a heterosexual family-centred model is fostered. Inseparable from this, it is also not the only site at which there is discernible a fear of the 'endlessly proliferating, ghastly body'.[71] Section 13(5), and its ideology, is supported by a number of other provisions within the Act. As with the Abortion Act, HFEA contains a conscience clause. Section 38 provides that no person who conscientiously objects to participating in any activity governed by the Act shall be under a duty to do so. Repeating the provisions of s.4 of the Abortion Act, the burden of proof of objection rests with the person claiming it. Unlike the abortion provisions, however, no reference is made to life-saving treatment.[72]

As with the abortion legislation, the provision of such a clause reflects the perceived nature both of the clinician and of the patient. The clause leaves treatment services and therefore those seeking such services as morally ambiguous. At the same time, the clinician's status as moral intermediary is affirmed. Given this designation of treatment services as morally ambiguous and the demarcation of the *morally correct* recipients of such services (through section 13(5)), s.38 may act to assert adherence to the pro-family ethos of the Act. Interestingly, the effect of ss.13(5) and 38 read together may act to locate such an ethos within the morality of the providers rather than the regulators. Yet, most tangibly, the conscience clause adds to the framework which attempts to ensure that the provision of treatment services is reserved for those who may be euphemistically defined as *fit* to parent. As Morgan and Lee note, s.13(5)

> effectively introduces a 'social' conscience clause, whereby consideration of the 'fitness to parent' of prospective applicants (and the effect of the section will be to ensure that they are all usually couples) will be to apply a prospective licensing system for parenthood similar to that used in adoption. If this is coupled with the 'conscience clause' as formally stated, s.38, and the exhortation to be issued in the Code of Practice (s.25(2)) ... an effective screening mechanism ... has been introduced.[73]

Beyond ss.13(5) and 38, the married or cohabiting heterosexual model of (assisted) reproduction is also asserted through securing the *legal* male presence. This male presence is perceived of as normalizing, bringing women within the realm of gender-appropriate behaviour, away from the monstrous challenge to cultural codes.

A male presence   Section 28(3) provides that, where a woman and her partner undergo a treatment service using donated sperm, the partner will be treated as the father of any resulting child. It has been noted that this provision is intended both to ensure that the child will not be left parentless should the woman die, and also, as Morgan and Lee write, to remove 'the spectre of large numbers of legally "fatherless children" from the legislation'.[74] The obvious effect of this may be to discourage men from agreeing to act as 'partners' for women without *recognized* partners for the purposes of s.13(5). Similarly, women may be discouraged from seeking such acting partners if the possibility exists that the man may later want to assert his legal fatherhood. This section will also mean that, with a lesbian couple, should the biological mother die the donor may have greater rights to custody than the surviving social parent. This would arguably fit within the general judicial presumption in favour of heterosexual parenting seen in cases such as *C* v. *C*.[75] While lesbian parents have managed to secure custody in cases such as *Re F*,[76] this appears only to be the case where there exists no other alternative apart from placing the child in care. The presumption in favour of heterosexual parenting exists notwithstanding a generally less overtly hostile response to legal applications from lesbian parents in recent years.[77] Building on the privileging of the heterosexual, and as with other provisions within HFEA, this section was also justified in terms of *the family*. According to Lord MacKay, s.28(3) may help to 'cement and strengthen the relationship with the informal family and reduce the risks of breakdown with its consequences for the child and, indeed, the taxpayer'.[78]

The desire for a male presence within assisted reproduction is also manifest in the response to the prospect of the use of sperm after the donor has died – so-called 'posthumous pregnancies'. The title is misleading but informative, suggesting a pregnant cadaver, a monstrous act of procreation. Again we can turn to *Frankenstein* and the Monster's desire for a monstrous mate: 'she might become ten thousand times more malignant than her mate … a race of devils would be propagated upon the earth'.[79] Considering the question of posthumous pregnancies, the Warnock Report advised: 'The use by a widow of her dead husband's semen for AIH is a practice which we feel should be actively discouraged.'[80] With embryos, the Committee recommended that the surviving partner should retain the right of use or disposal. Yet the Committee noted its hesitation: 'We make this recommendation notwithstanding our reservations about the possibility of posthumous pregnancies.'[81]

Responding to these reservations, and as the popularly supported case of Diane Blood informed the general public,[82] HFEA provides that sperm from a dead partner may only be used if there exists express consent to that end. Even with this requirement of written consent, the availability of posthumous pregnancies extends the desire for a male presence to almost macabre lengths in the priorities it reveals. As Millns noted before the Blood case, 'It appears that the spectre of a dead father figure is more readily acceptable than no father figure at all, or than a living parent who is in a same-sex relationship with the woman seeking treatment services.'[83] Millns' observation is very clearly placed in its wider context in the parliamentary consideration of single-parent families during the debate around s.13(5). Whilst the single-parent family was variously cast as the source of society's moral decay, a production line for juvenile delinquents and the cause of much child physical and sexual abuse,[84] Lord MacKay warned against such an absolute condemnation of the single parent: 'My Lords, I intervene only to contradict the assumption that one-parent families always result in disaster. One should consider the number of widows who have brought up the most successful families. It is hard but it is not impossible.'[85] Lord MacKay's statement extends the applicability of Millns' assertion that 'the spectre of a dead father figure is more readily acceptable than no father figure at all'. It is clear that the spectral presence of the male may provide a general validation as well as the more specific validation of suitability for treatment services where other women who are either single or in same-sex relationships are clearly constructed as unsuitable. The desire for a male presence appears so extreme as to privilege those who may provide a clinician with a macabre, disembodied and spectral presence over those who may seek treatment services with an embodied, corporal and supportive partner who happens to be the same sex.

Legislating for a male presence is also seen in s.4(1)(*b*), which provides: 'No person shall, in the course of providing treatment services for any woman, use the sperm of any man unless the services are being provided for the woman and the man together or use the eggs of any other woman except in pursuance of a licence.' The effect of this provision is to differentiate between artificial insemination by husband/partner (AIH/P) and artificial insemination by donor (AID) for the purposes of treatment licences. Under this provision, a licence is not needed for AIH/P. This creates a degree of legislative selectivity, as has been noted: 'it is apparent that this Act is not meant to be a comprehensive code covering all the legal and ethical issues to which the "reproductive revolution" has or may give rise'.[86] Although Morgan and Lee offer no explanation, it is worth returning to a previous statement by these commentators which recognized that the government's firm intention in introducing legislation was 'to place a restraint on the provision of certain modes of assisted conception to certain groups or types of women or couples'.[87] The decision to exclude AIH/P while bringing AID within regulatory control again asserts an idea of *fitness* to parent. The normalizing moral presence of the doctor is evoked with artificial insemination only where the sperm is donated. This therefore brings single women and lesbian couples who are seeking treatment services within the ambit of the legislation and, more specifically, within the ambit of s.13(5) and its ancillary provisions. This decision is amplified in its effect by the exclusion of AIH/P. This further defines appropriate models of reproduction. It maintains the pro-family intent and form of the legislation. There appears to be a tacit agreement with the sentiment expressed by the Earl of Lauderdale, where AIH/P was characterized as following the ethics of the household, while AID embodied the ethics of the farmyard.[88]

HFEA therefore provides a complex statutory system which regulates access to treatment services. Although access is limited, at its most visible, under a child welfare banner, the intention of the provisions appears clear. The provisions carefully construct and define the appropriate and inappropriate, the deserving and undeserving, those who fit within our gender codes and the monstrous who exist beyond these codes. The statutory system appears to give evidence to Smart's assertion:

> It would seem that the law is agnostic on the issue of whether women do all the caring for children, but it takes a strong view if women try to detach children from men and, by implication, from the nuclear family... [T]hese ... trends ... lend support to a particular family structure, namely one in which there is a heterosexual couple living together in a stable relationship, whether married or not.[89]

Within its support for the family to which Smart refers, the legislation and its enacting discourses are similar in their effect to those of the Abortion Act. Yet, as noted above, the new reproductive technologies have become enmeshed in new representations, new 'stories'. The regulation and discourses of these new possibilities have become imbricated in the monstrous narrative. It is worth reconsidering the following assertion by Smart:

> Where women resort to law their status is already imbued with specific meaning arising out of their gender. They go to law as mothers, wives, sexual objects, pregnant women, deserted mothers, single mothers and so on. They are not simply women (in distinction to men) and they are most definitely not ungendered persons.[90]

While Smart's statement remains valid, the 'Woman before the law' has the possibility of being perceived within a new gendered model. She may now be the Monstrous Mother empowered by technological possibilities. There is an element of historical continuity in this model, but our new technological and bioscientific fluency has filled this image with a new potency.

Conclusions

Frankenstein may be understood as a critique of the productive nature of scientific discourse. The Monster is, after all, 'scientific idea become ... bodily fact: an idea embodied'.[91] In conjunction with this, the novel illustrates the location of the monstrous within our discursive order. The monstrous may be understood both as a response to difference and as an essential defining negative (a pole of pejoration) in the creation of the useful and docile. As such, both woman *per se* and the woman who fails to fit within our cultural codes may be understood as monstrous – objects of fascination and horror. The preceding discussion illustrates how the defining of the monstrous and the assertion of appropriate gender behaviour is advanced within medico-legal discourses and practices. Bringing this and the preceding chapter together, it is clear that the development of medical technologies and their regulation both by medicine and by law is simultaneously an effect and cause of the association of ideas, the monstrous and the maternal.

The provision of treatment services, especially within the National Health Service, and their legislative support perpetuates the belief that infertility and childlessness are properly within the ambit of medical practice. Although the nomenclature is sensitive (the concept of treatment is tempered by the concept of service), infertility and childlessness are constructed within a disease model. Constructed as a disease, or even a disability, all infertile (and, importantly, childless) women should be brought within the curative/normalizing medical gaze. Women who are excluded from treatment (by s.13(5) and other provisions) remain outside this gaze. These women remain inherently diseased – monstrous. Just as Frankenstein's Monster was a product of science, so he also existed beyond it, removed by society defining him as monstrous. Medicine, and its legal regulation, clearly remain the locus at which women are brought into organic communication with the social body and regulated.[92] Importantly, such regulation is facilitated not only by the definition of disease but also by those it brings within treatment and those it leaves outwith.

In many respects, therefore, the discourses and practices of the new reproductive technologies repeat the debates which have proved historically enduring within consideration of the management of reproduction. The (female) body remains a site for the expression and resolution of anxieties. Michelle Stanworth has noted how the new reproductive technologies 'crystallise issues at the heart of contemporary controversies over sexuality, parenthood, reproduction and the family'.[93] Like the 'Aborting Woman' of the nineteenth and twentieth centuries, the 'Inseminating/Assisted Woman' becomes the point at which concerns converge. Yet the concerns that converge upon the female body seeking assisted conception are not only those of sexuality and reproduction. The body is written upon with other social, political and economic anxieties. As was noted above, consideration of appropriate gender behaviour becomes discussed in terms of welfare and the family. The female reproductive body is implicit in this. The degree to which this implicit body has become a repository, and perceived solution, for these and other anxieties is visible in a final plea in the House of Lords by Lord Ashbourne:

> We must get down to basics and this matter is one of the basics … . If we get the family right, all … other things will come right as a spin-off effect. Our prisons

will not be bursting; our rate of abortion will not be higher than anywhere else; marriages will not break down; and divorce will not be higher than anywhere else. The cause of the problem is that marriages go wrong. I recommend that the Government focus on the cause of the problem and do not spend their life trying to shore up the holes in the dyke as they occur.[94]

The female body and *Frankenstein* again form parallel texts. Frankenstein's Monster for Shelley and for her commentators has been the site for the expression and resolution of many fears and anxieties.[95] The subjects constructed within the 1990 legislation parallel this convergence of fear, anxiety and the monstrous.

As with other reproductive issues, the female body within the discourses and practices of the new reproductive technologies is constructed within and affirms a specific gender framework. On the peripheries of, but nonetheless essential to, that gender framework is the monstrous. The presence of this framework renders the new reproductive technologies less 'new' than they may at first appear as they construct and privilege a familiar model of female sexuality. As Millns observes: 'Those women deemed suitable for access to the technologies are precisely those who, prior to the reproductive revolution, would have been perceived as suitable mothers.'[96] The provisions are therefore clearly imbricated in the discourses of Woman and the maternal which have underpinned previous reproductive debates. Indeed, these discourses and the emphasis on heterosexual parenting have been strengthened, as Carol Smart concludes:

Reproductive technologies increase the opportunities for relatively privileged men and women to have children, but as long as the technology is contained within legal parameters that prioritize the patriarchal family, it does nothing to challenge existing notions of fatherhood and motherhood. In fact, in ideological terms, it adds to the celebration of the biological, nuclear family that affects us all.[97]

Notes

1   R. Braidotti, *Nomadic Subjects: Embodiment and Sexual Difference in Contemporary Feminist Thinking* (New York: Columbia University Press, 1994), 81. This duplicity is graphically seen in a pre-Biblical Persian creation myth retold by Frieda Fromm-Reichman: 'In [the] myth a woman creates the world, and she creates by the act of natural creativity which is hers and cannot be duplicated by men. She gives birth to a great number of sons. The sons, greatly puzzled by this act which they cannot duplicate, become frightened. They think, "Who can tell us, that if she can give life, she cannot also take life?". And so, because of their fear of this mysterious ability of woman, and of its reversible possibility, they kill her' (quoted in Adrienne Rich, *Of*

Woman Born: Motherhood as Experience and Institution (New York: W.W. Norton, 1976), 11).

2 Braidotti, *supra*, at 76.

3 Ibid., at 79.

4 Ibid.

5 Ibid., at 80.

6 M.A. Rubenstein, "'My Accursed Origin": The Search for the Mother in *Frankenstein'*, *Studies in Romanticism*, **15**, (1976), 165, at 193.

7 M. Homans, *Bearing the Word* (London: University of Chicago Press, 1986), 106.

8 For Margaret Homans, this apparent contradiction reflects the arguably masturbatory nature of Romantic ideology returning us to the analysis in the previous chapter: 'But if the demon is really a feminine object of desire, why is it a he? I would suggest that this constitutes part of Shelley's exposure to the male romantic economy that would substitute for real and therefore powerful female others a being imagined on the model of the male poet's own self. By making the demon masculine, Shelley suggests that romantic desire to do away, not only with the mother, but also with all females so as to live finally in the world of mirrors that reflect a comforting illusion of the male self's independent illusion' (Homans, *supra*, at 106).

9 Shelley, *Frankenstein* (London: Penguin Classics, 1992), 96–7.

10 P. Cantor, *Creature and Creator: Myth-Making and English Romanticism* (Cambridge: Cambridge University Press, 1984), 117.

11 Similarly, as Marc Rubenstein writes, the status of the maternal is suggested in the novel's narrative structure, a structure 'too complex, peculiar and interesting to be neglected' (P. Brooks, *Body Work: Objects of Desire in Modern Narrative* (London: Harvard University Press, 1993), 199): 'The concentric circles of narration which help us to locate this image of the mother and comprehend her significance also serve to isolate and entomb her. The mother is both degraded and feared' (Rubenstein, *supra*, at 189–90).

12 Braidotti, *supra*, at 80.

13 In Kenneth Branagh's *Frankenstein*, the parallel destinies of Elizabeth and the Monster's mate are made to converge as Frankenstein returns with Elizabeth's corpse to his Promethean machinery. Reborn hideously deformed, she learns of her own monstrosity in the face of the Monster. In a dramatic act of self-immolation, Helena Bonham Carter's Elizabeth dies again, burns as a witch, a body no longer salvageable. In this most modern telling of Shelley's *Modern Prometheus*, Elizabeth is both maternal virgin (filling the role left by Frankenstein's mother's death) and monster. Although it is appropriate and innovative, Branagh's rewriting in some respects plays upon James Whale's Frankenstein sequel, *The Bride of Frankenstein*. In this film of 1935, Whale cast the same actress, Elsa Lanchester, as both the witty and demure Mary Shelley and the infernal female monster. With a more explicit association of the monstrous and the feminine, *Andy Warhol's Frankenstein* sees the creation of a beautiful female monster – an object of sexual pleasure and experimentation. In one graphic scene, Frankenstein, while simultaneously having sex with and disembowelling his female creation, calmly and evenly tells his attendant, 'To know death you must first fuck life in the gall bladder.' For a history of the celluloid Frankenstein, see A.L. Lavalley, 'The Stage and Film Children of Frankenstein: A Survey', in G. Levine and U.C. Knoepflmacher (eds), *The Endurance of Frankenstein: Essays on Mary Shelley's Novel* (Berkeley: University of California Press, 1979), 243.

14 F. Leboyer, *Birth Without Violence* (New York: Alfred A. Knopf, 1975). For a discussion of this passage, see A. Rich, 'The Theft of Childbirth', in C. Dreifus (ed.), *Seizing*

Our Bodies (New York: Vintage Books, 1977); Boston Women's Health Collective, *Our Bodies, Ourselves*, 3rd edn (New York: Simon & Schuster, 1984); also K.P. Morgan, 'Of Woman Born? How Old Fashioned! – New Reproductive Technologies and Women's Oppression', in C. Overall (ed.), *The Future of Human Reproduction* (Toronto: The Women's Press, 1989), 60, at 67.

15 L. Hodges, 'Babe up in Arms', *The Times Higher* (3 November 1995), 19.

16 Ibid.

17 Ibid. While Haig, and others, have characterized the foetal–maternal hormonal relationship as one premised on conflict, others have presented this as a carefully mediated and regulated relationship controlled by the placenta. See L. Irigary, 'On the Maternal Order', in *Je, Tu, Nous: Towards a Culture of Difference* (London: Routledge & Kegan Paul, 1993), 37.

18 Braidotti, *supra*, at 81.

19 E. Ann Kaplan, *Motherhood and Representation: The Mother in Popular Culture and Melodrama* (London: Routledge & Kegan Paul, 1992), 210.

20 Ibid.

21 The idea of symbolic castration is not new within consideration of female reproductive behaviour, more specifically within male consideration of female reproductive freedom. As George Devereux wrote in his well known abortion study, 'abortion is indicative of a spiteful feminine aggression against the male, and represents a degradation and depreciation of his potency, and, more specifically, an attempt to castrate him and render him impotent. Thus the psychoanalytic thesis that the baby is unconsciously equated with the penis also receives indirect confirmation from the findings of anthropologists' (G. Devereux, *A Study of Abortion in Primitive Societies* (New York: The Julian Press, 1955)).

22 C. Vasseleu, 'Life Itself', in R. Diprose and R. Ferrel (eds), *Cartographies: Poststructuralism and the Mapping of Bodies and Spaces* (Sydney: Allen & Unwin, 1991), 55, at 60.

23 For a discussion of legislative protection of paternity, from the poor laws through to the Warnock Report, see C. Smart, '"There is of Course the Distinction Dictated by Nature": Law and the Problem of Paternity', in M. Stanworth (ed.), *Reproductive Technologies: Gender, Motherhood and Medicine* (London: Polity Press, 1987), 98.

24 Section 3(3)(*a*). Section 3(4) states that, 'For the purposes of subsection (3)(*a*) above, the primitive streak is to be taken to have appeared in the embryo not later than the end of the period of 14 days beginning with the day when the gametes are mixed, not counting any time during which the embryo is stored.'

25 Generally, s.15.

26 Schedule 2, para. 3(9).

27 See, sch. 2, para. 3.

28 As was noted in the preceding chapter, these prohibitions were extended to make illegal the use of foetal ovarian tissue by s.1(5)(6) of the Criminal Justice and Public Order Act 1995.

29 Section 11(2) and sch. 2, para. 4(2)(b).

30 Section 11(2) and sch. 2, para. 4(2)(b).

31 Section 11(2) and sch. 2, para. 4(2)(a).

32 Schedule 2, para. 3(7) and para. 3(8).

33 D. Morgan and R.G. Lee, *The Blackstone's Guide to the Human Fertilisation and Embryology Act* (London: Blackstone Press, 1991), 85–8.

34 Section 12.

35   '1. -(1) A licence under this paragraph may authorise any of the following in the course of providing treatment services–

(a) bringing about the creation of embryos *in vitro*,

(b) keeping embryos,

(c) using gametes,

(d) practices designed to secure that embryos are in suitable condition to be placed in a woman or to determine whether embryos are suitable for that purpose,

(e) placing any embryo in a woman ...

(2) Subject to the provisions of this Act, a licence under this paragraph may be granted subject to such conditions as may be specified in the licence and may authorise the performance of any of the activities referred to in sub-paragraph (1) above in such manner as may be so specified.

(3) A licence under this paragraph cannot authorise any activity unless it appears to the authority to be desirable for the purpose of providing treatment services.

(4) A licence under this paragraph cannot authorise altering the genetic structure of any cell while it forms part of an embryo.

(5) A licence under this paragraph shall be granted for such period not exceeding five years as may be specified in the licence.'

36   Morgan and Lee, *supra*, at 88.

37   Although the Act appears clearly predicated on a heterosexual model, clinical practice appears to vary greatly. Athena Liu, for example, provides the treatment guidelines/ policy statements for both St Mary's Manchester and the King's Assisted Conception Unit. While St Mary's clearly confines itself to providing services within the heterosexual model defined by the Act, King's Assisted Conception Unit states that 'We have no policy regarding our patients' relationships' (A. Liu, *Artificial Reproduction and Reproductive Rights* (Aldershot: Dartmouth, 1991), 167–8).

38   S. Millns, 'Making "Social Judgements that go Beyond the Purely Medical": The Reproductive Revolution and Access to Fertility Treatment Services', in J. Bridgeman and S. Millns, *Law and Body Politics: The Medical Regulation of the Female Body* (Aldershot: Dartmouth, 1995), 79, at 82.

39   B.K. Rothman, 'The Products of Conception: the Social Context of Reproductive Choices', *Journal of Medical Ethics*, **11**, (1985), 188, at 188–9.

40   Shelley, *supra*, at 159–60.

41   Ibid.

42   Morgan and Lee, *supra*, at 146. The recognition of a socioeconomic agenda is important, a reminder of the pro-procreative eugenic discourses for the middle and upper classes on both sides of the Atlantic in the nineteenth and early twentieth centuries.

43   Ibid, at 118.

44   *Report of the Committee of Inquiry into Fertilisation and Embryology*, Cmnd 9314 (London: HMSO, 1984), para. 2.11.

45   Revocation will most likely occur under s.18(1)(*c*). This provides that 'A licence committee may revoke a licence if it is satisfied ... that the person responsible has failed to discharge ... the duty under section 17 of this Act or has failed to comply with directions given in connection with any licence.' Section 17(1)(*e*) provides that 'It shall be the duty of the individual under whose supervision the activities authorised by a licence are carried on ... to secure ... that the conditions of the licence are complied with.'

46   It is worth noting that the effect of s.13(5) has, to an extent, been mitigated by the Human Fertilisation and Embryology Authority's Codes of Practice. See D. Cooper and D. Herman, 'Getting "The Family Right": Legislating Heterosexuality in Britain, 1986–1991', *Canadian Journal of Family Law*, **10**, (1991) 40, at 46–7.

47 M. Foucault, *Madness and Civilisation: A History of Insanity in the Age of Reason* (London: Tavistock, 1989), 272.

48 MacKay, HL Deb. vol. 516, col. 1098, 1990 (6 March).

49 G. Douglas, 'Assisted Reproduction and the Welfare of the Child', *Current Legal Problems* (1993), 54.

50 P. Brooks, *Body Work: Objects of Desire in Modern Narrative* (London: Harvard University Press, 1993), 220.

51 MacKay, HL Deb. vol. 516, col. 1098, 1990 (6 March).

52 MacKay, HL Deb. vol. 516, col. 1105, 1990 (6 March).

53 Steel, HC Deb. vol. 732, col. 1076, 1966 (22 July).

54 The media coverage of single women seeking treatment services is a good example of this, particularly the moral panic which emerged surrounding the prospect of artificial insemination by donor for so-called 'virgin mothers'; see *The Guardian*, 12 March 1991; also R. Silman (ed.), *Virgin Birth* (London: WFT Press, 1993).

55 The amendment was defeated by 61 votes to 60 (HL Deb. vol. 515, col. 787, 1990 (6 February)).

56 L. Doyal, 'Managing Conception: Self-Insemination and the Limits of Reproductive Freedom', *Policy and Politics*, **22**, (1994), 89. See also Cooper and Herman, *supra*.

57 See M. Thomson, 'Woman, Medicine and Abortion in the Nineteenth Century' *Feminist Legal Studies* (1995), 159.

58 MacKay, HL Deb. vol. 516, col. 1105, 1990 (6 March).

59 Ashbourne, HL Deb. vol. 515, col. 756, 1990 (6 February). David Wilshire, who introduced the final amendment to s.13(5), similarly claimed that the provision of treatment services to single women offended against the values of society and the 'biological facts of life [which meant] reproducing by means of a mother and a father' (Wilshire, HC Deb. vol. 519, cols 145–6, 1990 (15 May)). These sociobiological arguments, which were visible elsewhere, highlight the family as natural, and therefore other relationship structures as *unnatural* – monstrous.

60 Section 13(5) was only introduced during the report stage in the House of Lords. The current section made no mention of a need for a father until an amendment by David Wilshire MP in the report stage in the House of Commons.

61 Douglas, *supra*, at 58.

62 A similar critique of the child-centred welfare requirements of s.1(1) of the Children Act 1989 has been persuasively argued; see H. Reece, 'The Paramountcy Principle: Consensus or Construct?', *Current Legal Problems* (1996), 267; H. Reece, 'Subverting the Stigmatization Argument', *Journal of Law and Society*, **23**, (1996), 484.

63 MacKay, HL Deb. vol. 516, col. 1098, 1990 (6 March).

64 Human Fertilisation and Embryology Authority, *Codes of Practice* (London: HMSO, 1993), para. 3.3 (emphasis added).

65 [1988] 1 FLR 512.

66 Ibid., at 518–19.

67 Smart, *supra*, at 117.

68 HL Deb. vol. 516, col. 1103, 1990 (6 March).

69 Morgan and Lee, *supra*, at 147.

70 See S. Golombok and J. Rust, 'The Warnock Report and Single Women: What About the Children?', *Journal of Medical Ethics*, **12**, (1986), 182.

71 Kaplan, *supra*, at 210.

72 For a discussion of ss.4 and 38 and a possible conflict between the two, see Morgan and Lee, *supra*, at 177–81.

73 Morgan and Lee, *supra*, at 146.

74   Ibid., at 144.
75   [1991] 1 FLR 223.
76   [1983] 4 FLR 404.
77   See Reece, *supra*.
78   MacKay, HL Deb. vol. 516, col. 210, 1990 (20 March). This latter concern may be followed through into the subsequent creation of the Child Support Agency.
79   Shelley, *supra*, 160.
80   *Report of the Committee of Inquiry into Fertilisation and Embryology*, *supra*, at para. 10.9.
81   Ibid., at 10.12.
82   See *Independent on Sunday*, 6 October 1996; *The Guardian*, 19 October 1996, 14 January 1997.
83   Millns, *supra*, at 97–8.
84   See, for example, Phillips, HL Deb. vol. 515, col. 763, 1990 (6 February).
85   MacKay, HL Deb. vol. 516, col. 1104, 1990 (6 March).
86   Morgan and Lee, *supra*, at 119.
87   Ibid., at 118.
88   Lauderdale, HL Deb. vol. 519, cols 145–6, 1990 (15 May). Doyal makes a similar argument within the context of the legal regulation of self-insemination/AID (Doyal, *supra*).
89   Smart, *supra*, at 114 (reference omitted).
90   C. Smart, 'Law's Truth: Women's Experience', in R. Graycar (ed.), *Dissenting Opinions: Feminist Explorations in Law and Society* (Sydney: Allen & Unwin, 1990), 7.
91   Brooks, *supra*, at 220.
92   M. Foucault, *The History of Sexuality, Volume One* (Penguin: London, 1979), 104.
93   M. Stanworth, 'Reproductive Technologies and the Deconstruction of Motherhood', in M. Stanworth (ed.), *Reproductive Technologies: Gender, Motherhood and Medicine* (London: Polity, 1987), at 18.
94   Ashbourne, HL Deb. vol. 756, col. 7678, 1990 (6 February).
95   Immediately after publication of *Frankenstein*, the Monster became a strong political and satirical metaphor; see M. Butler, 'Introduction, in M. Shelley, *Frankenstein*, (London: Penguin Classics, 1992), 1; also M. Hindle, 'Introduction', in ibid., xI. Pertinently, in his 1974 Spanish film, *The Spirit of the Beehive*, Victor Erice uses the showing of James Whale's original *Frankenstein* in a Spanish village in the 1940s to associate the monstrous with Franco's Spain. See Lavalley, *supra*, at 279.
96   Millns, *supra*, at 82.
97   Smart, 'There is of Course the Distinction Dictated by Nature', *supra*, at 117.

8   Concluding Narratives: Applying the Past

Carol: (*Pause*) What is a 'term of art'?
John: (*Pause*) I'm sorry ...?
Carol: (*Pause*) What is a 'term of art'?
John: Is that what you want to talk about?
Carol: ... to talk about ...?
John: Let's take the mysticism out of it, shall we? Carol? (*Pause*) Don't you think? I'll tell you: when you have some 'thing'. Which must be broached. (*Pause*) Don't you think ...? (*Pause*)
Carol: ... don't I think ...?
John: Mmm?
Carol: ... did I ...?
John: ... what ...?
Carol: Did... did I ... did I say something wr ...
John: (*Pause*) No. I'm sorry. No. You're right. I'm very sorry. I'm somewhat rushed. As you see. I'm sorry. You're right. (*Pause*) What is a 'term of art'? It seems to mean a *term*, which has come, through its use, to mean something *more specific* than the words would, to someone *not acquainted* with them ... indicate. That, I believe, is what a 'term of art', would mean. (*Pause*)
Carol: You don't know what it means ...?
(David Mamet, *Oleanna* (London: Methuen, 1993), 2–3)

Introduction

The focus of this book was introduced in Chapter 1 as the discourses and practices which inhabit and invest reproduction and the reproductive body. In this first chapter the criminalization of abortion in the nineteenth century, the shift from *remedy* to criminal act, was located within the occupational assertion of medicine. The emergence of an albeit illusory consolidated medical opposition to abortion was revealed as motivated, in part, by a desire to criminalize not the act but the alternative and competing therapists.

197

Opposition to abortion provided a politically viable narrative through which to pursue legislation which went against predominantly laissez-faire governmental policies. Such a narrative was located in bioscience, written upon the body. Thus the manner in which the female body, and particularly the female reproductive body, may be read as a repository for social and economic concerns was introduced. More specifically, the chapter introduced the idea that narratives may inscribe the female body, defining and constructing the body and social relations.

Remaining with the medical campaign against abortion in the nineteenth century, Chapter 2 introduced the primary narrative it was intended to map. Within the parameters of the medical campaign it assessed the degree to which perceptions of gender may influence, and in turn be affirmed by, medical and state responses to reproduction. Medical opposition to abortion in this period was located within a more general opposition to emerging definitions of female economic and social participation. Medical opposition to abortion was, to an extent, indistinguishable from opposition to increased female access to higher education, employment and the medical profession itself. Importantly, the construction of the body became a primary method for justifying such opposition. This allowed the recoding of discrimination in the language and *objectivity* of science. In our sex–gender system the biomedical construction of the female body as weak, inherently pathological and dependent affirmed the desired characteristics of the female gender. Medicine contributed, located upon the body, a physical text telling of and legitimating exclusion, dependence and separate spheres. The body was constructed to locate it within desired social structures. The regulation of abortion in this period may therefore also be seen as inextricable from the emerging state interest in the body and the population. A shift in the modalities of power in this period enhanced medical calls for a greater degree of observation, regulation and control over reproduction and, more specifically, women's bodies.

The analysis of the nineteenth-century campaign provided in the first two chapters created a contextual backdrop for the analysis of the Abortion Act 1967 in Part II. Chapters 3 and 4 considered parliamentary responses to David Steel's Private Member's Bill and subsequent attempts to amend the legislation. Reading these responses, abortion in the second half of the twentieth century appears to remain an issue determined, to a large extent, by the perception of appropriate gender roles. Within the discourse of the parliamentarians, many of the narrative patterns read within the nineteenth-century discourses and practices were again evident. Although opponents and proponents of decriminalization appeared at first to be ideologically diametrically opposed, such opposition may be understood as in some respects superficial. Ideologically, there existed a fundamental commonality in terms of the perceived role of women. Both groups saw women as primarily bearers and rearers of children, contained within the private sphere of the home, economically and financially dependent. Having recognized this commonality, the possibility that a number of the proponents of reform assumed this position for political expediency must also be recognized. Yet within these parameters the nineteenth-century model of *separate spheres*, of mutually exclusive yet complementary roles, appears enduring. Whilst there existed this important commonality there was a conflict as to whether allowing limited access to abortion services would weaken or strengthen the existence of these separate spheres. Looking at the final provisions of the Act in this context, the failure to afford women access to abortion as of right, however qualified, becomes understandable. The determination of access to abortion services by two registered practitioners in accordance with the provisions of the Act allows a mediation of the *type* of woman receiving an abortion. In this way abortions for the *right* reasons and for the *right* sort of woman can be assured.[1]

One of the developments noted in consideration of twentieth-century abortion discourses, particularly after 1967, was a move towards a more *foetus-centred* focus within reproductive discourses. Chapter 5 suggested that this new cultural and biomedical *presence* was in part a result of the recoding of the narratives explored in earlier chapters. Narratives of gender that were once explicitly inscribed upon the female body have become displaced, investing instead the foetus. This argument was sustained in an examination of industrial foetal protection policies.

Consideration of these policies, which are broadcast as fundamentally motivated by concern for foetal well-being, again revealed a continuity of narrative with the preceding chapters. The chapter revealed that regard for the foetus is contingent and limited. Women are generally only excluded from workplaces which have historically been perceived as male, from industries which have a history of discrimination. No such exclusionary policies operate in industries which rely predominantly on female labour. Many of these latter industries involve exposure to foetotoxic chemicals at levels comparable to those found in the industries from which women have been excluded. Equally, women and not men are subject to exclusionary practices even though scientific studies suggest that at the preconception stage male exposure to the same toxins proves *at least* as potentially damaging to any subsequent foetus.

Inherent in the discourses and practices of industrial foetal protection are familiar narratives. The regulation of reproduction appears again determined by perceptions of gender, more specifically in this context perceptions of gender-appropriate employment. Gender narratives are once more written upon the body. The assertion that one needs to ask what mode of investment of the body is necessary for the functioning of society, what kind of body society needs, remains pertinent.[2] The familiar narratives that can be read within these policies have been recoded, retold, as governmental or corporate concern, civic duty or largesse.

In the last two chapters the increasingly energetic response to infertility and childlessness was interrogated. In Chapter 6, the new reproductive technologies and their governmental regulation were located within a history of masculine creation mythology and desire. Placing such developments within this context provided insights into both the masculine subject suggested by the emergence of these new possibilities and the status of the maternal within such (pro)creative projects. Ultimately, the analysis highlighted the circumvention of the maternal inherent in these masculine projects.

Chapter 7 returned to a reading of the discourses around the statutory regulation of reproduction. As with the Abortion Act 1967, the Human Fertilisation and Embryology Act 1990 appears framed within the narratives of gender which were formative in the regulation of reproduction in the nineteenth century. While the Act largely legitimates the creative desires of research scientists, the provisions for access to the more technologically advanced methods of assisted conception are less accommodating. Although the Codes of Practice have proved more flexible, the Act restricts access to the technologies within its ambit to those who fulfil a clearly prescribed model of gender behaviour. This model is one premised on heterosexuality and an active, visible male presence. A fear of technological possibilities, of a technologically liberated monstrous femininity, appears to motivate both the leeway afforded research and the privileging of access to fertility services for a particular group of women.

A Contemporary Focus

The introduction to this book asserted that an analysis of historic reproductive discourses could provide an interpretive aid for the analysis of modern reproductive issues. These issues, it is contended, are more readily understood when we are able to locate them within a continuity of desire. While preceding chapters go some way to drawing such interpretive parallels, here, by way of a conclusion, this is dealt with more explicitly. To achieve this, I consider a number of the recent cases which have concerned non-consensual Caesarian sections, looking briefly at similar and more expansive developments in the United States. In this way I aim to highlight the persistence of the two narratives, or more correctly narrative themes, that have emerged in the preceding chapters. Looking first at the legitimating narrative outlined in Chapter 1, it is contended that these cases are more readily understood if we contextualize medical responses to reproductive issues, and medical recourse to the law, as still involving issues of professional assertion and validation. Secondly, I reconsider the configuration of ideas: reproduction, gender and law, more specifically focusing on the way these cases may be located within a broader *technology of gender*.[3]

Re S[4]

On 12 October 1992, the High Court declared it lawful for a hospital to perform a Caesarian section without the consent of the woman involved. The decision of Sir Stephen Brown, the President of the Family Division, permitted the doctors to override the wishes of the woman and those of her partner. Both, described as Born Again Christians, objected to the Caesarian section on religious grounds. The operation was held to be necessitated by the foetus being positioned in a transverse lie with its elbow projecting through the cervix and the head being on the right side. Failure to perform the Caesarian section was seen to carry the 'gravest risk' of the woman's uterus rupturing.[5] With regard to both the woman and the foetus it was described as a 'life or death' situation.[6]

The woman had been in labour since midday of the Saturday and was, by the Monday when the case was heard, six days overdue. The High Court hearing took less than an hour. The court was contacted at 1.25 pm and the hearing started at 1.55 pm. Sir Stephen Brown's decision was made by 2.18 pm and the hospital was telephoned immediately. By this time, however, the foetus had died *in utero*. The brevity of the hearing may, in part, be explained by the fact that Mrs S was not represented.[7]

In granting the declaration sought by the Health Authority, Sir Stephen Brown P relied on two authorities. Reference was made to the case of *Re T (Adult: Refusal of Medical Treatment)*,[8] a decision of the Court of Appeal earlier in the year, which had held that an adult patient who was competent to decide had an *absolute right* to refuse to consent to medical treatment.[9] Lord Donaldson MR, after outlining this fundamental proposition, had stated: 'The only possible qualification is a case in which the choice may lead to the death of a viable foetus ... and, if and when it arises, the court will be faced with a novel problem of considerable legal and ethical complexity.'[10] Sir Stephen Brown P took this to mean that the question remained open, yet, as Michael Jones states, 'simply because there is no direct authority on the point does not necessarily mean that a question is open. It may be that the answer appeared so obvious that no one has had the temerity to argue the point.'[11]

In what was an extremely brief judgment, the President also made reference to the American case of *Re A.C.*,[12] asserting that it 'suggests that if this case were being heard in the American Courts the answer would be likely to be in favour of granting the declaration in these circumstances'.[13] This assertion is erroneous. *Re A.C.* (discussed below) does not validate, or support, compelled medical treatment against the wishes of a competent patient in order to save or benefit the life of a foetus. Rather, while the court had initially granted the declaration sought, this had, on appeal, been over-ruled. This was followed by the out of court settlement of a malpractice claim. Moreover, *Re A.C.* is seen as marking the conclusion of a decade of judicially sanctioned obstetrical intervention.[14] It is seen as very clearly stating that a competent patient cannot be compelled to undergo major invasive surgery, even if failure to do so will result in the death of the foetus.

Re S stood alone for a number of years as the only English case that had validated this form of intervention. However, there have more recently been a number of cases which have legitimated forced Caesarian sections.

Tameside and Glossop Acute Services NHS Trust v. *CH (A Patient)*[15]

On 5 January 1996, Wall J declared it lawful for the plaintiff NHS Trust to perform a Caesarian section on the defendant even if she should refuse her consent. The declaration also legitimated all clinically determined necessary/ancillary treatment in the management of the defendant's labour. This included the use of restraint in the event that it should become necessary. The order was both pre-emptive and precautionary. At the time of the application, the Caesarian was not held to be necessary, but it was believed that it might eventually become so. Similarly, at this time the defendant gave her consent to such a procedure, although it was feared this would be withdrawn. Owing to the unusual nature of the case, Wall J withheld his reasoning until 22 January.

On this date we were informed, through a judgment considerably longer than that handed down by Sir Stephen Brown in *Re S*, that CH was 41 years old, suffering from schizophrenia, and detained under the Mental Health Act 1983. She had two children and at the time of the application was in the thirty-eighth week of her pregnancy. While CH had at times refused prenatal investigation (aiding her characterization as difficult) it became apparent that since the thirty-first week of her pregnancy there had been intrauterine growth retardation, possibly caused by deficient functioning of the placenta. It was asserted by the consultant obstetrician and gynaecologist (referred to as Dr G) that if the pregnancy was allowed to continue for much longer the foetus would die *in utero*. Dr G planned to induce labour, but believed that the deficient placenta could lead to foetal distress necessitating an immediate Caesarian section. Because of the 'labile state' of CH, Dr G was afraid that the consent that had been given to the induction and Caesarian section would be withdrawn.[16] Whilst it was accepted that the death of the foetus *in utero* would not cause the defendant any physical harm, it was recognized that there were risks inherent in the Caesarian section and that the induction carried some risks to foetal health.

In seeking to grant the declaration sought, the court considered both the common law and statutory mental health provisions. In order to unravel the narratives within *CH* and subsequent cases, it is worth considering the court's reasoning in some detail. Under the common law the court had the jurisdiction to grant the declaration sought if the procedure was in the best interests of CH and if she lacked capacity. In terms of the issue of CH's capacity, there seemed to be a consensus in the medical opinion. Dr G 'was of the opinion that the Defendant had no understanding of what he was telling her about the baby, and was incapable of taking a decision'.[17] Dr M, the consultant psychiatrist, stated that CH was

incapable of making a balanced, rational decision about her treatment. She failed the three-fold test set out *In re C (Adult: Refusal of Treatment)* [1994] 1 WLR 290, 295D (that is to say firstly comprehending and retaining treatment information, secondly believing it and thirdly weighing it in the balance to arrive at a choice).[18]

Wall J accepted the evidence of both Dr G and Dr M and, applying the test set out in *Re C*, held that CH did lack the capacity to make a decision regarding the proposed treatment. With regard to whether a Caesarian section could be considered to be in the best interests of CH, whilst Dr G would not go so far as to say that a stillbirth would be detrimental to CH's mental well-being, he did feel that it would not 'benefit her schizophrenia'.[19] Dr R (a second consultant gynaecologist) and Dr M, however, were less ambiguously of the opinion that a Caesarian section would be in her best interests. Dr M described the likely effect of a stillbirth on the defendant:

In the short term one would anticipate a deterioration in her mental health and recovery would be impeded by the grieving process for the child. She would become increasingly paranoid and would blame us for the child's death. In the longer term the grief would endure and be complicated by the psychotic process ... . The effect on her treatment of a still-birth would be further to undermine the trust she has with the psychiatric services ... . The best interests of the patient lie in her producing a healthy child.[20]

Although WALL J accepted that CH lacked capacity and that a live birth would be in her best interests, he was reluctant, in the absence of judicial authority, to authorize the use of reasonable force to ensure treatment compliance. He therefore turned to the statutory provisions of the Mental Health Act 1983. Previous declarations founded upon s. 63 had authorized the use of reasonable restraint to facilitate treatment.[21] Having established the lawfulness of restraint under the 1983 Act and its Code of Practice, Wall J turned to the specific requirements of s. 63. This section provides that 'The consent of the patient shall not be required for any medical treatment given to him for the mental disorder from which he is suffering ... if the treatment is given by or under the direction of the responsible medical officer.'

In the case of *B* v. *Croydon Health Authority*, a declaration was sought that nasogastric feeding could lawfully be given without her consent to a patient suffering from a psychopathic disorder. B had a history of refusing to eat, which had led to dramatic weight loss. Hoffmann LJ held that forcefeeding was treatment *for* her mental disorder and as such could be given under the power conferred by s. 63 without B's consent. The case of *Re C (Adult: Refusal of Treatment)*, where a competent schizophrenic was held entitled to refuse an amputation of his gangrenous foot, on the grounds that 'gangrene was entirely unconnected with the mental disorder', was distinguished.[22] In response to Gordon QC, who had contended that food could not be considered treatment *for* mental illness, Hoffmann LJ had stated:

> It may be a prerequisite to a treatment for mental disorder or it may be a treatment for a consequence of the mental disorder, but it is not treatment of the mental disorder itself ... This is a powerful submission. But I have come to the conclusion that it is too atomistic ... a range of acts ancillary to the core treatment fall within the definition.[23]

In the case of B, force-feeding was required to treat a consequence of her mental disorder, namely, her weight loss. It is difficult to understand how this corresponds with the intention of this provision. As Lord Elton made clear in the House of Lords, this provision did not apply to 'borderline' or 'experimental treatments' but solely to 'perfectly routine, sensible treatment'.[24] Some of the treatments which could be characterized as borderline or experimental are provided with more stringent safeguards under ss. 57 and 58. In terms of s. 63, and the cases involving force-feeding, Phil Fennell has rightly noted: 'While one can envisage circumstances where it might be argued that force feeding is for the patient's benefit, it is hard to see it as "perfectly routine" and it raises sufficiently complex ethical issues to put it in the "borderline" category.'[25] Notwithstanding the obvious concerns regarding this expansive approach, Wall J adopted the *holistic* approach taken by Hoffmann LJ and held that a Caesarian section was treatment for CH's mental disorder – bringing it within the power conferred by s. 63. If, as Fennell contends, force-feeding may be characterized as raising sufficiently complex ethical issues to question the appropriateness of applying s. 63, a forced Caesarian section must clearly beg the same question. Nevertheless, whilst it could not be said that a Caesarian section was required to treat a consequence of CH's mental disorder, it was characterized as a prerequisite for the treatment of her mental disorder, Wall J stating:

> Firstly, there is the proposition that an ancillary reason for the induction and, if necessary, the birth by Caesarian section is to prevent a deterioration in the defendant's mental state. Secondly, there is the clear evidence of Dr M that, in order for the treatment of her schizophrenia to be effective, it is necessary for her to give birth to a live baby. Thirdly, the overall structure of her treatment requires her to receive strong anti-psychotic medication. The administration of that treatment has been necessarily interrupted by her pregnancy and cannot be resumed until her child is born ... the manner in which the delivery of the defendant's child is treated is likely to have a direct effect on her mental state.[26]

Thus giving birth to a live baby was deemed necessary to ensure that CH's mental condition would not deteriorate. Furthermore, it would avert a possible prolonged pregnancy and ensure that the administration of strong anti-psychotic medication could be recommenced sooner.

Norfolk and Norwich Healthcare (NHS) Trust v. W; Rochdale Healthcare (NHS) Trust v. C

These two cases were heard by Johnson J on the 21 June 1996. As with the preceding cases the order sought was granted.

At 9 o'clock on the morning of the application, W had arrived at the trust hospital's Accident and Emergency Department. She was in the last stages of pregnancy. Through the course of the day, and despite the late stage of her pregnancy, she denied she was pregnant. At 4.45pm, the application began before the court. The court learnt that W had a history of psychiatric treatment. She had also had three previous pregnancies, each culminating in a Caesarian section. The hospital sought authority to end the labour by a forceps delivery, or, if this should prove unsuccessful, by a Caesarian section. It was claimed that failure to deliver the foetus by these means would lead to foetal death. Unlike the circumstances of the *CH* case, the presence of a dead foetus in the patient was seen as a life-threatening possibility. There was also a secondary risk that the patient's old Caesarian scars would reopen, which would also threaten the life of the foetus and therefore the patient herself.

It was admitted that the patient was not suffering from a mental disorder within the meaning of the Mental Health Act 1983. Yet, relying on the application of *Re C (Adult: Refusal of Treatment)* by Wall J in *CH*, and the principle enunciated in *Re F* (that is, that there must be a necessity to act and that the action taken is such that a reasonable person would take it acting in the person's best interests),[27] Johnson J upheld the trust's request for authority to act.

The hearing of the above application by Norfolk and Norwich Healthcare (NHS) Trust was interrupted by Johnson J in order to hear a similar application in respect of a patient in a hospital in Rochdale. The application was interrupted at 5.15 pm. It was claimed that the Caesarian section which the second trust sought to legitimate had to be carried out by 5.30 pm if the foetus were to remain alive and the health of the woman were not to be endangered. Given the pressures of time, no psychiatric report was available. The only assessment of C's competence came from the consultant obstetrician. He informed the court that C's mental capacity was not in question and that she appeared to him to be fully competent.

Whilst Johnson J accepted the view of the consultant in relation to the first two elements of the threefold test relied on in *W* and *CH*, he believed that C was not able to properly weigh up the considerations that arose so as to make a competent decision.[28] As a consequence, Johnson J granted the declaration sought.

Having outlined *Re S* and three of the cases that have been heard since, it is possible to argue that these cases may be located within the analytical framework provided by preceding chapters. In order to illustrate this, to reveal the reproductive narratives I wish to consider, it is first necessary to turn to similar developments in the United States. Beyond helping to uncover these narratives, such a consideration also reveals the possibilities that exist for English law in this area. Following *Re S* some commentators had suggested that fears that we were to duplicate the American experience were unfounded, *Re S* being seen as such an obvious abberation that it could not possibly be followed or used as authority for any further foetal protection policies.[29] Whilst there has been no explicit reliance upon Sir Stephen Brown's ratio, the cases since *Re S* unfortunately leave such analysis redundant. It should also be emphasized that American law, like English law, does not recognize the foetus as a legal person.[30] Consequently, developments in the United States have all occurred within a similar jurisprudential framework.

American Intervention

On 22 January 1981, a petition came before the Superior Court of Butts County from the Griffin Spalding County Hospital Authority, seeking an order authorizing it to perform a Caesarian section, and necessary blood transfusions, upon the defendant.[31] A Caesarian section was held to be necessary as the woman was suffering from a complete placenta previa, the placenta lying between the foetus and the birth canal, a situation held to be virtually incapable of self-correction before birth. Expert evidence attested to the fact that there was a 99 per cent chance of the foetus dying, and the woman's chances of survival were put at 'no better than 50 per cent'. On the basis of her religious conviction, Ms Jefferson asserted that she would not require a Caesarian section and also refused any transfusion of blood. The order was sought with the aim of preserving 'the life of [the] defendant's unborn child', not that of Ms Jefferson. The court declined to grant the declaration sought.

A petition the following day from the County Department of Family and Children Services seeking the same declaration, but on the grounds that the foetus was a *deprived child* without proper parental care, was successful. The court relied on the state's interest in the life of the 'unborn human being', and the violation of the defendant's liberty was seen as 'outweighed by the State's duty to protect a living, unborn human being from meeting his or her death before being given the opportunity to live'.[32] Expanding on the balancing process that occupied the court, Hill PJ stated: 'we weighed the right of the mother to practice her religion and to refuse surgery on herself, against the unborn child's right to live. We found in favor of the child's right to live.'[33]

Ultimately, the order of the Superior Court, in terms of medical necessity, was a wasted exercise. The alleged 'impossibility' of the placenta previa correcting itself before labour began occurred. Jessie Mae Jefferson's assertion that she did not require a Caesarian section proved true: she gave birth naturally, by vaginal delivery, to her child.

Although the *Jefferson* case appeared a wasted exercise in terms of medical necessity, it proved valuable to those who sought greater control over the birth process. Although *Jefferson* is the only reported case of an application to authorize a forced Caesarian section before *Re A.C.*, it appears that at least 13 other such cases have occurred.[34] These cases have included situations where the pregnant woman has had her wrists and ankles forcibly secured with leather cuffs;[35] where the woman has been a non-American national;[36] where judicial authority has been granted over the phone;[37] and where doctors have carried out the operation without judicial authority[38] – strong echoes, ghosts, of the gynaecological barbarities of the nineteenth century.[39]

Whilst these cases all raise questions of physical integrity and autonomy there are clearly other issues involved. In terms of the 15 against whom orders were originally sought (13 being successful); seven (47 per cent) were black Americans, five (33 per cent) were African or Asian, and only three (20 per cent) were white Americans; 44 per cent were unmarried; and 27 per cent did not speak English as their first language.[40] In none of the cases was there material maternal morbidity or mortality reported, and only two of 14 infants (14 per cent) had important morbidity.[41]

These figures suggest discrimination on the grounds of race and, to a lesser, extent marital status: 80 per cent of the women treated were black, Asian or Hispanic, groups likely to suffer other forms of discrimination. The economic status of the women has also appeared to be a determining factor. All the women involved were in teaching hospital clinics, or were receiving public assistance. Doctors treating private patients would naturally be less inclined to subject their fee-paying clients to a court-ordered procedure. The suggestion of discrimination is further validated by the fact that the demands of the medical workers on the basis of necessity appear often to be of questionable worth. In three of the first five forced Caesarian sections, the women ultimately gave birth vaginally and without complications.[42] In each of the cases obstetrical intervention was said to be a necessity. Yet, as noted above, the incidence and legal status of non-consensual Caesarian sections in the United States have been affected by the case of *Re A.C.*

Angela Carder, white and middle-class, had been suffering from cancer since the age of 13. At the age of 28, and 26 weeks pregnant, she developed lung cancer. Against the wishes of Ms Carder, her partner and her doctors, the administrators of the George Washington University Medical Center in Washington, DC successfully sought an emergency order to perform a Caesarian section on the ground that she was dying anyway and the foetus could be saved. As with many of the preceding cases, the order was granted with haste and the Caesarian section performed. The foetus proved not to be viable, and Ms Carder died two days later. The court expressed its sympathy. Her death certificate listed the Caesarian section as a contributing factor in her death. The judge had acknowledged that the operation would probably shorten Ms Carder's life without necessarily saving the life of the 26-week-old foetus.

The District of Columbia Court of Appeals, on approving the decision of the lower court, stated that 'the trial judge did not err in his *subordinating* A.C.'s right against bodily intrusion to the interests of the *unborn child*'. Emphasis was placed upon the fact that the 'Caesarean section would not *significantly* affect A.C.'s position because she had, at best, two days left of sedated life'.[43] Therefore, Angela Carder lost the last two days of her life, and the possibility of a dignified death, as she was forced to undergo major surgery for the benefit of an unviable foetus. It is worth noting that the fact that she only had two days left was in part due to the hospital's earlier decision to withhold chemotherapy because of the dangers it posed to the health of the foetus. The District of Columbia Court of Appeals subsequently vacated its decision and reheard the case. The order previously made was overruled. It was held that a refusal of consent (by the patient or by substituted judgment) would be inviolable in 'virtually all cases'; the court continued: 'Indeed some may doubt that there could ever be a situation compelling enough to justify a massive intrusion into a person's body, such as a Caesarean section, against that person's will.'[44] Angela Carder's case has been seen as a landmark, a 'victory which marked a turning point in the United States in the struggle for reproductive autonomy'.[45]

Further Intervention

Non-consensual obstetrical intervention has not been limited to Caesarian sections. Court orders for both maternal and intrauterine blood transfusions, for example, have been sought in various states. In New York, a court granted an order compelling a woman to undergo a blood transfusion held to be necessary to prevent the death of her foetus.[46] The woman, 18 weeks pregnant, objected to the procedure on religious grounds. Two requests for forced intrauterine transfusions, held to be necessitated by Rhesus sensitization, have been granted in Colorado;[47] a third order sought in Michigan was denied. Two of the women were black American, the third Hispanic. Increased expertise in the field of foetal surgery leaves the spectre of further non-consensual invasive treatment.

Invasive intervention has also been coupled with court-ordered hospital detention. In Illinois and Colorado, orders have been granted against two black American women who, at 31 to 33 weeks of gestation, refused therapy for diabetes. The implications of this are considerable. In a 1987 study it was found that 46 per cent of heads of foetal–maternal medicine in the United States thought that women who refused medical advice, thereby endangering the life of the foetus, should be forcibly detained.[48] The medical advice refused was unspecified; it could include failure to consent to prenatal screening, foetal surgery, or restrictions on diet, sex, employment or leisure activity. Even broader grounds for detention seem possible. In Wisconsin, a pregnant 16-year-old was detained for the benefit of the foetus because she had a tendency to be 'on the run' and she lacked the 'motivation or ability to seek prenatal care'.[49] Again, it may be seen that the women against whom such orders are sought are economically and politically disadvantaged. These women may be the least able to provide resistance.

Judicial sanctioning of non-consensual treatment may be placed within a broader developing judicial role, within which the criminal law has become increasingly important. This has been evident in terms both of criminal regulation prenatally and of the use of postnatal prosecutions. In terms of

prenatal regulation, sentencing and remand have played an equally important role, the means and justification by which the women have been detained secondary to their actual detention. In 1980, a Los Angeles court
sentenced a woman convicted of a minor offence to imprisonment for the
duration of her pregnancy. This was done, not on the basis of standard
sentencing procedures, but in order to protect the health of the foetus.
Although the order was overturned on appeal, this occurred only after the
defendant had spent six weeks in prison.[50] Similarly, a District of Columbia
court, after convicting a woman of forgery, sentenced her to imprisonment
for the duration of her pregnancy after she was found to have used cocaine.[51]

Postnatal sanctions through the criminal justice system for injuries caused
prenatally have been more numerous. Women who have given birth to drug-
exposed neonates have been charged with a variety of offences, including
criminal neglect, delivering drugs to a minor and involuntary manslaughter.
In May 1989, Melanie Green of Rockford, Illinois became the first woman
in the United States to be charged with manslaughter for the death of her
baby. The child had died after being born with complications resulting from
prenatal cocaine use. She was also charged with delivering drugs to a minor.
All charges were dropped when a Winnebago County jury refused to indict
her.[52]

In July 1989, Jennifer Johnson was convicted of delivering drugs to a
minor by a County Court in Sandford, Florida.[53] Ms Johnson had used
cocaine while pregnant and traces of the drug were found in the child's
blood system. Whilst a charge of child abuse was unsuccessful, Johnson was
sentenced to 15 years' probation, attendance at a drug rehabilitation programme and mandatory prenatal supervision should she become pregnant
again. The court had convicted her by applying a statute typically used
against drug traffickers.[54]

In California, an obstetrician advised Pamela Rae Stewart to stay off her
feet, avoid sex and street drugs, and to go to hospital should she start to
bleed. On 26 September 1986, Stewart was arrested and charged with causing her son's death by failing to obtain adequate medical care during pregnancy. The arrest took place nine months after the birth of the child, and
more than seven months after his death. Ms Stewart was prosecuted on the
grounds that she had waited 'many hours' before seeking medical advice
after she had discovered she was bleeding vaginally and had experienced
uterine contractions. The prosecution also charged her with engaging in
sexual intercourse with her husband, and taking amphetamines and marijuana while pregnant. The District Attorney claimed the prosecution was
taking place because Ms Stewart 'didn't follow through on the medical
advice she was given'.[55]

On 26 February 1987, the court dismissed all charges: failure to follow a doctor's advice was held not to be illegal under the child support statute on which the prosecution had relied. Under the statute it is a crime for a parent to 'wilfully omit, without lawful excuse, to furnish necessary clothing, food, shelter or medical attendance, or other remedial care for his or her child'.[56] The prosecution failed notwithstanding a 1925 amendment extending the definition of 'child' to include the foetus. The irony of attempting to bring a prosecution under this amendment should not be lost, as Dawn Johnsen states: 'Ironically, the purpose of that amendment was to enhance the rights of pregnant women by expanding men's financial obligations under the statute to include the financial support of women pregnant with their children.'[57]

The attempt by the prosecution to rely on this amendment reflects a growing move to enact or interpret legislation to bolster this 'new prosecutorial trend'.[58] Family law provisions, for example, have been expanded retroactively to cover the prenatal period, allowing detention and surveillance if the foetus is believed to be in danger.[59] These provisions have also allowed courts to uphold petitions for the custody of the foetus,[60] and also for the removal of children on the basis of prenatal neglect.[61] In such cases prenatal conduct is seen as foretelling postnatal mistreatment. After the failure of an Illinois grand jury to indict Melanie Green for manslaughter, the state legislature expanded the protection afforded to neglected or abused minors to include 'any newborn infant whose blood or urine contains any amount of a controlled substance ... or a metabolite of a controlled substance'.[62] Several other jurisdictions have introduced similar statutes.[63]

Locating the Case Law

At the beginning of this chapter it was claimed that conclusions could best be drawn by highlighting the persistence of certain narratives. Preceding chapters provide a genealogy of narratives that have endured within consideration of the control or regulation of reproduction since the beginning of the nineteenth century. These narratives prove essential to our understanding of, and responses to, present-day reproductive issues. The first of these narratives is what could be referred to as the validating narrative of medicine. Although this will be dealt with as a distinct narrative, to a large extent this is an artificial exercise. As Chapter 1 and the above cases illustrate, gender is inextricable from this continuing occupational project.

Validating Medicine

The transformation in the organization of health care provision in the nine-teenth century was shown in Chapter 1 to be intimately tied to medical opposition to the common law status of abortion during this period. In fact, Chapter 1 suggests a directly causal link between the vocal (and politically directed) opposition to abortion and the rise of the regular physicians as the dominant health care providers. Legal protection of the regular physicians from competing therapists was attained through a claim to qualitatively superior knowledge. Medical legitimacy may therefore be understood as originating, in part, in the political manipulation of claimed knowledge regarding reproduction. This relationship between the attainment of medical power and a claim to knowledge supports Foucault's assertion of the synonymity of power and knowledge, his claim that:

> power produces knowledge (and not simply by encouraging it because it serves power or by applying it because it is useful); that power and knowledge directly imply one another; that there is no power relation without the correlative consti-tution of a field of knowledge, nor any knowledge that does not presuppose and constitute at the same time power relations.[64]

The assertion of knowledge to justify a privileged medical position, in other words to justify medical power, still focuses on reproduction. Increas-ing medical control of reproduction continues to assert the legitimacy of medicine's privileged position. Technological advances, regardless of effi-cacy, extend the range of medical practice, maintaining a fluid and unknowable body of knowledge. This is evident, for example, in the expo-nential growth in genetic science and medicine. Yet it is perhaps most clearly understood in terms of the new reproductive technologies considered in Chapters 6 and 7. This analysis may, in part, explain the prioritization of resources which has seen overwhelming investment in the new reproductive technologies, regardless of concern for their rate of success, and rather than in the development of alternative approaches to infertility.[65] In these terms, medical discourses still maintain a validating or legitimating narrative, as Michelle Stanworth clearly states:

> For obstetricians and gynaecologists, specific types of reproductive technologies may carry advantages quite separate from their impact on mothers and infants. Reproductive technologies often enhance the status of medical professionals and increase the funds they can command, by underpinning claims to specialized knowledge and by providing the basis for an extension of service. Such tech-nologies may, in addition, help a profession in its attempts to dominate other competitors for control of an area of work; the application of new forms of

technology has been one way that obstetricians have succeeded in reducing midwives to a subordinate status in the field of maternity services.[66]

Therefore claims of special (reproductive) knowledge, realized in technologically advanced procedures, have the same social, financial and political effects as claims to special (reproductive) knowledge had in the nineteenth century. Importantly, and as in the case of the medical challenge to the theory of quickening in the nineteenth century, medical claims of knowledge extend to claims of knowledge superior to that of the woman. Michelle Stanworth continues: 'Perhaps most significantly, new technologies help to establish that gynaecologists and obstetricians "know more" about pregnancy and about women's bodies than women do themselves.'[67]

Modern claims to a greater degree of knowledge than that of the pregnant woman are facilitated by reproductive technologies that are deployed once a woman has conceived. These technologies – a number of them visualizing the foetus – allow medicine to assert a knowledge which is perceived as more quantifiable, more valid, than the woman's experiential knowledge. These technologies intensify the degree of medical observation of reproduction and bolster the perception of medical knowledge as distant and inaccessible. In both these ways they secure and extend the market for medical expertise.

This tension between medical knowledge and the knowledge of the pregnant woman is an important element in the emergence of non-consensual obstetrical intervention. Where a conflict arises as to the perception of 'foetal well-being', it is important to note that doctors have sought recourse to the law to affirm the superiority of their knowledge. It is perhaps more important that in the majority of cases medicine's knowledge has been validated as superior and the court has sanctioned the procedure to which the woman has refused her consent. This validates the knowledge of the doctor and the technologies utilized. It also acts to extend medical practice, which becomes no longer determined by the parameters of consent.

Within this medico-legal relationship, the parameters of consent are further challenged in a recourse to medicine's historic construction of an association between the female reproductive system and mental instability. This was seen quite clearly in *CH*. Here the doctors' accounts of CH were privileged over the account delivered by the Official Solicitor almost to the point of exclusion. This was so even though these accounts differed dramatically. The Official Solicitor had characterized CH as fully aware of the problems involved in her pregnancy. CH becomes 'well orientated and clearly aware of the problems suffered by the foetus, in particular the inter-uterine growth retardation'.[68] It is clear from the Official Solicitor's report that CH understood the need to induce labour and the possibility that a deterioration in the foetus might have necessitated a Caesarian section. In response to this report, Dr M remained unconvinced, stating that he doubted CH's cooperation in the procedures. As Wall J recounted: 'He thought she saw the solicitor as an ally, whereas she saw psychiatrists and obstetricians as opponents.'[69] The Official Solicitor's report becomes an object of CH's psychotic paranoia. Wall J refers to it no further. This account of CH is marginalized notwithstanding the quite distinct impression we receive of her through it. There appears no tension between the two accounts: she remains within the court as Drs G and M portray her. The privileging of medical knowledge over a woman's own knowledge consequently led to her characterization as mentally unstable and the negation of the Official Solicitor's testimony which challenged this.

Whilst this case was located within an expansive interpretation of the Mental Health Act 1983, the cases of *C* and *W* fall outside this. As a result these cases have a potentially wider impact and for this reason should perhaps be viewed with more concern. As has already been noted, it was clearly stated that W was not suffering from a mental disorder within the meaning of the Mental Health Act. Nonetheless, Johnson J relying on the threefold test set out in *Re C* and relied on by Wall J in *CH*, claimed she was not competent to make the decision. The judge concluded that

> although she was not suffering from a mental disorder within the meaning of the statute, she lacked the mental competence to make a decision about the treatment that was proposed because she was incapable of weighing up the considerations that were involved. She was called upon to make that decision at a time of acute emotional stress and physical pain in the ordinary course of labour made even more difficult for her because of her own particular mental history.[70]

In *C*, the judge, following this same route, concluded: 'the patient was not capable of weighing up the information that she was given ... . The patient was in the throes of labour with all that is involved in terms of pain and emotional stress.'[71] The implications of these judgments are considerable. It is possible that women in labour (and perhaps earlier in pregnancy) may only have the capacity to withhold consent so long as they do not do so. Yet this diminishment in pregnant women's autonomy was already seen after *Re S* and before these more recent cases. According to Barbara Hewson, one effect of *Re S* has been that in some prenatal classes women are now instructed that they can no longer refuse obstetrical procedures which their doctor believes necessary.[72] As noted above, the concept of necessity appears unreasonably fluid in a medical context.[73]

While there is an important interplay here between medicine and the law, the law validating claims of specialized knowledge and consequently extending medical practice, this interplay becomes more important in terms of its wider effect when examined within the more complex configuration of reproduction, gender and law.

Reproduction, Gender and Law

The primary narratives that may be discerned within the medico-legal reproductive discourses considered in this book are those which concern gender. The consideration of abortion, foetal protection and infertility services demonstrates that in the regulation of reproduction there appears an almost inherent regulation of gender. The comparatively recent phenomenon of non-consensual obstetrical intervention and judicial intervention in the regulation of pre- and postnatal behaviour again demonstrates this.

This is perhaps most clearly seen in the rise of legal responses to what has been seen as maternal behaviour injurious to the foetus or child. As noted above, Pamela Rae Stewart was prosecuted, albeit unsuccessfully, for her failure to 'follow through on the medical advice she was given'.[74] In the case of *Grodin* v. *Grodin*,[75] the Michigan Court of Appeals recognized the right of a child, acting through his father, to sue his mother for her use during pregnancy of the antibiotic tetracycline, which had discoloured the child's teeth. Negligence was successfully claimed in the mother failing to 'seek proper prenatal care'.[76] Whilst this latter example may do no more than illustrate the degree to which reproduction has been constructed as a medical phenomenon,[77] and the foetal–maternal relationship realigned within a model of conflict, the case of Pamela Rae Stewart illustrates the regulation of gender within the interface of medical and legal discourses.

As noted above, Ms Stewart had been advised to stay off her feet, eschew sex and street drugs, and go to hospital should she start bleeding. Images of the Good Mother. Ms Stewart had sex, took marijuana and amphetamines, and left it several hours before seeking medical attention when she did start to bleed. Images of the Bad Mother. Although the District Attorney attempted to prosecute Ms Stewart, no such action was brought against her husband. Yet Mr Stewart had been a party to each of Ms Stewart's perceived failings. Mr Stewart took marijuana and amphetamines with his wife, had sex with his wife and delayed ensuring his wife attend the hospital. In addition to such coresponsibility, Stewart's husband physically assaulted her while she was pregnant. (One in 12 women in the United States are similarly assaulted by their partners during pregnancy.[78]) Failure to prosecute Pamela Rae's husband (or to introduce legislation against domestic violence) underlines the degree to which the involvement of the law in questions of reproduction will affirm dominant models of gender behaviour. Concern for the foetus again becomes limited and contingent with what could be called lifestyle intervention limited by gender bias. Pamela Rae Stewart was prosecuted, in part, because she failed to fulfil an idealized and largely middle-class model of appropriate gender behaviour. Mr Stewart's behaviour, on the other hand, proved more acceptable even if it was equally damaging to foetal health. These medicolegal narratives are reminiscent of the gender divisions of the nineteenth century – divisions which expected abstinence, sacrifice and compliance from the woman (she was 'patient, trustful, compassionate and timid'[79]) whilst the man could prove romantically reckless ('Sudden in impulse, brave, independent, fickle and eager after novelty.'[80])

Yet it is perhaps the image of *sacrifice* that is most important here. Maternal sacrifice is, after all, central to our iconography of not just motherhood but, in a culture of compulsory (productive) heterosexuality, also Woman. The idea of sacrifice was clearly seen in Chapter 5, where women were expected to sacrifice more highly paid jobs on the basis of possible adverse reproductive outcome. Pamela Rae was advised by her doctor not to work – advice that has similar suggestions of economic dependence, of *separate spheres*, of sacrifice. Sacrifice was also seen in consideration of the Abortion Act 1967. Abortion services were generally only construed as appropriately available when the woman had fulfilled her maternal role. The maternal role was often figured in the almost hallowed image of the 'Wearied Mother', an image inherently involving sacrifice. This figure was a 'married woman with too many children',[81] a 'poor, unfortunate woman driven to desperation'.[82]

Yet perhaps the clearest image of sacrifice is contained, paradoxically, within the cases of forced obstetrical intervention. In these cases – in the case of *Re S*, in the cases of *CH*, *W* and *C*, and perhaps most graphically in the case of Angela Carder – the pregnant woman is expected to sacrifice her legally protected right to autonomy. As with foetal protection policies, the regulation of reproduction places women outside the protection of basic legal rights. With foetal protection policies, the statutory anti-discrimination protection afforded American women was largely negated as defences to directly discriminatory policies were extended through judicial sophistry.[83] Here foetal identity negates a woman's right to deny consent to medical treatment, an expression of an individual's autonomy.[84]

As stated above, in *Re S*, Sir Stephen Brown P attempted to obviate the need for consent to medical treatment by referring to the 'open' question left by Lord Donaldson MR in *Re T*. Acknowledging the importance of bodily integrity, however, the courts have long recognized the right of the individual to refuse medical treatment – even when such treatment is seen by others as in the best interests of the individual, or where the individual will die without the treatment.[85] In the case of *Re F (Mental Patient: sterilis-*

ation), for example, Neill LJ stated that the right to refuse treatment existed 'even where there are overwhelming medical reasons in favour of the treatment and *probably* even where if the treatment is not carried out the patient's life will be at risk'.[86] The slight doubt included in this statement was not, however, included in the subsequent speeches given in the House of Lords in the case of *Airedale NHS Trust v. Bland*.[87] In *Bland*, Lord Keith stated that it was unlawful 'to administer medical treatment to an adult, who is conscious and of sound mind, without his consent. Such a person is completely at liberty to decline to undergo treatment, even if the result of his doing so will be that he will die.'[88] This view of the law was echoed by Lord Goff, who stated:

> it is established that the principle of self-determination requires that respect must be given to the wishes of the patient, so that, if an adult patient of sound mind refuses, however unreasonably, to consent to treatment or care by which his life would or might be prolonged, the doctors responsible for his care must give effect to his wishes, even though they do not consider it to be in his best interests to do so.

In such an instance, the 'principle of the sanctity of life must yield to the principle of self-determination'.[89] Both Lord Browne-Wilkinson[90] and Lord Mustill[91] gave concurring speeches.[92] Consent to medical treatment may therefore be understood as an embodiment of the fundamental precept of the common law that the liberty of the individual must be respected. Its jurisprudential significance is considerable. The principle of self-determination is generally protected as an essential prerequisite for autonomy: 'the body constitutes the major locus of separation between the individual and the world and is in that sense the first object of each person's freedom'.[93] As such the physical autonomy of the individual must be given primacy in terms of the rights that are afforded to the individual: 'the power of self direction as an embodied human being is even more substantively conditional of human worth and dignity than most of the political rights reputed to be basic in a liberal society'.[94]

Therefore, in the cases of *Re S*, *Re A.C.* and the others noted above, a woman's religious convictions, her perception of her pregnancy, her separation from the state in her right to physical self-determination and, in Harrison's words, her *human worth* are all negated, sacrificed.

Yet while the interface of law and medicine promotes the imagery and expectation of sacrifice it also affirms traditional views of gender in more prosaic ways. In this chapter such affirmation has been seen in the trend towards prosecuting women for drug use during pregnancy,[95] and what has been characterized as an unhealthy maternal independence. This independence has been both a general, almost nomadic independence[96] and a failure to submit to medical surveillance or control – apparently the most frequent motivation for recourse to the law. In the cases since *Re S*, for example, both W and CH were explicitly characterized as uncooperative.[97] The issue of cooperation, however, extends beyond a formal medico-legal relationship. Affirmation of gender roles has become, for pregnant women, increasingly difficult to avoid as behaviour during pregnancy has become increasingly subject to regulation, both medical and non-medical. Such regulation or discipline is ever more dispersed, with mounting prohibitions, warnings and concomitant social pressure to comply.

Conclusions

The chapters of this book have illustrated how medico-legal reproductive discourses may be understood as important sites at which dominant models of gender behaviour are constructed and reconstructed. As gender may be understood as a construct (the product of the 'deployment of a complex political technology'[98]), it becomes difficult to conceptualize it as neutral or inert. Indeed, gender has been conceptualized as 'systematically linked to the organization of inequality'.[99] Gender may therefore be read not only as a social position or relation[100] but also as a regulatory system through which social relations of inequality are constructed and maintained. This analysis can be developed further.

As has been noted above, gender as a relational system is predicated on the conceptual and rigid social opposition of the two biological sexes.[101] The construction of the biological sexes, of the physical habitats, therefore becomes a means of determining or regulating social relations. In these terms the construction of the body, within medico-legal reproductive (and other) discourses, itself becomes regulatory or disciplinary. These *technologies of gender* can be understood in the same context as that in which Foucault referred to technologies of sex: techniques that have developed since the late eighteenth century which allowed the bourgeoisie to continue its hegemony. Technologies of gender may be located within the same formulation of elaborate discourses and practices which construct, maintain and legitimate inequalities. While technologies of sex facilitate inequalities on the basis of class, technologies of gender maintain and legitimate sexual inequalities.

Although I have detailed how gender and gender inequalities are constructed and normalized within these discourses, this is not to say that medico-legal discourses are uniform or seamless, or indeed that they construct all women in the same way. Medico-legal discourses will be influenced, as other technologies of gender are influenced, by, amongst other things, race, class and geopolitical status. Again this is illustrated to an extent within the cases of non-consensual obstetrical intervention.

In the extract from the beginning of David Mamet's acclaimed play, *Oleanna*, which introduces this chapter, John talks of a 'term of art', an expression he is unsure of. He nonetheless suggests it means that 'which has come ... to mean something *more specific* than the words would, to some-one *not acquainted* with them ... indicate'. In this book I have suggested that reproductive issues have themselves come to mean something *more specific*. Reproduction and the reproductive body have become invested with meaning quite beyond that which the *words* themselves would suggest. Within the discourses of reproductive regulation many narratives are told. Here I have detailed two recurring and evolving narrative themes. These narratives are written upon the body, a physical palimpsest. The body itself becomes a 'term of art', or perhaps at least *artifice*.

The nature of the political investment of reproduction and the reproductive body, its many narratives and fictions, becomes increasingly important. The burgeoning science of assisted reproduction, and of reproductive medicine generally, provides a growing number of questions. These questions, and the questions we claim to have already answered, and the answers we afford, and have already afforded, must be located within a recognition of the investment of reproduction. Specifically, we need to show an awareness of the fact that medicolegal reproductive discourses and practices exist as influential *technologies of gender*. These discourses and practices justify and maintain sexual inequalities.

Notes

1 Of course there is, at times, a lack of continuity between this intention and the actual practice of the Act. This lack of continuity is particularly marked in practice outside the National Health Service.
2 M. Foucault, *Power/Knowledge: Selected Interviews and Other Writings 1973–1977*, ed. C. Gordon (Hemel Hempstead: Harvester Press, 1980), 58.
3 T. de Lauretis, *Technologies of Gender: Essays on Theory, Film and Fiction* (London: Macmillan, 1989), 3.
4 *Re S (Adult: Refusal of Medical treatment)* [1992] 3 WLR 806. For discussion of this and the other cases considered above, see M. Thomson, 'After *Re S*', *Medical Law Review*, **2**, (1994), 127; C. Wells, 'On the Outside Looking In: Perspectives on Forced Caesarian Sections', in S. Sheldon and M. Thomson (eds), *Feminist Perspectives on Health Care Law* (London: Cavendish, 1998); E. Fegan and P. Fennell, 'Feminist Perspectives on Mental Health Law', in Sheldon and Thomson, *supra*.
5 *Re S*, *supra*, at 807.
6 Ibid.
7 It should, however, be noted that Counsel appeared on behalf of the Official Solicitor as *amicus curiae*.

8   [1992] 4 All ER 649.
9   This assertion of patient autonomy may, however, be 'more apparent than real': see M. Wright, 'Medical Treatment: The Right to Refuse', *Journal of Social Welfare and Family Law* (1993), 204. Yet it should be remembered that the *legal* effect of consent is to make lawful that which would otherwise be unlawful. Withholding, or refusing, consent, therefore, is likely to make any unwanted treatment both a criminal and a civil offence, as Professor Kennedy states: 'If a patient who is aware of the nature of his condition and competent to make a decision refuses further treatment from his doctor then the continued treatment is unlawful as constituting a battery or a criminal assault' (I. Kennedy, 'The Law Relating to the Treatment of the Terminally Ill', *Treat Me Right* (Oxford: Oxford University Press, 1992), 315, at 320).
10   *Re T, supra*, at 649.
11   M. Jones, 'Treating Without Consent', paper given at Symposium on Consent to Medical Treatment (University of Liverpool, 7 April 1993), at 7–8.
12   [1990] 573 A.2d 1235.
13   *Re S, supra*, at 807.
14   This decade of forced obstetrical intervention started with the decision of the Supreme Court of Georgia in *Jefferson* v. *Griffin Spalding County Hospital* (1981) 247 Ga. 86, 247 SE 2d 457.
15   For a discussion of this and the two following cases, see C. Widdett and M. Thomson, 'Justifying Treatment and Other Stories', *Feminist Legal Studies*, **5**, (1997), 77. I am grateful to Ceri Widdett for sharing her mental health law expertise with me.
16   Page 5. All references are to the original judgment.
17   Ibid., at 7.
18   Ibid., at 8–9.
19   Ibid., at 6.
20   Ibid., at 9–10.
21   See, for example, *F.* v. *Riverside Health Trust* [1993] 20 BMLR 1.
22   [1994] 1 WLR 290.
23   *B* v. *Croydon Health Authority* [1995] 1 All ER 683, 688.
24   Elton, HL Deb., ser. 5, vol. 426, col. 1071 (1 Feb. 1982).
25   P. Fennell, 'Force Feeding and the Mental Health Act 1983', *NLJ* (3 March 1995), 319.
26   *Tameside and Glossop Acute Services (NHS) Trust* v. *CH (A Patient), supra*, at 21–2.
27   [1990] 2 AC 1.
28   *Rochdale Healthcare (NHS) Trust* v. *C.*, at 2. All references are to the original judgements.
29   See Jones, *supra*; also Kathy De Gama, who implies that the decision is important because it would fail to survive more authoritative judicial scrutiny. She states: 'The only comfort in this case is that [the] reasoning is so fatally flawed, it could not survive the scrutiny of the House of Lords' (K. De Gama, 'A Brave New World? Rights Discourse and the Politics of Reproductive Autonomy', in A. Bottomley and J. Conaghan (eds), *Feminist Theory and Legal Strategy* (Oxford: Blackwell, 1993), 114, at 122.
30   See *Roe* v. *Wade* (1973) 410 US 113, at 157–8, 162. See also *infra*, n.84.
31   *Jefferson* v. *Griffin Spalding County Hospital* (1981) 247 Ga. 86; 274 SE 2d 457.
32   Ibid., at 88.
33   Ibid., at 90.
34   V.E.B. Kolder, J. Gallager and M.T. Parsons, 'Court Ordered Obstetrical Interventions', *New England Journal of Medicine*, **316**, (1987), 1192. For a comprehensive

list of references, see J. Gallager, 'Prenatal Invasions and Interventions: What's Wrong With Fetal Rights?', *Harvard Women's Law Journal*, **10**, (1987), 9, at 11–12.

35 Gallager, *supra*, at 9–10.

36 Ibid., at 12.

37 Kolder *et al.*, *supra*, at 1193. This also occurred in the recent English case of *Re MB*. For a detailed consideration of this case, see Fegan and Fennell, *supra*.

38 R. Jurow and R.H. Paul, 'Caesarean Delivery for Fetal Distress Without Maternal Consent', *Obstetrics and Gynecology*, **63**, (1984), 596.

39 See B. Ehrenreich and D. English, *For Her Own Good: 150 Years of the Experts' Advice to Women* (Pluto Press: London, 1979).

40 Kolder *et al.*, *supra*, at 1193.

41 Ibid.

42 G.J. Annas, 'Protecting the Liberty of Pregnant Patients', *New England Journal of Medicine*, **316**, (1987), 1213.

43 (1987) 533 A.2d 611 (DC Ct. App.), per Nebeker AJ (emphasis added).

44 [1990] 573 A.2d 1235 at 1297.

45 De Gama, *supra*, at 122. Yet it should be noted that *Re A.C.* still allows the courts to override the wishes of a competent adult where there are 'truly extraordinary or compelling reasons'. As such it may not mark the end of forced Caesarian sections, even though the practice has been condemned by the American College of Obstetricians and Gynecologists. See K. Pollitt, 'A New Assault on Feminism', *The Nation* (26 March 1990), 409.

46 *In re Jamaica Hospital* (1985) 128 Misc. 2d 1006, 491 NYS2d 898 (Sup. Ct.). See also *Raleigh Fitkin-Paul Morgan Memorial Hospital* v. *Anderson* (1964) 42 NJ421, 201 A. 2d 537.

47 Kolder *et al.*, *supra*, at 1193.

48 Ibid.

49 *Wisconsin State Journal* (16 August 1985), s.3, 2.

50 *In re Steven S.* (1981) 126 Cal. App. 3d 23, at 30–31, 27, 178 Cal. Rptr. 525, at 526 (Ct. App.).

51 Cited in 'Rethinking (M)otherhood: Feminist Theory and State Regulation of Pregnancy', *Harvard Law Review*, **103**, (1990), 1325, at 1338.

52 Cited in D. Logli, 'Drugs in the Womb: The Newest Battlefield in the War on Drugs', *Criminal Justice Ethics*, **9**, (1990), 23, at 24.

53 'Rethinking (M)otherhood', *supra*, at 1330.

54 For a discussion of the constitutional implications of using drug legislation against pregnant women, or women who have used illicit drugs during pregnancy, see D.M. McGinnis, 'Prosecution of Mothers of Drug Exposed Babies: Constitutional and Criminal Theory', *University of Pennsylvania Law Review*, **139**, (1990), 505.

55 *The Los Angeles Times* (1 October 1986).

56 Cal. Penal Code 270 (West Supp. 1986).

57 D. Johnsen, 'A New Threat to Pregnant Women's Autonomy', *Hastings Center Report* (August 1987), 33, at 35.

58 McGinnis, *supra*, at 505.

59 The courts have sanctioned various forms of monitoring of maternal behaviour; for example, a Baltimore court ordered a woman, seven months pregnant, to enrol on a drug treatment programme, and to submit weekly to urinalysis until the birth of her baby: cited in 'Medical Technology and the Law', *Harvard Law Review*, **103**, (1990), 1519, at 1572.

60 See NJ Stat. Ann. 30:4C-11 (West 1981), this New Jersey statute appears to allow the

state to assume custody of an 'unborn child' on the ground that the behaviour of the mother is endangering the health or welfare of the foetus. See also *Jefferson* v.*Griffin Spalding County Hospital, supra.*

61   See *In re Baby X* (1980) 97 Mich. App. 111, NW2d 736, where a court denied a woman the custody of her newborn child on the basis of her prenatal 'abuse'. Evidence of the 'abuse' was obtained from the woman's medical records without her consent. See also *In re Ruiz* (1986) 27 Ohio Misc. 2d 31, 500 N.E.2d 935 (CP); *In re Danielle Smith* (1985) 128 Misc. 2d 976, 492 NYS2d 331 (Fam. Ct.).

62   Ill. Rev. Stat. ch. 37, para. 802–3(c) (1989).

63   See, for example, Fla. Stat. Ann. 415.503(9)(a)(2) (West Supp. 1990); Okla. Stat. Ann. tit. 10, 1101(4) (West 1987); Ind. Code Ann. 31–6–4–3.1 (West Supp. 1990).

64   M. Foucault, *Discipline and Punish: The Birth of the Prison* (London: Penguin, 1977), 27.

65   M. Stanworth, 'Reproductive Technologies and the Deconstruction of Motherhood', in M. Stanworth (ed.), *Reproductive Technologies: Gender, Motherhood and Medicine* (London: Polity Press, 1987), 10 at 11.

66   Ibid., at 13.

67   Ibid.

68   *Tameside and Glossop Acute Services (NHS) Trust* v. *CH (A Patient), supra,* at 11–12.

69   Ibid., at 10.

70   *Norfolk and Norwich Healthcare (NHS) Trust* v. *W, supra,* at 4.

71   *Rochdale Healthcare (NHS) Trust* v. *C, supra,* at 2.

72   B. Hewson, 'Mother Knows Best', *New Law Journal,* **142,** II, (1992), 1583.

73   Annas, *supra,* at 1213.

74   *The Los Angeles Times* (1 October 1986).

75   (1980) 102 Mich. App. 396, 301 N.W.2d 869.

76   Ibid., at 870. While third party liability is generally recognized for tortiously caused prenatal injury, no other state has extended this to maternal conduct. See *Stallman* v. *Youngquist* (1988) 125 Ill. 2d 267, 531 N.E.2d 355. The lower court found the mother liable for the congenital intestinal damage of the five-year-old girl involved. The damage resulted from a car accident suffered while the woman was pregnant (substantial weight being placed on the widespread existence of car insurance). This decision, however, did not survive appeal, and the court refused to recognize liability for unintentional infliction of prenatal injuries by the pregnant woman. The lower court's appreciation of the widespread existence of motor insurance (required in the United Kingdom by s. 143 of the Road Traffic Act 1972) was shared by the Law Commission in its recommendation that maternal liability should exist only in so far as the injuries sustained were the result of a motor accident. (See Law Commission No. 60, August 1974; also the enactment of this recommendation, Congenital Disability (Civil Liability) Act 1976, s. 2. The first case under this section did not come before a British court until May 1992, resulting in an award of £700 000 to a six-year-old child suffering from cerebral palsy following a car accident (*The Guardian* (20 May 1992)).

77   For a detailed account of the medicalization of reproduction, and pregnancy specifically, see A. Oakley, *The Captured Womb: A History of the Medical Care of Pregnant Women* (Oxford: Blackwell, 1984); also B. Ehrenreich and D. English, *For Her Own Good: 150 Years of the Experts' Advice to Women* (London: Pluto, 1979).

78   Pollitt, *supra,* at 416.

79   J. Crichton-Browne, 'Sex in Education', *BMJ* (7 May 1892), 949.

80   Ibid. See Chapter 2 of the present volume.

81 Short, HC Deb. vol. 732, col. 1163, 1966 (22 July).
82 Braine, HC Deb. vol. 747, col. 496, 1967 (2 June).
83 See M.E. Becker, 'From *Muller* v. *Oregon* to Fetal Vulnerability Policies', *University of Chicago Law Review*, **53**, (1986), 1219.
84 This occurs even when the foetus is without legal status. In English law, the foetus does not have a legal personality until it is born alive. (For a definition of 'born alive' in English law, see S.B. Atkinson, 'Life, Birth and Live Birth', *Law Quarterly Review*, **20**, (1904), 134; G. Williams, *The Sanctity of Life* (London: Faber, 1958), 19–23; also, more recently, the case of *Rance* v. *Mid-Downs Health Authority* [1991] 1 Q.B. 587, at 621, where it was stated that 'The meaning of "born alive" is clear ... [a child is] born alive if after birth it exists as a live child, that is to say breathing and living by reason of its breathing through its own lungs alone, without deriving any of its living or power to live by or through any connection with its mother.') The status of the foetus in English law was clearly stated by Sir George Baker P in *Paton* v. *British Pregnancy Advisory Service Trustees* [1979] Q.B. 276: 'The foetus cannot, in English law, in my view, have a right on its own at least until it is born and has a separate existence from its mother.' Baker P concluded that this 'permeates the whole of the civil law of this country' (ibid., at 279). See also the decision of the European Court of Human Rights in this case: *Paton* v. *United Kingdom* (1980) 3 EHRR 408, at 415. Similarly, in *B* v. *Islington H.A.* [1991] 1 QB 638, Potts J described the foetus as 'undefined in law and without status' (ibid., at 647). This refusal to recognize the foetus, or afford it rights, has also been seen in the failure of attempts to make the foetus a ward of court. See *Re F (In Utero)* [1988] 2 WLR 1297, involving an unsuccessful attempt by a local authority. The court unanimously rejected the proposition that a court could compel a pregnant woman to undergo any invasion on her liberty, Balcombe LJ stating: 'it would be intolerable to place any judge in the position of having to make such a decision without any guidance as to the principles upon which his decision should be based'. He continued, 'In such a sensitive field, affecting as it does the liberty of the individual, it is not for the judiciary to extend the law' (at 1307). See also Phillips (1987) 95 LQR 332; Lowe (1980) 96 LQR 29. For a discussion of the legal status of the foetus in American law, see J. Gallager, 'Prenatal Invasions and Interventions', *supra*, at 40–41; B. Gregoratos, 'Tempest in the Laboratory: Regulation of Medical Research on Spare Embryos from *in vitro* Fertilization', *Hastings Law Journal*, **37**, (1986), 977, at 987–90. Stevens J in *Planned Parenthood* v. *Casey* (1992) 120 L.Ed.2d 674, a case reaffirming the central finding of *Roe* v. *Wade* (1973) 410 US 113, reiterated the legal status of the foetus in American law. He further stated: 'as a matter of federal constitutional law, a developing organism that is not a "person" does not have what is sometimes called a "right to life"'. He concluded, 'This has been and remains a fundamental premise of our constitutional law governing reproductive autonomy' (at 738–9). For other jurisdictions, see *Dehler* v. *Ottawa Civil Hospital* (1979) 117 DLR 3d. 512; *Mathison* v. *Hofer* [1984] 3 WWR 343; *Borowski* v. *Attorney General of Canada* (1982) 130 DLR (3d) 588.
85 This is subject to statutory exceptions allowing for compulsory treatment, such as the provisions of the Mental Health Act 1983.
86 [1990] 2 AC 1, at 29 (emphasis added).
87 [1993] 1 All ER 821.
88 Ibid., at 860.
89 Ibid., at 866.
90 Ibid., at 881–2.
91 Ibid., at 889.

92   For American decisions on the right to refuse treatment, see *Bouvia* v. *Superior Court* (1986) 225 Cal. Rptr. 297, 179 Cal. App.3d 1127; *In re Conroy* (1985) 98 NJ 329, 486 A.2d 1209.

93   L. Tribe, *American Constitutional Law* (Mineola, New York: The Foundation Press, 1979), 15–9.

94   B.W. Harrison, *Our Right to Choose; Towards a New Ethic of Abortion* (Boston: Beacon Press, 1983), 194. For judicial recognition of these arguments in the context of refusal of treatment, see Robins JA in the Canadian case of *Malette* v. *Shulman* (1990) 73 OR (2d) 417: 'The right to determine what shall be done with one's body is a fundamental right in our society. The concepts inherent in this right are the bedrock upon which the principles of self-determination and individual autonomy are based. Free individual choice in matters affecting this right should, in my opinion, be accorded very high priority.' See also the recognition of the 'inviolability of [the] person' and 'human dignity and self-determination', in the American case of *Saikewicz* 370 NE2d 417, at 424; also *Pratt* v. *Davies* (1905) 118 Ill. App. 161, at 166, *aff'd* (1906) 224 Ill. 300, 79 NE2d 562.

95   Whilst women have been prosecuted for drug use during pregnancy, there have been no prosecutions for male drug use during the preconception stage. Male drug use during a partner's pregnancy may also prove damaging as a foetus may be exposed to foetotoxic chemicals carried in the seminal fluid. See J. Mason and R. Simon, 'Effects of Lead on Mammalian Reproduction', in V.R. Hunt (ed.), *Work and the Health of Women* (Boca Raton, Fla: CRC Press, 1976), 171.

96   See *Wisconsin State Journal* (16 August 1985), s. 3, 2.

97   *W, supra*, at 1; *CH, supra*, at 3.

98   T. de Lauretis, *Technologies of Gender: Essays on Theory, Film and Fiction* (London: Macmillan, 1989), 3.

99   Ibid., at 5.

100   Ibid.

101   Ibid.

Index